From Orality to Orality

Biblical Performance Criticism

DAVID RHOADS, SERIES EDITOR

The ancient societies of the Bible were overwhelmingly oral. People originally experienced the traditions now in the Bible as oral performances. Focusing on the ancient performance of biblical traditions enables us to shift academic work on the Bible from the mentality of a modern print culture to that of an oral/scribal culture. Conceived broadly, biblical performance criticism embraces many methods as means to reframe the biblical materials in the context of traditional oral cultures, construct scenarios of ancient performances, learn from contemporary performances of these materials, and reinterpret biblical writings accordingly. The result is a foundational paradigm shift that reconfigures traditional disciplines and employs fresh biblical methodologies such as theater studies, speech-act theory, and performance studies. The emerging research of many scholars in this field of study, the development of working groups in scholarly societies, and the appearance of conferences on orality and literacy make it timely to inaugurate this series. For further information on biblical performance criticism, go to www.biblicalperformancecriticism.org.

Books in the Series

Holly E. Hearon and Philip Ruge-Jones, editors
*The Bible in Ancient and Modern Media:
Story and Performance*

James A. Maxey
*From Orality to Orality:
A New Paradigm for Contextual Translation of the Bible*

David Rhoads
*Biblical Performance Criticism:
An Emerging Discipline in New Testament Studies*

Forthcoming

Joanna Dewey
Orality, Scribality, and the Gospel of Mark

Pieter J. J. Botha
Orality and Literacy in Early Christianity

FROM ORALITY TO ORALITY

A New Paradigm for Contextual Translation of the Bible

JAMES A. MAXEY

CASCADE *Books* • Eugene, Oregon

FROM ORALITY TO ORALITY
A New Paradigm for Contextual Translation of the Bible

Biblical Performance Criticism Series 2

Copyright © 2009 James A. Maxey. All rights reserved. Except for brief quotations in critical publications or reviews, no part of this book may be reproduced in any manner without prior written permission from the publisher. Write: Permissions, Wipf and Stock Publishers, 199 W. 8th Ave., Suite 3, Eugene, OR 97401.

Cascade Books
An Imprint of Wipf and Stock Publishers
199 W. 8th Ave., Suite 3
Eugene, OR 97401

ISBN 13: 978-1-60608-324-6

Cataloging-in-Publication data:

Maxey, James A.

From orality to orality : a new paradigm for contextual translation of the Bible / James A. Maxey

ISBN 13: 978-1-60608-324-6

xii + 222 p. ; 23 cm. —Includes bibliographical references and index.

1. Bible—Criticism, Performance. 2. Bible—Translating. 3. Bible, N.T.—Criticism, interpretation, etc. 4. Translating and interpreting—Camaroon. 5. Storytelling—Religious aspects—Christianity. 6. Oral Tradition. I. Title. II. Series.

BS2555.5 M28 2009

Manufactured in the U.S.A.

To Pam, Sam, Levi, Jane, and Lauren—
with great love and affection.

CONTENTS

List of Tables · viii
Acknowledgments · ix
Preface · xi

Introduction · 1

1 Translation as Contextualization · 19

2 Bible Translation in the Contexts of Africa · 49

3 Orality, Literacy, and Performance · 77

4 Literacy and Orality in Relation to the New Testament · 104

5 Biblical Performance Criticism and Bible Translation · 132

6 Bible Translation for Performance: A Case Study with the Vuté People of Cameroon · 167

7 Conclusion · 193

Bibliography · 197
Index · 217

LIST OF TABLES

TABLE 1: Foley's Oral-Written Spectrum · 96

TABLE 2: Literacy-Orality Continua · 115

TABLE 3: English Script of Vuté Performance for Mark 1:40–45 · 162

TABLE 4: English Script of Vuté Performance for Mark 2:1–12 · 186

ACKNOWLEDGMENTS

I AM GRATEFUL TO THE VUTÉ COMMUNITY FOR THEIR INstruction, guidance, and unfailing friendship. This extends beyond the Vuté community to my colleagues with the Evangelical Lutheran Church of Cameroon and the Yoko parish of the Roman Catholic Church. Secondly, I am grateful for the guidance of the professors at both the Lutheran School of Theology at Chicago and the Catholic Theological Union. Subjects explored have included a wide continuum, from Missiology to Anthropology, from New Testament studies to Contextual theologies. Thirdly, Lutheran Bible Translators has provided steady support of my work and research for twenty years—first in my MA in Linguistics and then in my PhD studies. I reserve my final acknowledgment of gratitude for my family. They have lived many of the experiences with me—from Africa and during my study program—that are discussed in this book. I thank them profoundly for accompanying me on this journey.

PREFACE

IN THE FOLLOWING PAGES I INTERTWINE TWO MAIN SUBjects: a proposal for an alternative paradigm for Bible translation as contextualization; a discussion of orality and biblical performance criticism as a methodology for biblical studies and its implications for translation. My research is exploratory and my findings are tentative. There is little public discussion of alternative paradigms for Bible translation, especially one associated with contextualization. My field research with translation of oral performances, both with my own and with the Vuté community in Cameroon, is in its early stages. There is a need for more experience with oral performances of biblical compositions.

Historically, critics linked Bible translation directly to literacy and evangelism, and (in)directly to colonial agendas. Those involved in Bible translation in recent centuries have often restricted their purview both in terms of communication media and theological imagination. This book asserts that such views are limited and do not reflect the rich theological heritage of Bible translation. Bible translation is presented in this book as an expression of contextualization that explores the neglected riches of the verbal arts in the New Testament. Beyond a historical study of media in antiquity, a renewed interest in oral performance informs methods and goals of Bible translation today. Such exploration is concretized in the NT translation work in central Africa among the Vuté people of Cameroon.

Contextualization as discussed in this study appreciates the agency of local communities—particularly in Africa—who seek to express their Christian faith in response to the results of human impoverishment. An extended study of African theologians demonstrates the ultimate goals of contextualization: liberation and identity. Bible translation exhibits how vernacular languages empower and equip these local communities to establish and maintain their identities by means of their cultures as articulated by their languages and also how such linguistic expression

Preface

subverts the dominant languages' control. Local communities create fresh pathways of not only responses to existing theological questions, but explore new inquiries of God and humanity.

Oral performance draws from all the senses by experiencing communication while performer, text, and audience negotiate meaning. Performance not only expresses identity but shapes it as communities express their faith in varied contexts. It is argued that the New Testament compositions were initially performed and not restricted to individual, silent reading. This understanding encourages a reexamination of how Bible translation can be done. Performance is not seen as a product but a process that infuses biblical studies with new insights, methods, and expressions. In the case study of the Vuté people of Cameroon, a New Testament translation project is reviewed as local performers exhibit their cultural values of the verbal arts in presentations of translated biblical passages informed by a renewed interest in the spoken word.

INTRODUCTION

From Orality to Orality

THE PAGES THAT FOLLOW TELL A STORY, A CIRCUITOUS story. Sometimes we think that things have always been the way they are. Many Christians in North America and Europe understand the Bible to be a literary production like many other books produced today. They understand that access to the Bible is uniquely available by literacy, a type of individual, silent, deciphering of written code. With such assumptions the transmission of the Bible into other parts of the world—for example Africa—has been accompanied by the agenda of literacy. This has been done with minimal attention to what is often a predominant part of everyday life: the verbal arts are often the means of communication. People speak and people hear. Important stories are artfully told, and communities participate in this storytelling that is part of who they are, their identity.

This book sets out to describe the ways in which the Bible—specifically the New Testament—was composed to be heard and to be experienced in a communal setting. This oral setting is not so different than the oral settings found in places such as Africa today. When this book's title states "From Orality to Orality," that is precisely what is intended: from the orality of the first-century Mediterranean world of the New Testament to the twenty-first-century oral contexts of much of the world today. The activities of Bible Translation[1] have for centuries presupposed literacy rather than orality as the predominant means of communication for the Bible's creation, transmission, and reception. I suggest that this understanding distorts both historical and anthropological evidence. The Bible was for the most part created, transmitted, and received in a predominantly oral context. This should affect how we go about Bible Translation today.

---

1. I capitalize the phrase Bible Translation to designate the academic discipline.

FROM ORALITY TO ORALITY

A central focus of this book is oral performance. The use of the word "performance" might distract people into thinking about disingenuous entertainment. Dramatic interpretation is what is meant. But there is more. Performance is a social activity in which community identity is shaped. Performance, therefore, can be understood as a verbal art as well as a social drama.[2] Performance is understood throughout this book as a sincere embodiment of communication. It is often modified by "oral" to indicate that although communication presupposes body movement there is a particular collaboration of the spoken word with such embodiment. Verbal art might be another appropriate phrase that communicates multi-sensory communication and reception. Oral performance in relation to Bible Translation is not an invitation for individual aggrandizing. The locale of performance may change the formality of presentation but biblical performances are conscious of the sacral nature of the experience.

A New Paradigm

For the past several centuries Bible Translation has been predominantly understood as a tool of evangelism. In more recent times, northern-hemisphere Christians have viewed their participation in Bible Translation in the southern hemisphere as a helping hand to those Christians. It was offered as a church growth or church maturity tool. In this twenty-first century, however, we recognize that such seemingly benevolent, neutral acts are called into question. In fact the larger structure—paradigm—of Bible Translation is being questioned in terms of the one-sidedness of who is doing Bible Translation and for what purposes.[3] This book offers an alternative paradigm of Bible translation. It is in a sense new, but only because we have forgotten our history. Bible Translation has never been simply a tool of evangelism or church growth. It has been a means of forming and sustaining a community's identity and, at times, of liberating a community from oppressive dominant structures. This book seeks to respond to twenty-first century critics of Bible Translation being an

---

2. Giles and Doan provide a very helpful discussion of what they mean by Performance Criticism in relation to biblical studies: Giles and Doan, *Twice Used Songs*, 12–16. In terms of social drama, Turner's work is helpful: *The Forest of Symbols*.

3. This notion of "paradigm" in regards to theologies was presented in Bosch, *Transforming Mission*.

Introduction

oppressive part of colonialism that denigrates the oral cultures around the world.

Understood from this new paradigm, Bible Translation is neither a neutral nor a simple activity. Moreover, Bible Translation is ideologically motivated.[4] The challenges and complexities of translation involve issues of power and issues of effective communication. All translation is interpretation. As a result, all translations reflect to varying degrees the social locations of those who are involved in the translation. Despite great acclamations of objectivity, this is not obtainable. Furthermore, modes of communication must not be understood as neutral. There have been significant studies of the differences between orality and literacy. Unfortunate binary discussions of these modes of communication have distracted researchers from the complexities of the potential interfaces between orality and literacy. Proponents of Bible Translation have vaunted the introduction of literacy by Bible Translation. The benefits of literacy should not be neglected. However, postcolonial studies have questioned whether the oral ethos has been sacrificed in this pursuit of literacy.[5] The situation ought not to devolve into another dichotomous discussion of literacy vs. orality. However, there is a significant myopia in ignoring the riches of oral communities. This has been particularly true with Bible Translation that has historically set its goal to a literary conversion of the population. Whereas literacy offers significant benefits, it should not be at the expense of oral appreciation.

As I returned to academia in the United States, I began to seek for myself a fresh missiological understanding of Bible Translation. Although such research was initiated for my own reasons, I soon began to see how many in America view Bible Translation in a limited way. Many individuals, churches, and organizations understand Bible Translation activities in Africa, South America, Asia, and the South Pacific as an instrument of

---

4. Ideologies—whether conscious or not—locate people socially, and when these people are involved in translation, these ideologies shape translations. As social constructions, ideologies, although perceived as neutral, involve power relations–relations of inequality. Such inequalities can be due to race, gender, economics, religion, ethnicity, sexual orientation, class, geographic location, colonial relations and so on; see Maxey, "Ideology and Bible Translation."

5. Postcolonial studies are an ever-broadening area of research and study. Fundamentally it uses the lens of power (generally understood as political) to examine history and human relations. An early work on the subject is Edward Said's *Orientalism*. Homi Bhabha's *The Location of Culture* also demonstrates a postcolonial approach.

evangelization with the goal of conversion to Christianity. Others view Bible Translation as a benevolent means to assist churches outside of North America and Europe to grow in the Christian faith. Another set of Americans (and Europeans) find Bible Translation to be an embarrassing (or detrimental) activity left over from an earlier era. My problem was that I was not satisfied with these limited views of Bible Translation. I needed an alternative; I saw that missiology needed another understanding of Bible Translation. The following chapters pursue such an alternative paradigm for Bible Translation.

Insights into these issues of Bible Translation come from understanding all Christian theologies as contextually shaped. Instrumental to the shaping of these theologies has been the Scriptures in a variety of languages. There is a dynamic relationship between the Bible and the people who engage in the Bible. The effects of this dynamic relationship are not limited to the people; the Bible itself is affected. The effects of such interactions benefit those of other social-linguistic groups. In this way the benefits to numerous groups can be viewed as mutual. Peoples of varied cultures and languages have shaped the way Bibles have been translated and Bibles have shaped the way people live out their faith. Furthermore, the expressions of faith extend to other communities of faith to challenge, diversify, and enrich all the communities involved. No longer can we understand Bible Translation as simply a gift to minority language communities. Christian communities elsewhere are in (desperate) need to experience how various communities articulate and live out their faith. In fact, given that the majority of the Christians of the world reside in the southern hemisphere, it is no longer accurate to limit Bible Translation to evangelization in these regions. Moreover, instead of an outdated accessory to contemporary discussions of contextual theologies, Bible Translation can be viewed as an integral part to how local communities construct local theologies.

An alternative paradigm for Bible Translation as contextualization responds to recent postcolonial critiques of missionary Christianity in general and the activity of Bible Translation in particular. Unfortunately, those from North America and Europe who are involved in Bible Translation in the southern hemisphere have not in general taken such critiques seriously. While discussions of new theories and methods of translation are being discussed by these translation agencies in terms of religious benefits, there is little dialogue concerning socio-economic challenges and discussions of power in the relationships between these agencies and host communities. My proposed paradigm of contextualization for Bible Translation seeks to listen to these critiques and respond to them in fresh ways.

Perhaps the most convincing argument for the contextual value of Bible Translation comes from those who use such translations. The agency of these communities is evident as they approach the Bible as a community of faith. This includes how they interpret and experience the Bible, and how they understand issues of power in relation to the Bible. Key to these issues is the notion of community. Whereas many Bible Translation associations from North America and Europe might envision individual access to the Bible as the goal, most of the world lives in community, with a collective sense of identity. In order to be contextually sensitive to this reality, community involvement in Bible Translation and the experience of the Bible become central.

The History of Vuté New Testament Translation

My familiarity with the variety of issues discussed in this book comes as a result of my experiences in Bible Translation for more than twenty years. Whereas this experience began in and has most recently returned to contexts of American educational institutions, the majority of my experience is a result of living in Cameroon, Africa during the period 1991–2003. I write about Bible Translation in Africa as a non-African. Yet, I can no longer understand myself as only American. My Vuté (VOO-tay) brothers and sisters have been influential, and their interactions with me have changed me. I retain aspects of an outsider, but I have also developed deep relationships that have resulted in responsibilities in the Vuté community that reflect a nuanced outsider-insider role. Such a role causes me to refrain from a simplified romantic view of life in Africa. At the same time, my experience permits me to appreciate the quality of agency of the Vuté community within the limits of historical and contemporary contexts of what I describe below as anthropological pauperization. This brief description of my social location and self-understanding is supplemented in chapter six.

Although called by the Evangelical Lutheran Church of Cameroon (ELCC) for the purpose of Bible Translation with the Vuté community, many other activities were related to this overall purpose. As an oral language, the Vuté community asked me to study their language to help them develop an alphabet and literacy program for their language. Besides the translation of the Bible, the community asked me to facilitate the translation of other materials: religious (liturgies, hymnbooks, catechisms), health, agricultural, and cultural materials, along with original literature in Vuté. We were invited to live in the town of Yoko, the political center of the Vuté community, a community spread over a wide geographic area. By April of 1992 I moved to Yoko with my wife and two young children. As the years went by, not only did my family grow by two more, but we grew more integrated into community life in Yoko. After ten years of living with the Vuté community we knew that the friendships—and in many ways the kinships—that were created were lifelong. In 2002 my family moved to the north of the country to the national offices of the ELCC in response to the request of the presiding bishop. My new role was to oversee sixteen translation and literacy projects of the ELCC—including Vuté. The challenges came from all directions: remote communities struggling to maintain their translation and literacy programs; demanding international partners who wanted financial accountability; a growing national church seeking the best way to use the riches of their diverse languages and cultures.

One way to trace the history of Bible Translation with the Vuté people is with the Gospel of Mark. The first efforts towards Bible Translation in the Vuté community can be attributed to two young Vuté Lutheran pastors who approached in 1969 the newly established Bible Society of Cameroon. Yet even this early request must be placed in the larger context of both the ELCC and the Yoko parish of the Catholic Church. Pastors Songsare and Kouri presented their request by making reference to their aunts and grandmothers in rural villages who were not able to follow the hymns and scripture readings in languages other than Vuté. Pastor Songsare later became President of the ELCC.[6] Once a provisionary alphabet was established, work began on the translation of Mark's Gospel. This eventually resulted in a 1988 test edition. Although exegetical help was provided by expatriates, the actual translation was done by Martin Yaya, at the time a local elementary teacher at the ELCC primary

---

6. This ELCC context is partially presented in: Lode, *Appelés à la Liberté*. For a history of Bible societies in Africa and more specifically in Cameroon, see: Schaaf, *L'Histoire et le Rôle de la Bible en Afrique*.

school.⁷ Soon after the printing of this test edition, Father Lachenaud, a French priest in the Vuté community, printed the three-year lectionary that included the translation work of several Catholic lay volunteers who translated lectionary lessons.⁸ I was involved in the remaining editions of the translation of Mark's Gospel. The first of these was a revision of the 1988 Yaya version that was done by Alfred Oumarou and Lazare Kouadjinlo and printed in 1997. This was the beginning of ecumenical translations with translators from both the Lutheran and Catholic churches. Slight revisions were made to Mark by Oumarou and his eventual primary Catholic counterpart, Jean Nogoadjéré. It was printed in a collection of all four Gospels received by the Vuté community in a celebration in December 1999. The feedback from these earlier translations was incorporated into the final manuscript of the entire New Testament that was published in 2007.

Translation Assumptions and Methodologies

I was the exegete for the past three editions of Mark's Gospel as well as the entire New Testament in the Vuté translation project of Cameroon. I present some of my presuppositions for this translation work below. Full-time translation began with me in 1997. Our first visit to the Vuté region was in 1991. In the interval between our arrival and full-time translation work, we concentrated on activities to learn the Vuté language and culture. It was primarily a time for us to build relationships with the Vuté community in general and the Christian communities in particular. Our focus on language learning helped us appreciate the intricacies of the language as well as build relationships. We spent over four years in this pre-translation phase.⁹ One of the important tools in learning the Vuté

---

7. Throughout this section the names of each of the Vuté translators are presented. This is intended to underscore that the translations were not done by expatriates (foreigners), but by representatives of the Vuté community. As an indication of the complexity of the task, Yaya translated in the central dialect but is himself from a minority northern dialect.

8. Father Lachenaud was involved in collecting the oral traditions of the Vuté people. Lachenaud, "Histoire Des Vuté d'après leurs traditions orales." The methodology for the lectionary translation consisted of the use of the common language *Français Courant* Bible, group discussions and some explanations by Father Lachenaud. One of the principal translators for this lectionary was Nicolas Mvoutsi, a retired nurse.

9. We spent eighteen months of this time in the USA where I finished up my MA in Linguistics culminating in a thesis on "Relative Clauses in Vuté."

language and culture was listening to and studying Vuté folktales. I noticed that certain Vuté were recognized by their communities for their gifted storytelling.

One of the accompanying activities of this pre-translation phase (as well as later phases) was the training of literacy teachers and the production of literacy materials. The question that we posed to ourselves was: What good will a translated New Testament do if the Vuté people cannot read their own language? It was assumed without any doubt that literacy was the only means of access to a translated New Testament. Our training in the USA, as well as workshops in Cameroon, reinforced this assumption. Only in the mid-1990s were methods for access to Scriptures through non-literacy ever discussed—and this only as ancillary to the essential written word. The results of the Protestant Reformation and the post-Gutenberg ethos were so well established in Bible Translation circles that there was not even an evaluation of the value of oral performance in conjunction with the translated New Testament except as a preliminary "pre-literate" stage.

While working with Oumarou and Nogoadjéré on translation we followed these basic steps: do an exegetical study of an entire New Testament book; draft a translation; revise the draft with comments from my study of the draft in comparison with the exegetical study notes; revision of draft with a representative group of reviewers;[10] test the revised draft with people in the representative community who had little prior contact with the translation;[11] have a Bible society representative check the most recent draft (in comparison to the Greek text). What is striking to me as I look back at these procedures is that almost every step involved an auditory reception of the text. This reality is in stark contrast to how I understood the ultimate goal of the translation: that all Vuté would have access to this translation by means of literacy. An auditory reception was considered second best. At times this blind spot was ridiculously evident, such as when we discussed the capitalization of certain (divine) words to distinguish them from common uses: for example, Spirit (as in God's Spirit) with spirit (human or anti-human). Sometimes a passage would need an explanatory note to help a Vuté understand cultural or religious

---

10. Most of these reviewers had access to the draft in written form but primarily heard the translation as they listened for unnatural phrases or wordings.

11. This testing was almost always done by the Vuté translators, who would read a passage aloud and then ask comprehension questions.

differences between first-century Palestine and the Vuté culture. This information was placed in footnotes. The translators and I knew that such notes would not be read in worship services at churches. They would only instruct a sophisticated reader and not a listening audience. These examples are meant to show that on a certain level the translators and I were aware of the literacy bias that accompanied our translation and how this bias was incongruent with the fact that most of the people would only hear the translation. Not once did I lead the translators into discussions of how the issues of aural reception might affect the translation. In fact, during my own training—both in Bible and linguistics for translation—I do not remember anybody indicating to me that the Bible was intended primarily to be heard in community and that this fact should shape the way that we do translation.

A distinct point should be made in relation to the above methodology and communication models. The presupposed communication model from which I taught translation principles in Cameroon has been described as the conduit or code model.[12] Numerous times when I explained this model I would draw two circles within two squares on the chalkboard. The squares represented distinct language differences (in this case Greek and Vuté). The "identical" circles represented the meaning contained within the linguistic forms. The task of the translator, according to this model, is to discover the meaning (note the singular) and remove it from its linguistic form and then transfer this identical meaning into a different linguistic form.

Several assumptions are made here in relation to communication: 1) one is able to separate meaning from form; 2) one is able to discover the meaning—assumed as the intended meaning of the original biblical author; 3) meaning is connected to the language and more specifically to the text. As I will demonstrate in the following chapters, these assumptions are misplaced. Form does shape meaning. Discovery of "the original meaning" proves to be elusive and often reveals as much about the exegete as it does the potential meanings (or range of meanings). Meaning is negotiated by an interpretive community in conjunction with authorial intention and text. Another difficulty with this model and method (beyond simply translation principles based on an overly simplified communication model) is that the issue of power is not overtly

---

12. Mojola and Wendland, "Scripture Translation in the Era of Translation Studies."

discussed. Whereas it was clear that the translators were Vuté people, there was an assumed benevolent neutrality towards my being the exegete, oftentimes the sole influence on how a biblical passage was explained. Clearly I was a white American male whose first language was English, but the conduit methodology seems to presume that despite such particularities I was able to remain objective in my understanding and exegetical instruction. In reality I was far from objective. I approached the Bible as a modern American influenced by my Protestant middle-class background. For example, demon possession was an exotic spiritual hypothesis—this differed greatly from the Vuté cultural understanding of the spirit world and its everyday impact and realities. This capacity for my cultural bias was especially true in terms of the assumed goal of literacy for access to the translation and minimal esteem towards community-based oral performances.

Literacy Bias with Workshops

To exemplify how a literacy bias played out in translation expectations, I relate below several workshops in which I was involved. The background for these workshops included the challenge of getting the Vuté community more interested in using their newly translated Scriptures. We thought that disinterest in the translated Vuté New Testament was due in part to the Vuté community's view that the scriptural texts did not address the daily concerns of the community. We decided to respond to this concern by holding a workshop in December 2000. This workshop included famed Vuté storytellers and various church leaders. For several days, numerous Vuté folktales were performed, recorded, and written down. Each tale unfailingly ended with a moral lesson that was comparable to a biblical lesson. First, a performer would present his or her story in an animated manner. The story was often accompanied by dance, song, the playing of the local "thumb piano," gestures, and a variety of vocal styles coming from the single performer who "played to the crowd." The audience responded in laughter, clapping and joining in with the performer's singing. Both the audience and the performer recognized that despite the jovial atmosphere, the folktales were communicating important moral values for Vuté communities. The next step was the writing down of the story—done by one of the few "scribes" who had mastered the tone-marking system of the language. This reduction

Introduction

to writing demonstrated the difficulty of expressing all that the performer had said or done. Instead of a multi-dimensional performance, there was a two-dimensional linear series of letters on a blackboard. The third phase for each moral lesson was the search in the newly translated New Testament (pre-publication) text. Various passages were suggested that corresponded in content to the folktale's moral instruction. Usually a single passage was chosen to represent this message and was then read aloud. The reading was often hesitant, monotone, and starkly different from the earlier performances.

The stated goal of the workshop was to demonstrate that the moral lessons included in the traditional folk stories were also contained in Scripture. This goal was met, and the participants were all satisfied with this correlation and how it also supported the value of their folktales. It was only later, after reflection, that perhaps an even more profound lesson was being presented in this workshop. The workshop was heavily biased to the written text. Comparison of the orally performed folktales and the printed New Testament permitted an assessment of the common moral lesson. The enormous disparity in liveliness in the dramatizing of these two presentations—the performance of the folktale and the reading of the scriptural text—was not commented on. Perhaps the workshop participants had grown accustomed to this disparity and understood it as the cost of literacy. Somehow the written biblical text—with the same moral lesson—elicited greater respect than the oral presentation. A literary bias seems to explain this denigration of the oral folktales. Could one imagine the biblical text being performed in like manner as the folktale? These are the same biblical texts that were at one point in history oral compositions, performed in public, in interaction with the audience. The biblical message presented with the power of the spoken word, addressing a specific occasion and an audience, had been instrumental in the transformation of the hearers in early Christianity. Could not such a method be utilized with the Vuté people? Although the community seemed uninterested in their language's written form, they eagerly performed and attended oral performances. Neither the workshop participants nor the facilitators ever considered such issues.

Another workshop—this time for songwriters—presented similar valorization of orality. In this workshop, the ultimate goal was not to have a written artifact, but rather lively music involving many communities. For several years the Catholic parish in the central town of Yoko had facilitated a songwriters' workshop for its composers throughout the region. In the spring of 1999, a joint Lutheran-Catholic workshop was held. The French priest, Father Lachenaud, who had already lived twenty-five years among the Vuté, insisted that the Vuté language be used in worship services. He had also recognized the love of music that the Vuté people demonstrate—music vastly different from European or North American hymnody. The 1999 workshop was the first opportunity for the composers to use the newly translated and tested Gospel of Luke. Four parables from this Gospel had been chosen and sent in advance to the participants who collaborated with their co-composers in four groups. Two of the participants were blind. Interestingly, this physical limitation was no handicap to their songwriting. In fact, these two blind composers were often the quickest to master the lyrics of the songs, the lyrics being a passage from Luke. At the end of the workshop, four new songs had been composed and learned by the twenty participants. These songs were recorded on audiocassettes and distributed to the participants along with a booklet of the lyrics not only of the four gospel songs but also of the dozen other original compositions that had been presented and learned by the participants.[13]

The intention of the workshop was not only the composition of new songs, but that these participants would return to their villages to teach others the new songs and that they would be performed in worship services. Indeed this is what happened in the Catholic Church.[14] Since the songwriting workshop has been going on for years in the Catholic Church, many of the gospel texts for Sunday worship are already composed into song. Most often, at the moment in the liturgy when one is to hear the Gospel, a musical performer comes forward. She or he sings through the Gospel with the congregation joining in on refrains of the text. However, these newly composed songs were also sung in other contexts. It was not unusual when I was walking through a neighborhood to see a child playing or a woman preparing a meal and to hear them sing one of the newly composed songs from Luke's Gospel. Nor was it uncommon to hear these songs being sung as people were going to or coming from their fields. As the children gathered water early in the morning

13. Curiously, it was I who offered to transcribe, print, and provide written copies of these orally-composed songs. None of the participants made this request. After all, they had already memorized the songs.

14. Use of these songs in the Lutheran church is sporadic.

Introduction

and late in the afternoon, snatches of the songs could be heard echoing from the surrounding hills. The melodies are catchy—they are Vuté melodies. And the lyrics are retained. They are words from Scripture. No books are used; no paper is held. It is the sound of the voice, weaving a tonal and melodic fabric of song in the Vuté language, a song that echoes God's Word.

One other context in which these songs were performed was during a celebration of the printing and distribution of the four Gospels of the New Testament in Vuté. On the first evening of this two-day festival an ecumenical concert was held. As the municipal football field filled with observers, the Lutheran and Catholic choirs exchanged newly composed Scripture songs. Between the choir sets, stage-show presentations based on gospel texts were presented. One of these dramas was the parable of the ten virgins. The ten storm lanterns' flames were accentuated by the evening shadows. Humor and African dance were added to this performance as the actors spoke forth the words of the gospel story. The audience of several hundred was captivated by the use of the Vuté language and the animated presentation.

The following morning during the worship service, two soloists led both choirs in that Sunday's gospel text: Mark 1:1–8. The two choirs joined in with the refrain from the prophecy of John the Baptist. This event was held to celebrate the writing and printing of part of the New Testament in the Vuté language. Curiously, the participants and the audiences commemorated this written document in a very oral fashion. Songs were sung; dramatic performances were presented. As the crowds listened and sang along with the new compositions, they were hearing and internalizing the message of the Scriptures. When the crowds witnessed the plays and participated by laughing and clapping—all the time straining to see the activities on the stage—they were witnessing in a dramatic way the message of the Scriptures.

I have described these workshops and events to demonstrate that while I was oblivious to issues of aural reception and its potential impact on New Testament translation, I was often witnessing oral performances in both traditional settings and in newly contextualized settings in the Christian church. These experiences remained detached from my translation work until I began my formal doctoral studies and began to understand the impact of written biases on New Testament and missiological studies. In time, my research into contextualization models and

New Testament methodologies that take orality seriously led me to understand how my understanding of Bible Translation has been severely handicapped by a literacy bias. This book has been an initial step into the theoretical considerations of integrating oral performance with Bible Translation.

This book encompasses several disciplines of study. To identify its methodology as interdisciplinary privileges the separation of categories of knowledge. I would prefer to understand this work as an example of the necessary breadth of research needed to address the complexities of today's world. A missiological discussion of Bible Translation requires a plethora of skills. Divisions of theology and biblical studies cannot be maintained. Textual study cannot monopolize research that requires anthropological research. In the remaining pages of this introduction I highlight major sections of each of the chapters.

Chapter Review

Chapter 1 understands Bible Translation as an expression of God's nature—especially through creation and incarnation. This theological assertion becomes the support for looking at theology—all theologies—as contextual theologies. Once the contextual nature of theologies is explained, I then present Bible Translation as contextualization. As stated above, this is an innovative alternative to past views of Bible Translation. Discussions of Bible Translation are notorious for giving facts, figures, methods, and principles. What I want to make clear is that Bible Translation is a theological activity—a contextually-shaped theological activity. This is not simply an assertion about contemporary realities, rather, I attempt throughout this early chapter to demonstrate historically the theological paradigms of the use of the Bible and the ways of doing Bible Translation. The chapter closes with an anticipation of the centrality of orality in this proposed paradigm of Bible Translation as contextualization.

Chapter 2 narrows the scope of this study geographically to the culturally-diverse continent of Africa. In this book, Africa represents the southern hemisphere in the shift of Christianity from a predominantly northern-hemisphere movement to the south. If contextualization is the model to be used for Bible Translation, then it seems important to hear

Introduction

from those in a specific context what are their interests and concerns. Fundamentally there is an agreement throughout Africa regarding the religious-social-political consequences of the relatively recent history of colonialism on the continent. From this condition we hear several expressions of contextual theologies: Translation, South African Black, Womanist, Reconstruction, Inculturation Hermeneutics, and Ordinary Readers. We will look at each of these types of contextual theologies in order to understand what the Bible is and its role in the theological methodology. These roles of the Bible vary—from the Word of God, to an instrument of colonial domination, to an object of power, to a dialogical partner with local communities. These understandings influence how the proponents of these theologies view Bible Translation. It seems that a new era of discussion is emerging that looks at Bible Translation as more than a technical exercise. In this new era, theologians seek to understand the missiological and theological implications of Bible Translation. In these discussions, we hear the voices of Africans on the subject of orality and its relation to the Bible. Their contributions confirm that any paradigm of Bible Translation as contextualization in Africa must consider the centrality of orality. The chapter closes with an initial composite presentation of what such a paradigm needs to consider:

- Bible Translation is not a neutral activity but is ideological;
- Bible Translation presupposes a theology of language that gives preferential option to local languages;
- modes of communication are not neutral—literary and oral affiliation shapes Bible Translation;
- the hermeneutics of Inculturation / Ordinary Reader, when informed by the realities of oral performance, offer Bible Translation several insights in regard to social relevancy.

Chapter 3 begins an in-depth study of issues of orality, literacy, and performance. The disciplines that inform this chapter are classical studies, cultural anthropology, sociolinguistics, and folklore studies. With a renewed interest in orality and its relation to literacy, the chapter investigates cognitive and social implications for communication media. I argue against the notion of a binary great-divide understanding of the relationship of orality to literacy. Rather, it is more helpful to understand that there are various forms of interface of these modes of communication. Sociolinguistics helps us understand the technical distinctions in communication that accompany their different strategies.

In anticipation of later chapters, I introduce the subject of ethnopoetics, a discipline that addresses how to translate and transcribe oral performances while seeking to maintain the artistic value of such verbal art. Such an endeavor recognizes that the task of translation extends beyond interlingual to intersemiotic translation. Several folklorists offer methods and tools to that end. However, a structural analysis and presentation of performances that does not engage in the social functions of such experiences is held in question. Oral performances are effective because they presuppose oral traditions that are shared by performers and audiences. Performances connect identity-shaping traditions to audiences. Each of these non-biblical researchers offers help in understanding the biblical material as transcriptions of performances that assume important community traditions.

Chapter 4 underscores that Bible Translation must be solidly rooted in biblical studies. Bible Translation efforts that neglect the centrality of biblical exegesis and theological research might demonstrate skill in linguistics but they risk capitulating to theologically unrefined agendas. Bible Translation as contextualization seeks to be as sophisticated as possible in taking into consideration both historical and current research of biblical studies. This chapter demonstrates this aim by looking closely at recent research on literacy and orality in regard to the New Testament. The interplay of media in the first century becomes the lens for looking at the New Testament composition, transmission, and reception. The results of historical research into communication of this period counter the anachronistic print bias projected by much of modern research. I argue in this current research project that although there is an interface of media, the first-century culture is accurately described as predominantly oral. I review New Testament compositions in terms of the structural and social impact that results from this context. Structurally, one finds that these texts were composed to be heard and that such compositions align themselves with rhetorical strategies. Intentional aesthetic qualities to evoke transforming emotions and allegiances reveal that the structures of New Testament compositions have social agendas. A number of gospel passages and Pauline epistles are reviewed to demonstrate both the structural and social awareness of this oral character. My own studies of Philemon and 1 Corinthians supplement such findings as extra-textual issues of social memory and identity are discussed. Biblical studies infused with insights from orality support a view of Bible Translation that is both liberating and concerned with issues of community identity.

Chapter 5 recognizes that although great progress has been made with orality studies in relation to New Testament research, there is an advantage in understanding such communication with the use of the eclectic methodology of Biblical Performance Criticism. Whereas it is true that New Testament texts were composed to be heard, it is insufficient to limit such reception to the ear. The eye is also involved as performers embodied the communication through gestures, body posture, facial expressions and proximity to the audience. Even the visual sense is not adequate to portray the experience of performance. Biblical Performance Criticism understands that the performance event also includes interaction with the audience as well as the material and social contexts surrounding performances.

This chapter argues that Biblical Performance Criticism promises positive reconfigurations of established biblical criticisms as they take into consideration the performative nature of the biblical texts. Three methodologies are discussed: Audience-response criticism (a revision of reader-response criticism), ethnopoetics, and ideological criticism. Beyond the contribution of a limited number of researchers in this regard, I present my own findings from my experiences of performing Philemon and 1 Corinthians 15:1–11 in Greek and the first half of Mark's Gospel in English. Understanding these compositions as intended for performance serves to challenge many of the established translation theories and procedures. I present some of these issues as I seek to address these challenges. These include the notion of a singular meaning and the location of meaning, the questionable validity of separating form from meaning, the challenge of scripting performances, the tension between fidelity to a source text and loyalty to a host community, and the issue of authority—whether emanating from a text or community tradition.

Chapter 6 presents a case study of the Vuté translation project. I present oral performance as a method and goal for Bible Translation. In my field research, I have worked with Vuté translators and performers in the preparation for performance of five passages from Mark's Gospel. These lively descriptions of Jesus' healings, exorcisms, and resurrections were re-translated by the experienced Vuté translators whose recent activities culminated in the publication of the Vuté New Testament. Once draft translations were ready, community-recognized performers were added to the group and these gifted artists contributed to the selection of passages for each performer along with the various contexts in which they would perform them. Later, I studied the video-recorded performances. I contrast numerous differences between the published translation and the performance translation and between the transcripts and video footage of the actual performances. There is considerable liveliness in these performances that is not evident in the published translation. Furthermore, the performers and audiences combine their efforts to create an experience centered in the biblical text that demonstrates a contextualized presentation of Mark's stories. These performances demonstrate the influence that each of us—as exegete, translator, performer, and audience—has on the translation process. The experience demonstrates a lively encounter with the Bible in which performer, audience, and text are transformed.

My aspiration in writing this book is that its research and presentation will broaden the view of Bible Translation in the twenty-first century. At the same time there is an enduring impact of oral performances that offers to enliven and engage both communities and the disciplines involved in Bible Translation. As representative of the southern hemisphere, I present the contexts of Africa, contexts that must be heeded if the Bible is to remain relevant to the challenges confronted. This book invites the reader to enter into the mutually rewarding activity of Bible Translation as contextualization.

1

TRANSLATION AS CONTEXTUALIZATION

Introduction

THIS CHAPTER IS EXTENSIVE IN THE BREADTH OF MATERIAL that it covers. Its purpose is to place Bible Translation in the larger picture of discussions of mission, contextualized theology, and a selective history of Bible Translation. More provocatively, I present in this first chapter a proposal for understanding Bible Translation within a new paradigm: Bible Translation as contextualization. It is new in the sense that discussions of Bible Translation generally have not been extended beyond evangelization or church growth. The proposed alternative paradigm responds to current global discussions of identity and ideologies and in this way models contextualization. Instead of ignoring the critiques against and indifference towards Bible Translation, this chapter engages directly such challenges. The goals of this chapter will be met if the reader begins to understand Bible Translation as a theological activity that has the capacity to mutually shape and be shaped by a community's expression of its faith in a contextually relevant way.

Bible Translation in History

When we look at the history of the world Christian movement, a subject threads its way ubiquitously throughout the centuries. Its presence is as widespread as its acknowledgment is muted. Even those who present the world Christian movement's history to us are surprised when it is pointed out to them that a consistent activity in mission is Bible Translation. Bible

Translation's sustained role throughout history, however, is by no means singular. The agents and benefactors are multiple throughout the world and their aims, methods, and results are as varied as the languages they speak. Nevertheless, those who have recognized the impact of translation in Christianity perceive themes in which these activities can be grouped. One such theme has been rarely documented. It has been with the rise of postcolonial studies that questions have been posed that permit one to ask if Bible Translation is inherently connected to a colonial agenda, supported by theologically conservative views of the Bible. In response to such inquiries and supplementary to previously perceived views of Bible Translation, I present here a missiological interpretation of Bible Translation as contextualization.[1]

The first fundamental statement, therefore, is that Bible Translation is a theological enterprise.[2] Moreover, it should be understood as a prime example of contextual theology. This activity underscores what has been argued since the 1960s: theology is always contextual. This contextual understanding calls into question a singular universal Christian theology. This change has permitted us to see that the contexts in which theology is done shape the theology. Our first task, then, is to describe this development of contextualization. Contextualization may be a recent word in theological discussions of the past generation, but the concept itself has been central to Christianity from its beginning. The concept accentuates the relationship of faith to its context, whether it is the socio-economic structures or the culture. In the twentieth century this concept has evolved in theological discussions, shaped by the ecclesial contexts of its dialogue. One way to understand this dialogue is to look more closely at several mission conferences within Christian traditions: Roman Catholic, Evangelical, and Conciliar Ecumenical. These conferences have discussed several important twentieth-century topics, including for our current purposes, the subject of Christianity's relationship to culture and the varied understandings of contextualization.

---

1. The use of different terms—inculturation, liberation, and contextualization—in this paper is determined by the specific context of the discussion. The broader, overarching term is contextualization, whereas inculturation is generally used when the reference is specific to issues of culture. A correlate to inculturation, likewise subordinate to contextualization, is liberation, used in discussions of domination.

2. Arichea, "Theology and Translation," 40.

Discussions of Contextualization: Conferences

One can say that there was a suspicious silence on the subject of culture for the first half of the twentieth century in mission conferences. It is suspicious because it seems that everybody (from the North) had a clear notion of what was meant by the term "culture." Culture at the end of the nineteenth century was a term used in the singular to denote a universal (European) culture.[3] Culture and civilization were interchangeable. In regard to mission, the goal in the early part of the twentieth century was to bring culture (civilization) to the uncivilized. The view was that the indigenous people of the South did not possess culture. Whatever way of life they did have was looked upon as innately evil. Mission meant for many the destruction of these evil practices, rituals, and customs.[4] With the beginnings of field research in anthropology in the early twentieth century, there was a turn from this classical, universal (and singular) notion of culture to an understanding of multiple cultures.[5] Although not yet a topic of mission conferences, missionaries were demonstrating a new appreciation for indigenous cultures. Their customs were not categorically dispelled as bad, but the languages and cultures were potential means of communicating the Gospel. The following paragraphs sketch the development of thinking in Roman Catholic, Evangelical, and Conciliar circles to the relationship of Christianity to its contexts.

Vatican II (1962–65) was a historic moment in Christianity. It was at Vatican II that culture began to be discussed theologically as having value, moving beyond a mono-cultural view. This followed a more optimistic view of humanity itself: "the human person . . . can achieve true and full humanity only by means of culture."[6] In regards to missionary activities, "whatever goodness is found in the minds and hearts of men

---

3. Young, "Culture and the History of Difference."

4. This of course is a generalization with many exceptions. Lamin Sanneh (in *Translating the Message*) describes how missionaries upheld indigenous culture and language through Bible Translation. Such a view of indigenous culture through translation occurred, in a sense, despite the missionaries' conscious view of culture. It should also be noted that certain missionaries valued the indigenous cultures and learned from their local structures and utilized such structures in evangelization. People such as Henry Venn and Rufus Anderson are nineteenth-century examples whose view of indigenous culture was not entirely negative; see Bevans and Schroeder, *Constants in Context*, 42.

5. Malinowski, *A Scientific Theory of Culture and Other Essays*.

6. Scherer and Bevans, *New Directions in Mission and Evangelization*, vol. 3, 6.

[sic], or in the particular cultures and customs of peoples, far from being lost is purified, is raised to a higher level and reaches its perfection for the glory of God..."[7]

This higher view of culture and a recognition of "God's preferential option for the poor" led to the Second General Conference of Latin American bishops in Medellin in 1968.[8] The Medellin conference broadened discussions of the relationship of Christianity to culture by lifting up the socio-political and economic context in Latin America as critical to understand the relationship of Christianity to culture. This was the public beginning of the rejection of the notion of a universal theology. The participants of the Medellin conference refused to accept this notion of a dominant universal theology. Not only were people to be liberated from socio-political and economic oppression, but from theological oppression as well.

Evangelicals became more and more concerned with the direction that mission discussions were going after the integration of the International Missionary Council in the World Council of Churches in 1961 in New Delhi. In 1974 many of these Evangelicals gathered together in Lausanne, Switzerland, to begin what has become known as the Lausanne Movement. In the ensuing document on the conference, the Lausanne Covenant, the reflections of Evangelicals on Christianity's relationship to culture, demonstrated a more positive, yet ambiguous view of culture. "Under God, the result will be the rise of churches deeply rooted in Christ and closely related to their culture. Culture must always be tested and judged by Scripture. Because men and women are God's creatures, some of their culture is rich in beauty and goodness. Because they are fallen, all of it is tainted with sin and some of it is demonic. The Gospel does not presuppose the superiority of any culture to another, but evaluates all cultures according to its own criteria of truth and righteousness, and insists on moral absolutes in every culture."[9]

In 1978 the newly emerging Lausanne Movement met in Willowbank, Bermuda, for a "Consultation on Gospel and Culture." At this consultation Evangelicals further laid out their understanding of the relationship of Christianity to culture. The approach proposed—based on

---

7. Ibid.
8. Scherer, *Gospel, Church and Kingdom*, 206–7.
9. Scherer and Bevans, *New Directions in Mission and Evangelization* 3, 7.

Nida's translation theory—was the Dynamic Equivalence model.[10] This model was further articulated the next year by one of the participants, Charles Kraft, in his book *Christianity in Culture: A Study in Dynamic Biblical Theologizing in Cross-Cultural Perspective*.[11] The point of similarity between these models of contextualization and translation is the concept of a transfer of an objectified source meaning into a receptor culture/language. The focus of the transfer is not the form (culturally or linguistically) but "the meaning." At this point in the discussion it is this kernel of meaning, separated from the form, transferred into another form, that I wish to emphasize. Further analysis of this translation theory will be discussed in the following chapters.

As for the Conciliar Ecumenical movement, it was not until 1973 that the subject of culture came to the focus of the Commission on World Mission and Evangelism (CWME) in Bangkok. The Southern churches of Africa, Asia, Latin America and the South Pacific were just as indignant as the Roman Catholic participants were in Medellin in 1968. The Bangkok participants were claiming that not only their personal identities but also their cultural identities were neglected in past missionary efforts. "The one faith must be at home in every context and yet it can never be identical with it . . . Christ has to be responded to in a particular way."[12] For the conference participants from the South, inculturation was a "matter of life or death."[13]

Following this meeting, the World Council of Churches (WCC) assembled in Nairobi (1975) and pushed the Bangkok discussion even further. "It maintained that the cultural context can disclose something *new* and *original* about the confession of Jesus Christ in particular confessional contexts . . . We need each other to regain the lost dimensions of confessing Christ and even to discover dimensions unknown to us before."[14] This insight underscores what was being hinted at in the Roman Catholic and Evangelical conferences: diversity of cultures is not a curse to Christianity but a richness to be celebrated. For it is when people of all cultures freely celebrate their faith in God through Christ that the

---

10. Nida and Taber, *The Theory and Practice of Translation*.
11. Kraft, *Christianity in Culture*.
12. Scherer and Bevans, *New Directions in Mission and Evangelization*, vol. 3, 8.
13. Gittins, *Life and Death Matters*; Shorter, *Toward a Theology of Inculturation*.
14. Scherer and Bevans, *New Directions in Mission and Evangelization*, vol. 3, 8–9.

mystery and beauty of the church is portrayed. The following CWME in Melbourne (1980) and the ensuing WCC assembly in Vancouver (1983) reinforced the need for peoples of all cultures to free themselves from colonial restraints in regard to worship and theological reflection. "Too many churches are still imprisoned by forms and structures inherited from other countries and are thus not free to establish such signs of the kingdom of God as to make use of their own cultural context."[15]

Scherer and Bevans note the points of consensus among the variety of conferences in each of the Christian traditions. Listed here are the points of growing consensus.[16]

1. Culture is now recognized as an indispensable component in evangelization and in the life of each local church.

2. We now agree that the uninformed and heedless equation of the gospel with Eurocentric culture in the period of colonial missions was a serious aberration.

3. Contextualization, or inculturation, is recognized as the proper way of implanting the church in an unevangelized area.

4. The gospel must be neither captive to local culture nor alienated from it. This implies a tension between gospel and culture and calls for a self-critical and prophetic stance on the part of the local Christian community.

5. Finally, the horrendous practices of identity politics and ethnic genocide, tragically misguided abuses of gospel and culture in our time, have been soundly condemned.

Whereas the above points ring true to a more accommodating stance towards the relationship of Christianity to people's cultures, they also betray several misunderstandings. As mentioned above, the subject of "culture" is often essentialized as the discussions are separated from the people who enact, reflect, and embody their cultural behaviors. Furthermore, although the noted conferences above suggest an openness to the voices from the southern hemisphere, oftentimes the approach is still "from above." This approach from above reflects a mentality of "bringing" contextualization to a specific context rather than a grassroots,

15. Ibid., 9.
16. Ibid., 12.

organic flourishing of Christianity within the local communities, from below. As a result, much of the discussions remain in the theoretical realm without concrete examples of how local communities express their contextualized theologies.

Discussions of Contextualization: Literature

Parallel to these conferences several pieces of literature from a variety of Church traditions contribute to our understanding of contextualization. Bevans' book *Models of Contextual Theology* helps to categorize the numerous approaches of contextualization by describing six models: translation, anthropology, praxis, synthetic, transcendental, and countercultural.[17] Selections of these models are discussed below.

Robert Schreiter's seminal work, *Constructing Local Theologies*, was later complemented by its sequel, *The New Catholicity*.[18] Schreiter utilizes several disciplines (generative linguistics, semiotics, anthropology, communication theory) in his presentation of his synthetic model of contextualization. The key subjects to these works include: culture, authentic Christian identity, the relation of tradition/Scripture to local theologies, syncretism, catholicity, and globalization. Schreiter's semiotic approach to culture leads him to a three-fold definition of culture: "First, culture is 'ideational,' providing a grid by which the world can be interpreted, and according to which life can be lived. Such a grid includes beliefs, values and codes of conduct; it provides the culture's basic 'worldview.' Second, culture is 'performance'; every culture has ritual ways by which its basic worldview can be expressed and through which members of the culture are bound together. Third, culture has a 'material' dimension; every people has distinctive language, food, clothing, music, etc."[19]

Schreiter comprehensively addresses the tensions that are noted by all those writing about contextual theologies. There is a balance between a local theology being particular to a given culture and yet still considered a continuation of Christianity. This is where the notions of

---

17. Bevans, *Models of Contextual Theology*.

18. Schreiter, *Constructing Local Theologies*; Schreiter, *The New Catholicity*.

19. Schreiter, *The New Catholicity*, 29. Semiotics has been an approach to culture in anthropological circles since the mid-1960's. Examples of such work include: Turner, *The Forest of Symbols*; Geertz, *The Interpretation of Cultures*.

tradition/Scripture, syncretism and catholicity are addressed. Schreiter presents church tradition/Scripture as an example of earlier contextualized theologies. Although he admits that there is something particular to Scripture, Schreiter does not insist on making Scripture the sole criteria of a local theology's authenticity. Catholicity (from the Greek *kata holon*—"according to wholeness") is an important dialogical partner with inculturation. Authentic, culturally relevant theology must also somehow fit into the whole; it must be catholic. This balance is difficult enough without taking into consideration the broader backdrop of globalization. It is this challenge of globalization that motivated Schreiter to write the sequel to constructing local theologies.[20] Local theologies are also a part of the larger global network now. This globalization process risks obliterating the particularities of cultures and, as a result, local theologies. Yet, at the same time, local cultures cannot avoid the fact that they are a part of the global market, global communication, global Christianity, and so on.

In *Life and Death Matters*, Anthony Gittins begins his discussion of inculturation as "the way in which God's message is communicated with humanity, given the twin assertions of God's transcendence and humanity's cultural and linguistic variety."[21] With a thorough understanding of culture's dynamic nature, Gittins continues his definition of inculturation as "the way in which particular communities or cultures receive the revelation of the Gospel of salvation in Jesus Christ, then assimilate it and express it."[22] The result of such inculturation is not limited to expressions of worship or some vague notion of "the Gospel," but "inculturation must be nothing less than the transformation of everything."[23] Gittins develops an analogical examination of inculturation with generative linguistics. This serves to differentiate surface-level changes in behavior with deep-structure transformations.[24] Furthermore, these transformations occur within the core values of local communities' cultures as they are challenged and enhanced by Christian faith. "[T]he life of faith and worship is not simply a copying or reiteration of past forms but the creation of something new, meaningful, comprehensible, and enlightening."[25]

20. Ibid., xii.
21. Gittins, *Life and Death Matters*, 20.
22. Ibid., 25.
23. Ibid., 26.
24. Gittins, "Beyond Liturgical Inculturation," 53.
25. Ibid.

Gittins insists that inculturation should not be co-opted into another programmatic initiative: "Inculturation happens not when 'faith is inserted', but when faith is embodied—incarnated and expressed in the life of the faithful."[26]

Evangelical reflections on contextualization have remained similar to its initial statements presented at the conference in Willowbank in 1978. Most published literature has remained very close to Kraft's book on the Dynamic Equivalence model.[27] Paul Hiebert as an anthropologist-missionary has been instrumental in helping Evangelicals to appreciate the tools of anthropology for the purpose of mission. He has written numerous articles as well as an anthropological textbook used by many Evangelical schools. The article I wish to focus on, "Critical Contextualization," demonstrates the great concern Evangelicals have with remaining faithful (to the Scriptures) and thus avoiding syncretism.[28] Hiebert cautions against extremes of contextualization that, in his opinion, can lead to syncretism. This term is understood by Hiebert as heresy. Historically, the challenge of authentic Christianity in regard to inculturation has been syncretism. Whereas anthropologists view syncretism as a neutral result of acculturation—cultures encountering each other—it has been predominantly treated as taboo in the twentieth century among most Christian theologians.[29] Schreiter challenges this understanding, however, by stating that all theologies are syncretistic to some degree.[30] This assertion permits discussions of syncretism to be approached without a priori negative assessment.

In a recent WCC document under the section "Called to incarnate the gospel within each culture" is a grouping of eleven paragraphs that are understood to present the WCC's view of the relationship of gospel to culture.[31] The first section (par. 45–47) reviews the statements on culture since the Bangkok conference in 1973, continuing on to the Canberra

---

26. Ibid., 70.

27. Kraft, *Christianity in Culture*. A more recent presentation of this model is found in Shaw and Van Engen, *Communicating God's Word in a Complex World*.

28. Hiebert, "Critical Contextualization," 104–12.

29. Stewart and Shaw, *Syncretism/Anti-syncretism*.

30. These discussions are followed up in: Schineller, "Inculturation and Syncretism," 50–53; Schreiter, "Defining Syncretism," 50–53.

31. *Mission and Evangelism in Unity Today,* under section C: "Mission Paradigms for Our Times," sub-section 3. http://www.wcc-coe.org/wcc/what/mission/m-e-in-unity.pdf.

(1991) and Salvador (1996) conferences. Each of these paragraphs reiterates the centrality of culture in considering religion. Paragraphs 48–51 discuss the incarnational theological support for inculturation. As well, there is a clear voice that not all of cultural expressions are good; certain aspects of culture are harmful to the people of that culture. Following the principles of inculturation, with concern for identity of particular cultures, one culture's identity should never be lifted up to the suppression of another's identity. Paragraphs 52–53 discuss the variety of ways that the gospel enters into a culture along with the ways that it is displayed within a culture. In this view, inculturation into a community can take many forms; evangelistic approaches to other cultures also must take a variety of forms, sensitive to the context. A holistic gospel—avoiding dualistic concepts—for example, spiritual vs. material—must be presented to cultures.

The final two paragraphs (54–55) discuss the issue of syncretism. After giving several notions of syncretism, a guiding principle is stated: "The quest then is whether a specific inculturation helps or hinders faithful witness to the gospel in its fullness." The challenge of syncretism had already elicited in Salvador the need for an intercultural hermeneutics. There is then listed certain criteria (stated previously in the report from Salvador) for "assessing . . . the appropriateness of particular contextual expressions of the gospel." These include: faithfulness to God's self-disclosure in the totality of the scriptures; commitment to a lifestyle and action in harmony with the reign of God; openness to the wisdom of the communion of saints across space and time; relevance to the context.

The point that I suggest the reader keep in mind from the presentation above of various church conferences and literature discussions of contextualization is that people express their Christian faith in diverse ways as they are shaped by their contexts. People involved in God's Mission lift up the richness of diverse cultures and anticipate discovering God actively participating in these varied cultures. Whereas there are differences of opinion as to the extent and ways that contextualization ought to occur and still remain faithful to the Scriptures and Christian tradition, all church traditions recognize the central importance of contextualization.

Translation as Contextualization

Contextualization and the Bible

The most direct example of contextualization and the Bible is to note that the Bible itself is already contextualized. The individual authors lived and composed in specific situations and addressed specific issues of their day. In the New Testament this contextual effect is seen with the four Gospels. Each of the gospel writers presented contextually their story of Jesus. However, even with one single author—the apostle Paul—we see a variety of ways in which he contextually communicated, taking into consideration his audience and their backgrounds. We need look no further than the Bible to view a contextualization of God's message.[32]

A critical difference between a translation model and an anthropological model of inculturation is based upon the starting point. As indicated above, the translation model starts with Scripture in order to exegete the message to be translated into the culture. With the anthropological method, the starting point is the culture, to understand the "web of meaning" within the host culture. Another way of articulating the difference is that the translation model intends to *bring* God's good news to the culture; the anthropological model seeks to *discover* God's good news within the culture. Such a distinction reveals each model's view of culture: corrupted by sin (translation model), reflection of God's image (anthropological model). Each model has its strengths and weaknesses. For example, the anthropological model by itself has difficulty in critiquing culture due to the relativistic nature of the model.

On the one hand, the role of the Bible in the translation model, as primarily supported by Evangelicals by means of Dynamic Equivalence theory, would suggest that Bible Translation is by necessity limited to a conservative understanding of contextualization. On the other hand, the anthropological model's starting point of culture holds Scripture as subordinate to culture. This would suggest that the contributions of Bible Translation to contextualization are peripheral. Are these two roles the only ones available to Bible Translation in regard to contextualization? Andrew Walls, one of the most influential missiologists of the twentieth century, states: "Bible translation as a process is thus both a reflection of the central act on which the Christian faith depends and a concretization of the commission which Christ gives his disciples. Perhaps no other

---

32. This view of the contextual Bible is presented in Shaw and Van Engen, *Communicating God's Word in a Complex World*; Rhoads, *The Challenge of Diversity*.

FROM ORALITY TO ORALITY

specific activity more clearly represents the mission of the Church."[33] Walls is referring to the central act of the incarnation as a theological depiction of translation. He in turn describes Christianity as "infinitely translatable."[34] How has such an assertion played out in the history of the world Christian movement?

Historical Patterns of Bible Translation

Here I present two patterns for the early eras of Bible Translation. This notion of missiological patterning in conjunction with Bible Translation was first suggested by Andrew Walls. Two major models of Scripture use have been followed throughout history: that of Wulfila, who developed an alphabet and translated the Bible into Gothic and also trained an elite class to read it; and that of Patrick, who required believers to use the Scriptures in Latin, not their vernaculars. For many centuries it was Patrick's pattern that prevailed, however, in the last century the shift has been towards that of Wulfila."[35] Walls' patterning distinguishes either the use of the vernacular or the use of a second, regional language that is not the mother-tongue of the local community. This is a helpful linguistic distinction. Yet, what are the missiological aims and impact of such patterns?

Cyril and Methodius (echoing Walls' description of Wulfila) demonstrate one pattern.[36] They developed linguistic tools—the alphabet—to translate the Scriptures and other Church materials into a language that was spoken in every-day life by the community. Initially this community was not Christian, and so such endeavors by Cyril and Methodius were understood to be evangelistic in nature. This pattern becomes predominant in the modern missionary era with the Bible Society movement and continues to the present. A second pattern can be described as an activity of church growth, in which an already existing Christian community benefits from Christian materials in a language that is not necessarily their own. It is exemplified by Latin and Syriac—two languages which

---

33. Walls, "The Translation Principle in Christian History," 28.
34. Ibid., 22.
35. Stine, *Bible Translation and the Spread of the Church*, viii.
36. A summary of Cyril and Methodius' activities can be found in Irvin and Sunquist, *History of the World Christian Movement*, 367–69.

were at an early point the vernacular of the local community.[37] However, over time, these languages became the official church languages for the West and East, respectively. These languages soon became the language of Scripture and liturgy for people whose first language was different from what was being spoken in the church context.[38] The purported benefit to such a pattern was the unity—or catholicity—that was exemplified by the fact that one could travel a great distance and still participate in a liturgy that was recognizable. These languages often take on the role of "sacred language." They are perceived as having inherent religious value, a language of God.[39] The discussions above concerning the tension between a universal theology and local particular theologies are reflected in this issue of language.

The second pattern (sacred language) does not insist on the use of the vernacular in translation. It may involve those who have learned the language of translation, but their mother tongue is not the focus of translation. This pattern distances itself from the incarnational nature of Christianity. In the cases of Latin and Syriac, they became a dominating language over the vernacular.[40] Thus the issue of domination is introduced not only into Christian history but also, more particularly, into that of Bible Translation. Such linguistic domination has been described by the African novelist, Ngũgĩ Wa Thiong'o. Through several of his books, most notably in *Decolonizing the Mind: The Politics of Language in African*

---

37. By 400 CE the entire New Testament was translated into Syriac (with most of the Old Testament)—known as the Peshitta. Syriac became the *lingua franca* for the Eastern Church; see ibid., 277–78.

38. "For nearly a thousand years, the Vulgate was used as the recognized text of Scripture throughout western Europe. It also became the basis of pre-Reformation vernacular Scriptures, such as Wycliffe's English translation in the fourteenth century, as well as the first printed Bibles in German (1466), Italian (1471), Catalán (1478), Czech (1488), and French (1530)." Metzger, *The Bible in Translation*, 35. See also Orlinsky and Bratcher, *A History of Bible Translation and the North American Contribution*.

39. Such a view is similar to an Islamic understanding of Arabic. The distinction between Islam's view of language and that of Christianity has been thoroughly argued by Lamin Sanneh in *Translating the Message*. However, a similarity between the two is recognized in this second pattern, when a non-vernacular language becomes the religious language of a community and potentially a language of domination.

40. It should be understood that there are language situations where a local community has additional access sociolinguistically to a trade or regional language, or a "language of wider communication." The use of such a language is different than an oppressive refusal to acknowledge a minority language, thus forcing those speakers to communicate in a dominant language.

Literature, he describes the enforced use of the dominant (colonizing) language as "the cultural bomb."[41] Language is understood as synecdoche to culture; that is in this case, language represents the larger world of culture.[42] "Language, any language, has a dual character: it is both a means of communication and a carrier of culture."[43] Ngũgĩ understands language as affiliated with identity (a central issue of contextualization as well). "The effect of a cultural bomb is to annihilate a people's belief in their names, in their languages, in their environment, in their heritage of struggle, in their unity, in their capacities and ultimately in themselves."[44]

There are two decisive features that distinguish the two recognized patterns of biblical translation: first, the use of biblical translation in the context of a Christian community (or as a means of evangelism to non-Christians); second, the use of the vernacular language or a dominating language in translation. My questions here echo the issues of contextualization. Are there only two ways of understanding the activity of Bible Translation? Is Bible Translation only to be understood as a tool of evangelism or as a means for edification? An accompanying question: is Bible Translation unilateral in its benefits? Must the advantage of such endeavors only be to those who receive the Bible in their language? Could it not be that those who appropriate their vernacular language translation can offer new insights into Christian theology, directly as a result of such translation work? Translation then would become a mutual conversation of Christians from the North and South with the Scriptures. Such questions and assertions suggest that we need to understand how a biblical translation is used in missiological endeavors.

Translation as Mission[45]

Most discussions about Bible Translation focus on the statistics of languages in which Scriptures are translated or the histories of translation projects are portrayed somewhat neutrally. In this section I want to present a more theologically-toned reflection of Bible Translation. In doing

41. Ngũgĩ, *Decolonizing the Mind*.
42. Appiah, "Topologies of Nativism," 55.
43. Ngũgĩ, *Decolonizing the Mind*, 13.
44. Ibid., 3.
45. Taken from Smalley's book, *Translation as Mission*.

so, I will incorporate conversation partners from the fields of historical theology, postcolonialism, and anthropology, as I pursue a missiology of Bible Translation for the twenty-first century.

As background, I mentioned in the contextualization section how the Evangelical *Lausanne Movement's* position with contextualization was articulated by one of its participants, Charles Kraft. In accordance with such an approach, the translator remains suspicious of the culture and holds to the critical importance of beginning with the Scriptures as the ultimate point of departure. Although a greater appreciation has been shown for culture and its contribution to theology, authors such as Kraft and Hiebert have continued to place the starting point of inculturation with Scripture. Each of these has considered the study of the "target" culture as important, but in the end the process involves dynamic translation.[46] The evaluation of whether such inculturation is acceptable depends on its faithfulness to the Scriptures. Critical also to this process of translation is the role of the outsider—to assure fidelity. There are several points that problematize this interpretation of translation as mission. There seems to be a naïve acceptance of Scripture as beyond cultural influence itself.[47] Kraft's view of Scripture permits such theologians to make Scripture as the unique point of departure, and the ultimate judge to a theology's fidelity. Such an approach places the translator or the expatriate-outsider theologian in the role of determining, by their understanding of Scripture, whether other theologies are acceptable. In the end, this approach to translation as mission is unilateral in its communication of theology. It marginalizes the local cultures and communities who ought to be recognized as the agents of theologizing; it also ultimately excludes the local communities from determining the acceptability of a theology, reserving that role to the outsider theologian.

People are questioning what appear to be magnanimous gestures of Bible Translation. Whereas Bible translators have insisted on the objective nature of both translation methods and Bible Translation in mission, this objectivity is questioned from postcolonial studies. Gosnell Yorke, a former UBS translation consultant, has stated, "Bible translation, to a

---

46. Hiebert, "Critical Contextualization"; Gilliland, *The World among Us*; Shaw and Van Engen, *Communicating God's Word in a Complex World*.

47. This contextual variation is evident in the Synoptic gospels. It is even more apparent with one sole author, St. Paul. This one individual contextualizes his messages according to his audiences; see, Rhoads, *The Challenge of Diversity*.

large extent, is ideologically driven."[48] Randall Bailey and Tina Pippen are editors of the *Semeia* volume titled "Race, Class, and the Politics of Biblical Translation."[49] The editors state clearly their position: "When evangelism and conversion are goals of translation, the claim has been that these goals are theological and not political. The articles in this volume reveal how 'translation as evangelism' functioned ideologically as a tool of colonization."[50] Addressing the false notion that translation is an objective activity, they continue, "To argue that the translation process is objective and that either Dynamic Equivalence or formal equivalence are not guided by these ideological sets, but are two forms of objectivity, is untenable in the face of this evidence."[51] One of the contributors, Robert Carroll, states that "the fundamental problem is to be found in the practice of 'dynamic equivalence' translation."[52] He explains, "Every translation of the Bible is an attempt to provide as accurate a translation as possible *within the constraints set by the prevailing ideology of the group translating and publishing the Bible.*"[53]

Perhaps the most prevalent voice heard on this subject is R. S. Sugirtharajah.[54] His position in terms of translation is clear: "Translation, thus, is more than a mere linguistic enterprise. It is a site for promoting unequal relationships among languages, races, religions, and peoples. It brings into focus the manipulative position of a translator."[55] Sugirtharajah adds: "By privileging written texts as the valid medium for sacred communication, missionary translations devalued the orality and rhetoric of hearing. In trying to render word for word, translators failed to take note of the function the words had in Indian thinking."[56]

Sugirtharajah has written extensively on biblical studies from a postcolonial perspective. As a result, he has also discussed the role of Bible Translation, dedicating several chapters to the subject in *Postcolonial*

---

48. Yorke, "Bible Translation in Anglophone Africa and her Diaspora," 153; Yorke, "Hearing the Politics of Peace in Ephesians," 113–27.

49. Bailey and Pippen, "Race, Class, and the Politics of Biblical Translation."

50. Ibid., 3.

51. Ibid., 5.

52. Carroll, "Cultural Encroachment and Bible Translation," 47.

53. Ibid., italics original.

54. Sugirtharajah, "Textual Cleansing," 7–19.

55. Ibid., 9.

56. Ibid., 12.

Criticism and Biblical Interpretation.[57] Sugirtharajah understands Bible Translation as "implicated in diverse imperialist projects."[58] His critiques include the missionaries' view of these languages as exotic but deficient and their efforts to domesticate and reshape them to both European and biblical standards. He suggests that missionaries held an ambivalent approach as both "dismissing and embracing."[59] However, I think Sugirtharajah understands the effects of translation as unilateral, where "the translators remedy was to convert and baptize these languages into 'a Christian sense.'"[60] Such a comment portrays languages as inherently static rather than understanding the dynamics people of adjusting language to varied contexts. Furthermore, it disempowers the indigenous language communities, suggesting that they are impotent to shape foreign concepts to their own categories. Comprehending Bible Translation as solely an evangelistic tool, Sugirtharajah pleads, "Biblical translation has to move beyond the narrow understanding of mission as a simple revival of a textualized biblical faith that is intolerant, smug and superior."[61] Anticipating an important component of my proposed paradigm for Bible Translation, he problematizes the dominance of biblical languages: "The fundamental fault of translators is that they preserve the state of established biblical languages instead of allowing these languages to be powerfully affected by languages other than the biblical ones . . . In other words, biblical languages have to be transformed and rendered more open to the claims of other languages and cultures."[62] Opposed to translation that supports the status quo, Sugirtharajah presents his aim of translation: "In the postcolonial context, the role of translation is to subvert meanings, grammatical arrangements, and linguistic practices."[63]

Such critiques echo anthropological critiques of the missionary movement in general. Perhaps the most extensive anthropological examination of issues of colonialism and Christian mission comes from John and Jean Comaroff's two-volume set *Of Revelation and Revolution.*[64] The

57. Sugirtharajah, *Postcolonial Criticism and Biblical Interpretation.*
58. Ibid., 156.
59. Ibid., 161.
60. Ibid., 160.
61. Ibid., 172.
62. Ibid., 172–73.
63. Ibid., 177.
64. Comaroff and Comaroff, *Of Revelation and Revolution*, 2 vols.

FROM ORALITY TO ORALITY

Comaroffs describe a missionary collusion with colonial efforts in southern Africa, specifically with the southern Tswana, and the Tswana's own resistance efforts to such colonization. Amid such theses as Christian mission propagating a hegemonic, universalizing ethos with the aim of a worldwide Christian commonwealth, are the particularities of issues accompanying Bible Translation efforts with the southern Tswana. Missionaries comprehended the crucial importance of indigenous languages in the communication of their message as the "key to the civilizing mission."[65] In so doing they accepted that such languages were able to convey the meanings that they wished to communicate. Placing this value on the vernacular was coupled with the technology of literacy. The Comaroffs describe this importance of literacy as exemplary of the "textualized faith . . . of early Christianity."[66] In this way, "the written language became a sine qua non of Christianity and civilization."[67] At the same time, missionaries recognized how language with the southern Tswana had an illocutionary force, a use of language that under certain circumstances changes reality, a function that portrays speech as having "the magical power of words."[68]

Perhaps the most sustained counterargument to the Comaroffs and others who view Christianity as an accomplice of colonization is Lamin Sanneh. Sanneh's research has sought to counter such a negative portrayal of missionaries in general. In particular, he argues that biblical translation has been beneficial to receiving communities. He accuses the Comaroffs and others of holding a priori assumptions about missionary motives, assumptions that cannot be supported by empirical facts. To counter this, Sanneh's research involves the historical impact of the Bible Translation enterprise on cultures—African in particular. Such research looks at Africa in terms of its first contact with Christian missionaries and their endeavors to translate the Scriptures. Sanneh has shown in several of his books and articles the central value placed on languages and their cultures. Such high value is demonstrated in accepting these languages as viable means of God's revelation. Furthermore, in discovering already existing names for God in these languages, Bible translators

---

65. Ibid., vol. 1, 215.

66. Ibid.

67. Ibid., 223.

68. Ibid., 226. This view of language as event is supported by speech-act theory; Austin, *How to Do Things with Words*.

trusted God's Spirit when the speakers of these languages began working out their understanding of God in relation to the Scriptures and their own traditions. Sanneh has written extensively on the cultural impact of the tremendous effort of Bible Translation. Countering the general anthropological critique of missionaries as destroyers of culture, Sanneh argues that these cultures were enriched through vernacular translations. Such enrichment came about often despite the missionary's own cultural ethnocentrism. "The missionary sponsorship of Bible translation became the catalyst for profound changes and developments in language, culture, and ethnicity, changes that invested ethnic identity with the materials for a reawakened sense of local identity."[69]

Sanneh claims that Africans were not simply recipients of Christianity but that they were themselves agents of change. In conjunction with this cultural impact of Bible Translation, Sanneh indicates its theological effects. "Bible translation has thus helped to bring about a historic shift in Christianity's theological center of gravity by pioneering a strategic alliance with local conceptions of religion."[70] It is in regard to this notion of indigenous theology where Sanneh spends considerable time presenting examples of the use of indigenous names for God. In his view, such an approach automatically created a climate for indigenous theology. Sanneh is not proposing that there are no distinctions between Christianity and indigenous religions; rather, he argues, an approach that uses indigenous language and categories will be more indigenously acceptable. "Bible translation enabled Christianity to break the cultural filibuster of its Western domestication to create movements of resurgence and renewal that transformed the religion into a world faith."[71]

Throughout Sanneh's presentation, we begin to understand an alternative way of viewing Bible Translation. This alternative paradigm will not limit the subject of Bible Translation to facts and figures about the people and languages who have participated in translation. Following Gerald West's suggestion, there is a deeper understanding of translation: "Translation in this sense is much more than a technical discipline; it is a metaphor for forms of inculturation."[72]

---

69. Sanneh, "Domesticating the Transcendent," 70.
70. Sanneh, *Whose Religion is Christianity?* 10.
71. Ibid., 130.
72. West, "Mapping African Biblical Interpretation, 46.

FROM ORALITY TO ORALITY

Typology of Theologies

I follow up on West's suggestion above by pursuing a theological foundation for an alternative paradigm of Bible Translation in this section. Bevans and Schroeder introduce a typology of theologies into their analysis of the history of mission as well as their articulation of their proposed theology of mission for the early twenty-first century.[73] This typology is argued to be evident from the beginning of the Church and is played out in historical contexts up to the present day. Bevans and Schroeder utilize two theologians, Justo González and Dorothy Sölle, to distinguish between the three historical typologies.[74] Whereas González presents these theologies from an historical perspective by focusing much of his presentation on early Christianity, Sölle reflects from a systematic theological view with an emphasis on a modern (nineteenth-twentieth century) perspective, although she acknowledges these theologies are lived out throughout the centuries. The following brief summary of their findings begins with González's summary of the three theologies. Next is a review of how both authors present each theology's use and view of Scripture.

González presents three theologies that are linked to individual second-century theologians and schools. The person affiliated with type A (Sölle's "Orthodox") is Tertullian, who was located in Carthage. Significant to this theology are the importance of Roman law and the denigration of the Greek philosophy in relation to Christianity. Curiously, Tertullian's thinking is markedly shaped by Stoic philosophy, a philosophy whose "final goal of wisdom is to discover the law of the universe and to live according to it."[75] Type B theology (Sölle's "Liberalism") is associated with Origen and the school of thought of Alexandria. One of the predominant features of Alexandria is the Hellenistic influence in each sphere of life. For Origen the Platonic philosophical pursuit of immutable truth and a renewed moralism guided his articulation of his reflections on Christianity. The knowledge of such truth "does not come to us through sensory perception, but from two sources in agreement with each other: reason and revelation."[76] From the school of Antioch

---

73. Bevans and Schroeder, *Constants in Context*.
74. González, *Christian Thought Revisited*; Sölle, *Thinking about God*.
75. González, *Christian Thought Revisited*, 6.
76. Ibid., 11.

and Asia Minor comes Type C (Sölle's "radical/liberation") theology which is connected to Irenaeus. González presents this theology as the oldest of the three theologies. Distanced from the context of platonic philosophy and Roman law, this theology focuses on perceiving God's acts in the events of history. Such a theology is interested in the daily life of Christians and how their faith interacts with the institutions of culture (politics, economy, religion, and so on).

Type A theology uses Scripture, as did Tertullian, like a legal text, in the fashion of a lawyer. It seeks proof texts that make clear what God expects of humanity. In this way it is seen as a moral code. González notes Scripture's twofold function in Type A theology: "(a) as a proof of Christian orthodoxy (which is the principal use of prophecy in this context); and (b) as a guidebook to tell us what we are to do in order to please God and reach heaven."[77] Sölle goes on to describe this approach as "literalism" which is a consequence of one's understanding of the origin of the Bible as revelation "remote from the relativity of history and lived in an absolute sphere."[78]

Origen's Type B use of Scripture follows the Alexandrian tradition of Philo's allegorical interpretation of the Hebrew Scriptures. Although a text could be interpreted literally, a more enlightened approach "seeks to discover a symbolic meaning in a text."[79] Following Type B's theological premises as indicated by Sölle—"the validity of science, the historicity of religion, and the unity of culture and religion"[80]—one's view of Scripture begins with historical criticism of the text. In the liberal view of Scripture, "the experience of scientific and historical truth stands over against the revealed truth of scripture."[81]

In Type C's view, Scripture is taken seriously as a narrative of God's participation in history. Given this historical view, González presents three aspects of Type C's scriptural hermeneutics: 1) the events in the Bible are taken as real (without allegorizing them); 2) those passages which are intentionally allegorical ought to be interpreted by the larger non-allegorical context; 3) although the events recounted in the Bible are

---

77. Ibid., 51.
78. Sölle, *Thinking about God*, 23.
79. González, *Christian Thought Revisited*, 53.
80. Sölle, *Thinking about God*, 13.
81. Ibid., 29.

real, they have a meaning which goes beyond themselves.[82] Type C theology understands "the historical and socio-historical context of the Bible is fundamental."[83] The key perspective in this liberation view of Scripture is that of "the poor" and that Scripture is written for the poor. "We must read the Bible in the context of the poor, in the light of its effect among the poor and the way in which it changes the life of the poor."[84]

These studies are complementary in presenting from the second century to the present three theologies that have shaped Christianity and that in turn have been shaped by their various contexts. If Type C/liberation theology has been muffled throughout history, it is clear that since the 1960s it has developed into a predominant view for many theologians and Christians. Nevertheless Type A theology (demonstrated by Evangelicals) and Type B theology (still recognized in Academia) continue to offer their views.

I propose that Type C theology offers an alternative understanding of Bible Translation. Such a proposal allows for Bible Translation to be understood neither as simply a conservative translation model of contextualization nor as a liberal peripheral element to the anthropological model. The third option is to see Bible Translation as a means of liberation. Such liberation comes about by the theological praxis of the Scriptures being translated not only *into* indigenous languages but also into its opposite: *from* the indigenous cultures. These translations contribute to Christianity's understanding of God's activity in the world, an activity of liberation. This liberation comes about culturally and theologically, resulting in an affirmation of the identity of people as God's people.

A New Paradigm: Translation as Liberation

In their parallel work of theological typologies, Sölle and González discuss the uses of the Bible and the different theological perspectives. From the perspective of type C, Scripture is connected to history and is committed to the liberation of the poor. "The poor" are defined as those who are oppressed. In type C theology, mission is approached through the presentation of God's rule as proclaimed by Jesus and his ministry.

---

82. González, *Christian Thought Revisited*, 56.
83. Sölle, *Thinking about God*, 38.
84. Ibid., 39.

Translation as Contextualization

Jesus does not define God's rule; instead, he demonstrates it through riddles, healings and exorcisms, and his ministry of inclusivity. We are given insight into Jesus' view of God's rule as we study Jesus' behavior in the Gospels.[85] To remain faithful to the spirit of Jesus' ministry, such a dialogue ought to be in the language that is most accessible to the hearer or reader. As type C theology seeks the liberation of those who are oppressed, it seems to me that linguistic oppression has been overlooked. The "world languages" of Europe determine to a great extent how theology is done and which questions are posed. With ninety percent of the world's population having at least a portion of Scripture translated into their languages, the ten percent minority remains significantly neglected. This ten percent includes over four hundred million people and more than two-thirds of the world's languages.[86] From a linguistic perspective, these minority-language speakers are the poor. Not only are they generally poor socially, economically, and politically, but they are oppressed religiously by the confines of theological reflection that is in languages not their own. Bible Translation in these minority languages becomes a means of liberation for these people. "The spectacle of a translated Bible, proceeding as divine oracle in the accents of native speech, being at the same time novel and patriotic, empowered victim and marginal populations."[87]

González and Sölle admit that Type C/Liberation theology has not always been welcomed throughout history. In fact, it appears to have gone underground for extended periods. Nevertheless, it has been a consistent thread of theology since the beginning of Christianity. By the 1960s Type C theology was again (re)surfacing. The subject pertinent to our present discussion is Bible Translation. I am arguing that although Type A and B theologies have been active in the history of Bible Translation; there is a third theology which is also an important component of biblical translation. Can this be seen in history?

Glimpses are recognized with the archetype of Type C, Irenaeus, who "warned that it was now difficult to write in Greek because he had

---

85. These indicators for understanding God's Reign are presented in Bevans and Schroeder, *Constants in Context*, 305–22.

86. These statistics are taken from a web site of Wycliffe Bible Translators, USA: http://www.wycliffe.org/wbt-usa/trangoal.htm, accessed October 27, 2006.

87. Sanneh, "Domesticating the Transcendent," 85.

been preaching so long in the local language."[88] In the eighth century a bishop in China, Adam, was not only translating Christian literature into Chinese, but he also participated in the translation of Buddhist *Sutras*. "[I]t appears that for the purpose of communicating the Christian Message, and for the deepening of their own faith-life in the Messiah, they employed Buddhist terms, expressions, and symbols."[89]

A century later, one can perceive a similar liberative use of the vernacular. "One of the truly remarkable pieces of medieval Christian literature is the Heliand (Savior), a tale of the Gospel written by a poetic monk who attempted to let the Gospel 'sing' in the culture of the Saxons."[90] "He rewrote and reimagined the events and words of the Gospel as if they had taken place and been spoken in his own country and time, in the chieftain society of a defeated people, forcibly Christianized by Charlemagne: the Saxons."[91] The Heliand offers several insights not only into the inculturation of the biblical narratives, but also into a promising reconstitution of medium. This work was heard rather than read in a contextually appropriate location. "The audience of the Heliand was probably to be found in mead hall and monastery. The epic poem seems not to have been designed for use in the church as a part of official worship, but is intended to bring the Gospel home to the Saxons in a poetic environment in order to help the Saxons cease their vacillation between their warrior-loyalty to the old gods and to the 'mighty Christ.'"[92]

The most dramatic historic example I suggest is the Protestant Reformation of the sixteenth century. The prevailing Latin language was not only dominating Church activities, but was also determining the categories of theology. Martin Luther's translation of the Bible into German was an act of linguistic liberation. It ushered in an era in which the German language—as inspired by the biblical translation—began to present fresh categories of theology. "Every new step in biblical discovery or translation seemed to be the occasion if not the cause of another development in Protestantism."[93] "The victory of Protestant Christians and Luther's

---

88. Norris, *Christianity*, 19.

89. Bevans and Schroeder, *Constants in Context*, 105–8; cf. Irvin and Sunquist, *History of the World Christian Movement*, 320.

90. Norris, *Christianity*, 98.

91. *The Heliand: The Saxon Gospel*, trans. Murphy.

92. Ibid., xvi.

93. Escobar, "The Role of Translation in Developing Indigenous Theologies," 85.

Translation as Contextualization

German Bible in much of the region was a high water mark in the development of the German language. Luther's Bible can be studied not only as an important religious document, but also as the printed book that created the modern German mother tongue."[94]

Such a linguistic reformation is noticeable as well in English. John Wycliffe is accredited with the translation of the first complete English Bible. "Just as Martin Luther's version had very great influence upon the German language, so too the Wycliffe Bible was well received by the people and influenced greatly the development of the English language."[95] William Tyndale's translation of much of the Bible from the original Hebrew and Greek (Wycliffe translated from the Latin) demonstrated a translation that was "free, bold, and idiomatic."[96] Each of these translations, along with several others, was a precursor to the King James Authorized Version. Fifty biblical scholars worked on the KJV translation from 1604–1611. "Its grandeur of phrasing and the deep slow music of its rhythms—far more evident here than in any Bible the sixteenth century had produced—were conscious embodiments of regal glory."[97] The story of this English Bible is interwoven with the shaping of not only the English language and the nation of England but also with the British Empire.[98]

Another way to understand this third model of Bible Translation is to look at how contemporary liberation theologians are using the Bible. Curiously, the Latin American emergence of liberation theology was in a context using the language of the conquistador. Similarly, Black theology is articulated in the language of their oppressor. These modern expressions of Type C theology, therefore, differ greatly from Reformers' use of vernacular Bible translations. Samuel Escobar, a leading Evangelical theologian, comments on this: "Like the existence of living forms of Christianity, the promise of a new indigenous theology is closely linked to the availability of Scripture in the language of the people."[99] Yet, Escobar waits in expectation: "It is yet to be seen in these lands what is going to be the effect of Bible Translation on the large native communities that

---

94. Norris, *Christianity*, 153.
95. Metzger, *The Bible in Translation*, 57.
96. Ibid., 59.
97. Nicolson, *God's Secretaries*, xiv.
98. McGrath, *In the Beginning*; Sugirtharajah, *The Bible and Empire*.
99. Escobar, "The Role of Translation in Developing Indigenous Theologies," 88.

have kept a singular cultural identity in spite of centuries of Iberian and Westernized domination."[100] "I think there are reasons to believe that the rise of indigenous churches and indigenous theologies, facilitated by the existence of Scripture in the Andean languages, will have a deep and lasting social impact."[101]

A New Paradigm: Translation as Inculturation

Inculturation represents a second component, with liberation, in this paradigmatic shift of Bible Translation as contextualization. "Incarnation is translation" is a forceful theological statement about translation.[102] God's Word is articulated in human form. The effects to such an event are mutual: Christ's becoming human affects humanity, and humanity has influenced Christ. The incarnation-translation dynamic issues forth a mutual transformation. The translation of Scriptures transforms languages, cultures, and people. Likewise, as the Scriptures are "enfleshed" in new languages and cultures, they become transformed. "New translations, by taking the word about Christ into a new area, applying it to new situations, have the potential actually to reshape and expand the Christian faith . . . Translatability of the Scriptures potentially starts *inter*actions of the word about Christ with new areas of thought and custom."[103] This is a significant reciprocity that is not usually discussed in studies of Bible Translation.

In her recent book, *The Bible at Cultural Crossroads: From Translation to Communication*, Hill combines a critique of Dynamic Equivalence theory with a presentation of a general model of communication, Relevance theory.[104] Through empirical research she discusses how biblical translations shape the understanding of theological categories. Whereas she asserts that the use of key terms in translation, over a long period of time, can introduce foreign concepts into a culture, she is hesitant in her arguments to affirm the reciprocating dynamic of local categories that can contribute to Christianity's broader understanding of itself and the

---

100. Ibid., 92.
101. Ibid., 94.
102. Walls, "The Translation Principle in Christian History," 27.
103. Ibid., 29.
104. Hill, *The Bible at Cultural Crossroads*.

Bible.[105] Yet, to understand the Bible as static is to view it from a Type A theology. It is only from a perspective of Type C that we can appreciate the dynamic quality of the Bible to transform and to be transformed.

From the perspective of linguistics, the Sapir-Whorf hypothesis may help us to appreciate how vernacular translations can contribute to a broader understanding in Christianity.[106] This hypothesis was built on the anthropological research of Franz Boas and his field research with the Hopi Indians. This linguistic-worldview connection has continued to be researched and empirically documented in cognitive linguistics as exemplified by Lakoff's *Women, Fire, and Dangerous Things: What Categories Reveal about the Mind*.[107] This argument has led to further precision about issues of code switching. From this perspective, translation does not make an identical transfer; rather, there is semantic overlap from one language to another. This hypothesis indicates to me the merit of what Sanneh, Walls, and others have suggested: language does influence worldview. Postcolonially, people such as Ngũgĩ and Musa Dube recognize that discussions of language incorporate more than a communication code.[108] Such discussions pertain to the culture, and thus the identity of individuals and communities. If there is any value to the Sapir-Whorf hypothesis, it seems to me that the expression of Christian theology (and Bibles) in vernacular languages is an opportunity for the global Church to become enriched by indigenous culture and language. Such "vernacular hermeneutics" support a paradigm shift in Bible Translation that responds to postcolonial critiques through liberation and inculturation. "The vernacular hermeneutics which privileges indigenous culture as an authentic site for doing theology, and which focuses on native characteristics and ideas, does not rank as highly as liberation theologies . . . Vernacular hermeneutics is postmodern in its eagerness to celebrate the local, and postcolonial in its ability to disturb and dislodge the reigning imported theories."[109]

Historically one recognizes the importance of Bible Translation and language in the shaping of theological thought. "It would be difficult to

---

105. See, however, Hill, *The Bible at Cultural Crossroads*, 45.

106. Sapir, 'The Status of Linguistics as a Science"; Whorf, "Science and Linguistics."

107. Lakoff, *Women, Fire, and Dangerous Things*.

108. Ngũgĩ, *Decolonizing the Mind*; Dube, "Consuming the Colonial Cultural Bomb," 33–59.

109. Sugirtharajah, *Vernacular Hermeneutics*, 12.

overestimate the importance of the influence exerted by the Latin versions of the Bible and particularly by Jerome's Latin Vulgate . . . The theology and the devotional language typical of the Roman Catholic Church were either created or transmitted by the Vulgate. Both Protestants and Roman Catholics are heirs of terminology that Jerome either coined or baptized with fresh significance—words such as salvation, regeneration, justification, sanctification, propitiation, reconciliation, inspiration, Scripture, sacrament, and many others."[110] Over time, however, this theological shaping has taken on a normative character in theology.

Recognition of a dominant linguistic position is evident in the German language as well. In a recent historical study, James C. Russell's *The Germanization of Early Medieval Christianity: A Sociohistorical Approach to Religious Transformation* looks at the cultural effects on Christianity.[111] In relation to Russell's treatment of the distinctive missiological patterns in the East and West, Robert Schreiter summarizes Russell's thesis: "[Christianity] adopted a policy of temporary accommodation to a highly vital society that enjoyed high levels of group solidarity (as compared to the anomie of the Mediterranean world). This temporary accommodation led to a transformation of Christianity itself, a transformation that from the tenth century onwards flowed back into Italy to become the cultural standard in Rome. And from Rome, it spread throughout the West."[112]

I suggest that there has been a similar shaping of theological thought in Christianity due to the German language domination in the past centuries. Russell observes: "For at least the preceding millennium, from the coronation of the Saxon King Otto I as the Holy Roman Emperor by Pope John XII on February 2, 962, to the opening of the Second Vatican Council by Pope John XXIII on October 11, 1962, the religio-cultural orientation of popular Roman Catholicism was predominantly European and largely Germanic."[113] The influence is certainly culturally based, but even more precisely, linguistically shaped. Even in today's massive changes due to world Christianity, the German language is regarded as essential for academic theological reflection. Just as Latin shaped the early theological reflections, so too have the European languages shaped (and

---

110. Metzger, *The Bible in Translation*, 29–30.
111. Russell, *The Germanization of Early Medieval Christianity*.
112. Schreiter, *The New Catholicity*, 66.
113. Russell, *The Germanization of Early Medieval Christianity*, vii.

limited) the articulation of Christian theology. In today's world, however, theological shaping is occurring in many cultures beyond Europe and its languages.[114] "Bible translation has thus helped to bring about a historic shift in Christianity's theological center of gravity by pioneering a strategic alliance with local conceptions of religion."[115]

Bible Translation and Orality: A Preview

Throughout much of the modern history of Bible Translation, an accompanying technology has been assumed: literacy. Postcolonial critiques of Bible Translation implicate the introduction of writing into the colonial agenda in oral societies. Anthropological studies have inquired about the interface of literacy and orality in such contexts. In addition to my proposal that Bible Translation be recognized missiologically by the paradigm of liberation and inculturation, I suggest that literacy not be the presupposed medium for biblical translation. Such a suggestion is not primarily in response to recent postcolonial critiques of affiliations with literacy. Rather, my proposal's source is twofold. First, the anthropological model of contextualization suggests that one discover what is already available in a given context. Oral communications continue to be predominant throughout much of the world—even when literacy is available. Second, historically the first-century world consisted of a predominantly oral setting in which the New Testament was composed. The presentation of a Type C paradigm of Bible Translation that values this oral ethos as a site for theology is presented in the following chapters.

Conclusion

Bible Translation concisely reflects the dynamics of the incarnation. Yet this reflection has been perceived in a limited way through history either as a tool of evangelism or as a means for church edification. Postcolonially, Bible Translation has been understood as a method of subjugation. These options do not exhaust the possible theological models, because liberation has consistently played a role in Bible Translation.

---

114. World Christianity and its demographics are discussed in such works as: Jenkins *The Next Christendom*; Sanneh, *Whose Religion Is Christianity?*

115. Sanneh, *Whose Religion Is Christianity?* 10.

FROM ORALITY TO ORALITY

The linguistic liberation that is offered from the dominating languages and cultures of today by one's own language is exemplified throughout history. Furthermore, the dynamic mutual transformation that occurs in Bible Translation offers World Christianity a diversity of theologies, shaped by their contexts, and articulated in their translations. Such liberation and inculturation are demonstrated in the next chapter as we focus in on the issues of African theologies and their relation to issues of Bible Translation.

2

BIBLE TRANSLATION IN THE CONTEXTS OF AFRICA

Introduction

AT THE BEGINNING OF THE TWENTIETH CENTURY THE MAjority of adherents to Christianity resided in the northern hemisphere. By 1970 the beginning of a global shift in the center of Christianity was being recognized. At that time David Barrett projected 350 million Christians in Africa by the year 2000—from nine million in 1900.[1] Today the majority of Christians live in the southern hemisphere—almost 400 million in Africa! Such a global shift in World Christianity has been recognized by several historians and missiologists.[2] Beyond sheer numbers such a shift to Africa offers insights into Christianity that present possibilities to enrich World Christianity. This is to say that an intentional look into Africa presents an understanding of contextual theologies and issues of Bible Translation that promise to be beneficial beyond Africa.

Following our introduction in the previous chapter of an alternative paradigm for Bible Translation as contextualization, this chapter looks at how several African theologians view issues of contextual theologies. The continent of Africa exemplifies the plurality of Christian theologies as local communities reflect and respond to their contexts. This pluralism

---

1. Barrett, "AD 2000—350 million Christians in Africa," 39–54; quoted in Bediako, "Epilogue," 243.

2. Walls, "Towards Understanding Africa's Place in Christian History"; Bediako, *Christianity in Africa*; Jenkins, *The Next Christendom*; Sanneh, *Whose Religion Is Christianity?*

expands our understandings of Christianity in general and in relation to the Bible and its effects upon and through language in particular. Although the modern voices of African theologians are relatively recent, it would be impossible to represent here what has become a myriad of approaches from the continent. Nevertheless, several emerging theologies in Africa are presented: Translation theologies, South African Black theologies, African Feminist/Womanist theologies, Inculturation theologies, and Ordinary Readers theologies.[3] Throughout this chapter these theologies are examined in terms of their use of the Bible and, when possible, of how Bible Translation plays a role in them. In relation to this last subject, the study continues with a presentation of a continuing dialogue on issues of Bible Translation and postcolonialism in Africa. As a forecast to later chapters, the subject of orality as presented by African theologians is discussed. The chapter closes with my statement of a composite approach to Bible Translation that incorporates various concerns noted by African theologians. Throughout these discussions of African theologians I often refrain from my own comment on or critique of their views. This has been done expressly to permit African theologians—at least those who are published—to determine the topics of discussion.[4] Furthermore, these topics demonstrate how Africans are discussing these subjects; this helps avoid to some degree a presentation of Africa based solely on my perspective and opinions.

Early Voices of African Theologians

It is appropriate to begin with those who may be considered first-generation (published) African theologians of the twentieth century. By the 1960s African scholars were seeking to have their voices heard in relation to the Bible. Early writings and conferences focused on the viable contribution that Africans could make to biblical studies. They focused on how Africa itself was found within the Bible, thus legitimizing Africa in some way. There was also discussion of how African culture could serve as a type of Hebrew Scriptures as the backdrop for the New

---

3. Maluleke, "Half a Century of African Christian Theologies," 4–23; Maluleke, "The Bible and African Theologies," 165–76.

4. Most African theologians on the continent remain unpublished; they are "oral theologians." I am very aware of the ideological filter of using only published theologians for this study.

Testament and African Christianity. Nonetheless, the criticisms and methods of biblical studies used by African scholars initially reflected their European and North American training. As well, the writing for their research was predominantly in the European languages.

Perhaps the early voices of African theologians were best represented in the Jerusalem conference in 1972 on *Black Africa and the Bible*.[5] The conference and its published articles set out to persuade European and North American theologians of the appropriateness of African theologies. Numerous articles discuss how Africa itself is positively included in the Bible. The central role of the Bible in African theologies is underscored. Yet the presentations remain predominantly within the categories established by Europe and North America. Africans who were trained in these northern institutions display able dexterity in applying these methods to Africa. John Mbiti and John Pobee demonstrate early approaches to African theologies that lay the groundwork for later discussions. Not only is the centrality of the Bible in theology underscored, but both of these Africans lift up the importance of vernacular languages—albeit in articles and books written in European languages and following predominantly European categories of theology. Pobee surmises in *Toward an African Theology*: "Ideally, African theologies should be in the vernacular. Language is more than syntax and morphology; it is the vehicle for assuming the weight of a culture. Therefore, this attempt to construct an African theology in the English language is the second best, even if it is convenient if it should secure as wide a circulation as possible."[6] Mbiti's comments on examples of what he provocatively called "pure theology" demonstrate his links to the notion of an objective theology whereby a theologian can disassociate oneself from one's social location. At the same time, Mbiti lauds the contextual contributions of vernacular languages. "In this way, the Bible in the local language becomes the most directly influential single factor in shaping the life of the church in Africa."[7] Nonetheless, pursuit of vernacular theologizing had not yet begun.[8]

---

5. Mveng and Werblowsky, *Black Africa and the Bible*.
6. Pobee, *Toward an African Theology*, 23.
7. Mbiti, *Bible and Theology in African Christianity*, 28.
8. "I do not know, however, to what extent they are actually utilizing translations of the Bible in African languages. Many of them are, in any case, well versed in the biblical languages of Hebrew and Greek, in addition to European languages like Latin, English, French and German. We are forced by circumstances to write our theology in essential

FROM ORALITY TO ORALITY

Another important conference occurred in 1977 in Accra, Ghana. A firm declaration of the centrality of the Bible in theology is made: "The Bible is the basic source of African theology, because it is the primary witness of God's revelation in Jesus Christ. No theology can retain its Christian identity apart from scripture."[9] Nevertheless, the collection of papers presented in Accra demonstrates an early epistemological break with Western theologies. It states clearly that all theologies are ideologically motivated—none is neutral. At the time of the conference, apartheid was still enforced in South Africa and as a result much of the black theology addressed issues of race and white supremacy as well as other struggles of class, gender, and poverty. It is perhaps from this conference that theologians began to clarify a distinction of sources for theologies in Africa. The starting place for doing theology was distinguished as either the Bible or the contexts of the theologians.[10] Mbiti and others would hold to the Bible as the primary source for doing theology whereby contextual additions are appropriate steps toward relevance. An alternative understanding of the source—or, more appropriately, the sources—of theology is the contexts in which theologies are done. This contextual understanding has been historically and geographically determined to a large extent and is further distinguished in Africa by understanding the aim of theology as that of inculturation and/or liberation.[11] Early examples of inculturation replicated New Testament efforts—specifically the book of Hebrews where the author interprets Jesus' activities and roles to rituals found in the Hebrew Scriptures. This occurred most often with Christologies. Jesus was understood as an Ancestor, as a Healer, as a Chief, etc.[12] Other early inculturation efforts involve African views of ecclesiology.[13] These early inculturation themes are distinguished from South African theologians' struggle for liberation. Efforts by Desmond

---

'foreign languages' which, for some of us, are our working languages at least in academic matters. Serious theological research and output in African languages (at least in those into which the Bible has been translated) still waits to be done." Ibid., 60–61.

9. Appiah-Kubi and Torres, *African Theology en Route*.

10. A simple dichotomization cannot be maintained; there is a tension with these two points on a continuum. Theologians interpret the Bible through the lens of their contexts.

11. Martey, *African Theology*.

12. Schreiter, *Faces of Jesus in Africa*.

13. Mugambi and Magesa, *The Church in African Christianity*.

Tutu and Alan Boesak borrowed heavily not only from South American liberationists, but also from James Cone's Black Theology.[14] These early liberation theologians were dissatisfied by inculturation methods that, they argued, did not take seriously oppressive political and economic structures.

Anthropological Pauperization

Emmanuel Martey looks to unite these apparently disparate African theologies by understanding liberation and inculturation as legitimate responses to essentially the same problem—anthropological pauperization: humanity's impoverishment due to colonialism and domination.[15] Historically these two hermeneutics differ in their early stages in Africa: inculturation (after going through several phases of adaptation, indigenization, inculturation) addresses the "religio-cultural" issues of contexts in "independent" (sub-Saharan, but non-southern Africa), whereas liberation addresses the socio-political issues of contexts in southern Africa. However, given apartheid and neocolonialism of the present and colonialism of the past, these hermeneutical approaches have more in common than has been presented often by African theologians. From this point of view, Martey asserts: "The main emphasis of this study is that such a tension is not necessary, since in the African theological reality, the two foci are not contradictory but complement each other."[16] In Martey's study we come to understand an appreciation for the linguistic diversity in Africa and its role in response to anthropological pauperization. "If language, as we have established, is at the very heart of culture, and if it is impossible for an authentic African cultural revolution to take place using a foreign language, then African writers, including theologians, must take African languages seriously."[17] Furthermore, this African linguistic diversity has the capacity to contribute to creative understandings of Christianity. "Undeniably, the riches of African culture lie hidden in

---

14. Tutu, "Whither African Theology"; Boesak, *Finger of God*; Cone, *A Black Theology of Liberation*.

15. The "African Report" presented at the Second General Assembly of EATWOT held in Oaxtepec, Mexico, in 1986 in Abraham, *Third World Theologies*, 35.

16. Martey, *African Theology*, xi.

17. Ibid., 45.

African languages, waiting to be uncovered. Language can be said to represent a key that offers African theologians enormous opportunities for discovering the culture of African people... Each language is a distinctly new way of 'experiencing' the truth, implying that linguistic pluralism is an index of religion, culture, and sociopolitical diversity."[18]

Contemporary African Responses to Contextualization

Having presented the centrality of liberation and inculturation for African theologians from the examples above, I turn to several important contributing voices for this chapter. Each of them represents models of contextual theologies and the Bible's role in such theologies.[19] A translation model is supported by Kwame Bediako and critiqued by Tinyiko Maluleke. Womanist theologies are articulated by Mercy Amba Oduyoye and Musa Dube. Inculturation and Ordinary Readers approaches are evident in the writings of Gerald West. Each of these voices contributes to my argument for a paradigm of Bible Translation as contextualization.

Kwame Bediako

Bediako not only contributes to issues of contextualization but he is especially articulate on the use of vernacular languages and vernacular Bible translations in doing theology.[20] He echoes the foundational understanding of Christianity of his mentor, Andrew Walls, when he asserts that the Christian faith is "infinitely translatable."[21] Bediako's early work demonstrates a serious engagement in both African cultures and Christian history and theology. He parallels the second-century dynamic context of Christianity with Africa's contemporary discussions. In the second century, Christians were struggling for identity in the context

---

18. Ibid., 44–45.

19. Many other African theologians could be discussed in this section, including: Ela, *Repenser la Théologie Africaine*; Magesa, *Anatomy of Inculturation*; Mugambi, *From Liberation to Reconstruction*; Mugambi, *Christian Theology and Social Reconstruction*; Kobia, *The Courage to Hope*; Dedji, *Reconstruction and Renewal in African Christian Theology*; Getui and Obeng, *Theology of Reconstruction*; Getui and Theuri, *Quests for Abundant Life in Africa*; Villumstad, *Social Reconstruction in Africa*.

20. Although not discussed in this chapter, Lamin Sanneh is a strong voice that parallels the assertions of Bediako.

21. Walls, "The Translation Principle in Christian History," 25.

Bible Translation in the Contexts of Africa

of dominant cultures. Similarly, African Christianity in the twenty-first century seeks to establish its identity as African in the context of both colonial and neocolonial influences.[22] With identity as the aim, Bediako's work promotes inculturation for Africans to discover and maintain their identity as African Christians. Central to inculturation is the valorization of the African languages and worldviews. "The ability to hear in one's own language and to express in one's own language one's response to the message which one receives, must lie at the heart of all authentic religious encounter with the divine realm. Language itself becomes, then, not merely a social or a psychological phenomenon, but a theological one as well."[23] Vernacular biblical translation, therefore, aligns itself with this pursuit.[24]

An example used often to demonstrate this principle in the early church is Acts 11:20, where the Greek language influences the title of Jesus. This title is not articulated in the Jewish context of Messiah (or even the Greek translation of Christ), but as the Greek title *kyrios* ("Lord"). The creation of new categories of theology is not limited to the original biblical languages. "[S]uch an enhanced appreciation of the exegetical significance of the translated Scriptures will be an effective response to what appears as to be a sort of 'Bible deism' that suggests that after God spoke in Hebrew, Aramaic, and Greek, he ceased to speak to humanity in any other language."[25]

Understanding Bible Translation in the paradigm of inculturation and liberation is supported by Bediako's insights. "[S]ince we are dealing with a translatable faith and translated Scriptures, mother tongues, new languages, and the potential for new idioms become central and are crucial in opening up fresh insights into our common understanding of the doctrine of Christ."[26] One recognizes the critical importance

---

22. "My own studies in the formative stages of modern African theology brought me to the conclusion that the issue of identity lies at the heart of the process by which the Christian theological enterprise is actually carried forward." Bediako, *Christianity in Africa*, 256.

23. Ibid., 60.

24. "Mother-tongue Scriptures, accordingly, come to constitute an irreplaceable element, among others, for the 'the birth of theology'"; Bediako, "Biblical Exegesis in the African Context," 17.

25. Ibid., 22.

26. Bediako, "The Doctrine of Christ and the Significance of Vernacular Terminology," 111.

of the Scriptures available in languages of Greek, Latin, Syriac and European languages. The first biblical translation for Christians—the Greek Septuagint—demonstrates how translations shape one's theology.[27] Such a dynamic of theological shaping is by no means unilateral. The languages and contexts in which translations appeared influenced these very translations and their use. "But translatability and the impact of the translated Scriptures also ensure that the 'world of experience' can be expanded in the other direction, leading occasionally to startling and novel ways of participating in the Scriptures, shaped, in such situations, by the cultural world of experience of the reader or hearer."[28]

Vernacular Bible Translation, therefore, not only offers mutual contributions to fresh theological insights, but it also becomes an activity of liberation in the face of global linguistic domination. In today's context of globalization, the translation principle must not be muted by being satisfied with theological articulation in global languages. "To the extent that the church should be tempted to capitulate to this attrition of cultural worlds of meaning represented by languages [due to globalization], the church will deprive itself of the opportunity for new theological insights."[29] This liberation is not only political but intensely personal. "To learn and understand in the vernacular had a significance within the universal relevance of the Christian faith: the sense of liberation—spiritual and intellectual—was tremendous."[30]

A word of caution: a correlation of vernacular Scriptures with inculturation and liberation overly simplifies a rather complex relationship. Recent history instructs us that the presence of vernacular Scriptures in a community does not ensure an engagement by the community with these Scriptures. Furthermore, participation in forming these Scriptures does not result automatically in inculturation or liberation. "The state of the churches in their relation to the traditional worldview presents a rather paradoxical picture: the churches which have a longer historical connection with the society, and a profound vernacular heritage, appear to be less effective in meeting the spiritual and psychological needs of

---

27. "[I]t was the Septuagint that proved decisive in shaping the mind of the church in relation to its own self-understanding." Bediako, "Biblical Exegesis in the African Context," 16.

28. Ibid., 18.

29. Ibid., 19.

30. Bediako, *Christianity in Africa*, 51.

their members for most of whom the traditional worldview continues as a potent element in their understanding of reality."[31] Bediako clarifies that it is not simply the presence of vernacular Scriptures that assures an integration of the biblical message and African Traditional Religions. Churches with Scriptures available in the vernacular can fail at such integration. He states: "It is the failure to read the vernacular Scriptures from the standpoint of the traditional worldview and in the light of its realities."[32] It appears to be that such a worldview position of engagement in the Scriptures is demonstrated with African Initiated Churches (AIC). David Barrett's *Schism and Renewal in Africa* investigated these religious movements that are distinguished from churches in Africa that were initiated by expatriate missionaries.

> Up to this point the missions had had the same absolute control over the scriptures as they had exercised over the church. They alone had access to the Hebrew and Greek sources; their interpretation was final. But with the publication of African translations, a momentous change took place: it now became possible to differentiate between missions and scriptures. Through these scriptures, God, Africans perceived, was addressing them in the vernacular in which was enshrined the soul of their people; but a large proportion of the missionary force still had not learned the vernacular and addressed them in foreign tongues. The vernacular scriptures therefore provided an independent standard of reference that Africa Christians were quick to seize on."[33]

Bediako's writing contributes significantly to my proposed paradigm alternative of Bible Translation as contextualization. The culturally appropriate engagement of vernacular Scriptures offers a mutual dynamic to the shaping of African theological articulation as well as the shaping of biblical categories by African agency. Dominant theological questions and categories imposed by speakers of foreign languages are relieved of their oppressive duties. In their places are local questions and novel approaches to responses. The contributions of vernacular Bible translations are not limited to African localities but offer to World Christianity keen insights into Christianity and its theologies.

---

31. Ibid., 68.
32. Ibid., 70.
33. Barrett, *Schism and Renewal in Africa*, 127.

FROM ORALITY TO ORALITY
Tinyiko Maluleke

My purpose for including Tinyiko Maluleke in the review of African theologians is that he represents a second generation of South African theologians. He is primarily concerned with issues of liberation. Furthermore, he engages the work of those participating in inculturation and specifically critiques the works of Bediako in the process.[34] By discussing Maluleke, I am able to access South African liberation theologians and biblical scholars and their critique of inculturation efforts by non-South African theologians.

Maluleke argues against four dualisms held by Bediako. First, Maluleke does not accept the clean separation that his opponents suggest between Christianity and colonialism. Whereas Bediako acknowledges missionaries' complicity at times in colonialism, he does not understand Christianity as a religion being involved in such colonial activities. Maluleke's critique of this view can be explained by stating that Christianity is inherently hegemonic; it is not simply benevolent as portrayed by Bediako. A second critique by Maluleke is the distinction Bediako makes between the missionary transmissions of the message (Gospel) on the one hand and the indigenous assimilation of the message on the other hand. This is a difference between what was intended and what was appropriated. Bediako alludes to the agency of Africans and their ability to assimilate the Gospel in different ways than intended by missionaries. Maluleke's third critique involves the distinction between Gospel and Christianity. He asserts that Bediako attempts to remove responsibility from Christianity by insisting that Christianity has not always promoted the Gospel, which, by its very nature, would never be oppressive. In each of these first three critiques Maluleke asserts the inherent oppressive nature of Christianity. Bediako, in turn, distinguishes successively the Gospel from Christianity; the intentions of Christian missionaries from the African agency in reshaping the missionaries' Christianity; and, a distinction between the colonial agendas of (some) Christians to the inherent liberative nature of Christianity.

A fourth critique challenges the equation of the Bible with the Word of God. It is in this fourth critique that Maluleke especially follows

---

34. Maluleke as a theologian has been considerably influenced by the South African biblical scholar Itumaleng Mosala. Mosala, "The Use of the Bible in Black Theology"; Mosala, *Biblical Hermeneutics and Black Theology in South Africa*.

Mosala's earlier arguments. Mosala, expressing a Marxist materialist approach, finds the naming of the Bible as the Word of God as a means of restricting the ability of scholars to critique the Bible itself. Mosala states that before the Bible can liberate people it must first be liberated itself. It is this fourth argument of Maluleke's that demonstrates a significant division throughout the African continent as theologians either view the Bible as equal to the Word of God (i.e. as beyond critique) or they have a view that permits a critique not only of how the Bible is used, but also of the very content of the Bible itself. "The failure to problematize the relationship between African theologies and the Bible on the one hand and the relationship between the Bible and Christianity on the other is a serious shortcoming in many Black and African theology proposals— Bediako and Sanneh's included."[35] Maluleke suggests that Africans need to utilize ideological criticisms—such as feminist and postcolonial—not only in the neocolonial contexts but with the Bible itself. "It seems to me that the way out of Biblical entrapment is not to take flight, but to confront, not only the Bible, but all other sources and interlocutors of theological discourse precisely at a hermeneutical level."[36] In sum, my understanding of Maluleke's argument of the Bible is as follows. Maluleke suggests that African theologians should approach the Bible as many in Europe and North America do in Academia. It is literature to be studied through various criticisms—perhaps most importantly by ideological criticism.

Maluleke's critiques of Bediako challenge an optimistic view of Christianity in Africa. The critiques also question how people read the history of Christianity in Africa. This is especially pertinent to my proposal of a paradigm of Bible Translation as contextualization. Bediako offers much support to such a paradigm by supporting the doing of theology in vernacular languages. However, Maluleke's critiques may question the validity of viewing Bible Translation positively. Nonetheless, Maluleke seems to value the use of vernacular languages in Africa to articulate a "truly African" view of life. His unpublished doctoral thesis, titled "'A Morula Tree Between Two Fields': The Commentary of Selected Tsonga Writers on Missionary Christianity," suggests support for vernacular language use.[37] I accept Maluleke's assertion that the Bible cannot be

---

35. Maluleke, "Black and African Theologies in the New World Order, 11.
36. Ibid., 14.
37. Maluleke, "'A Morula Tree Between Two Fields.'"

accepted as neutral. It is important to determine the actors in the drama of the Bible in Africa. Agency and agendas are critical to the Bible itself as well as to whether the Bible is used for life or death. My paradigmatic proposal places agency significantly with Africans. Likewise, accepting that translation is interpretive, it views African agency as asserting their theological agendas in the realm of translation. I discuss further these issues in later sections.

Mercy Amba Oduyoye and Musa Dube

Oduyoye challenges the Western (male dominated) approach and findings of theology.[38] She also challenges the feminist (white) works (e.g., Schüssler Fiorenza) that may not be able to encompass so called "double colonization," whereby women experience domination due to bias of both gender and race.[39] Oduyoye in feminist fashion not only reads the biblical text against the grain to critique the patriarchal agendas but also looks for inspiration to African cultures and African Traditional Religions (ATR). Her approach is distinct from many African male theologians who do not apply the same hermeneutic of suspicion to African cultures and ATR as they might to the biblical text. Oduyoye examines issues of purity and defilement within the cultures and understands them as patriarchally-biased, marginalizing women. Whereas Oduyoye's early work focuses on the biblical text for much of her literary resources, her later work looks at African oral traditions with folktales, narratives, proverbs, and so on. She applies her feminist hermeneutic to these resources as well to show how many of these are also biased in favor of a patriarchal system. Another of Oduyoye's resources is the AIC.

The leadership roles that many women in these AIC play are lifted up as exemplary. Nonetheless, there are challenges to Oduyoye's work—many of which are articulated by Pemberton. In general, Pemberton shows great respect for Oduyoye as the "Mother of Circle Thinking." Yet there are many ambiguous elements in Oduyoye's work. As a feminist critic, Oduyoye uses the very framework that she is often criticizing—an Enlightenment model of critical thinking. The ambiguity continues in

---

38. My experience with Oduyoye's work through her books *Hearing and Knowing* and *Daughters of Anowa* is also supplemented by Carrie Pemberton's work on *Circle Thinking*.

39. Dube, *Postcolonial Feminist Interpretation of the Bible*, 113.

Oduyoye's treatment of both Scripture and ATR. At times these sources support Oduyoye's purposes, yet elsewhere they are contrary to her efforts. Furthermore, the very women of the AIC that Oduyoye lifts up as examples would have difficulties with Oduyoye's views of the Bible as well as her critique of cultural views of purity.

Musa Dube is a prominent African woman biblical scholar today. She opens her book on *Postcolonial Feminist Interpretation of the Bible* with a story of the Bible and the Land: "When the white man came to our country he had the Bible and we had the land. The white man said to us, 'let us pray.' After the prayer, the white man had the land and we had the Bible."[40] Issues of Land and its resources is a critical component of Dube's work. To a great extent Dube is informed by Mosala and Maluleke's work. She understands that the Bible is a site of struggle and oppression that must be liberated. In her book, Dube utilizes postcolonial theory in a study of biblical passages, as well as literary works. She notes that the Bible continually discusses liberation of the people of God in the context of oppression of others. The Exodus precedes an invasion of the "promised land," whereby indigenous communities already living there are dehumanized as the Other and the people of Israel use God-ordained violence to remove them. In the New Testament, Dube challenges the "Great Commission" in Matthew 28:18–20 as being a similar divine carte blanche for the subjugation of others. Dube refuses such domination and suggests interdependence. The Bible, for Dube, has historically been an instrument of abuse—not only because the missionaries have used it with their colonial agendas, but because the Bible itself is a colonizing document. Leaning heavily on Ngũgĩ Wa Thiong'o's discussions of the "colonization of the mind," Dube discusses how various literary works, including the Bible, have been used to colonize Africa—not through guns and wars, but through books and languages.[41]

Yet Dube's work is not simply a reaction to history. Her work is proactive and subversive. "[P]ostcolonial is not about dwelling on the crimes of the past and their continuation, but about seeking transformation for liberation."[42] Subversion is to take place with genre and language. Dube writes: "On these grounds, decolonizing literary practitioners do not,

---

40. Ibid., 3.
41. Ngũgĩ, *Decolonizing the Mind*.
42. Dube, *Postcolonial Feminist Interpretation of the Bible*, 16.

and in my opinion, cannot, confine themselves to analyzing representations of the imperial constructions, or even spinning subversive hybrid re-readings of the colonizer's text. Rather, they must always insist on new spaces for cultivating new contextual and international readings-writings, which are both decolonizing and depatriarchalizing."[43] Dube supports her assertions from portions of her research on Botswana women as a demonstration of "hearing God afresh, in a new space—one that operates outside the oppressive structures and their symbols."[44] In Dube's research of certain women leaders of AIC, she finds for herself the critical hermeneutic for African women. "In short, the challenge at hand is how to seriously, responsibly, and effectively use the fact that 'God never opened the Bible to us,' yet we still hear God speaking to us as women and in our situations."[45] Dube's views of the Bible in Africa are further discussed below in relation to Bible Translation in Botswana.

At this point I want to assure that the discussion of African theologians does not deter the reader from the main thesis of this book: Bible Translation as contextualization. Whereas I discussed in the first chapter an alternative paradigm of Bible Translation that follows contextual theologies, I am attempting in this current chapter on Africa to demonstrate concretely a variety of contexts on the continent of Africa. Given the proposed paradigm, these contexts must inform how one understands Bible Translation. The optimistic view of the Bible as represented by Bediako is tempered by Maluleke's concerns of oversimplifying the relationship of missionaries, the Bible, and Africans. I press this subject by including feminist views of Christianity in Africa and more specifically their views of the Bible. My proposed paradigm takes into account these varied African contexts. Having given this reminder of the overarching theme, I pursue in the following sections more detailed discussions by African theologians that become integral to Bible Translation as contextualization.

Gerald O. West

Gerald West, as a white South African biblical scholar, has consistently located himself in the liberation struggles of Africa. He recognizes the

---

43. Ibid., 116.
44. Ibid. cf. Dube, "Readings of *Semoya*," 111–30.
45. Dube, *Postcolonial Feminist Interpretation of the Bible*, 123.

colonial and neocolonial influence on the continent and particularly the oppressive structures of apartheid in South African society and in the guild of biblical studies. Whereas numerous scholars recognize the influence of the Bible on Africa with the hundreds of Bible translations, West challenges us to understand this relationship between the Bible and Africa as more of a transaction, a mutual exchange whereby Africa influences the Bible. "While the Bible has been used for purposes of oppression and imperialism, both because of the ideologies of those who have used it and because of the ideologies intrinsic to it, ordinary Africans have at a deeper, often hidden, level negotiated and transacted with the Bible, and partially appropriated the Bible by relativizing, resisting, and modifying it with uncanny creativity."[46] Thus West recognizes the agency—subjectivity—of African hearers and readers whereby they were not simply recipients of the Bible but appropriators.[47] West recognizes the contribution of Mosala, Maluleke, and others who question the idea of equating the Bible with the Word of God; however, he also suggests that "ordinary readers" may be expressing this equation with a more complex comprehension. "More precise analysis of 'the Bible as power' is imperative; it does not help to label those we disagree with as guilty of a 'Word of God' approach to the Bible."[48]

This analysis must not dichotomize issues of liberation and inculturation, nor attempt to separate biblical scholars from theologians. "Issues of Africanness, ethnicity, and culture cannot be separated from the complex matrix they share with issues of race, class, and gender."[49] Nor is this complexity limited to professional theologians; ordinary readers are central to West's proposal of how to understand the Bible in the African context. He recognizes the value of Bediako's vernacular proposals but also asserts the importance of research done by African American theologian Vincent Wimbush.[50] "If Bediako and Wimbush are right in their respective arguments—that translation into the vernacular loosens the control of the missionary on the message and that the hermeneutic strategies that local communities adopt in order to appropriate the

---

46. West, "On the Eve of an African Biblical Studies," 99.
47. West, "African Biblical Hermeneutics and Bible Translation."
48. West, "On the Eve of an African Biblical Studies," 113.
49. Ibid., 112.
50. Wimbush, "The Bible and African Americans."

message for themselves are foundational—then more careful analysis of such transactions would be extremely valuable."[51] Perhaps this combination can be understood as an attempt to avoid a reification of vernacular languages by asserting the agency of local communities in the appropriating of the Bible in their own languages.

West pursues this community agency in his work with ordinary readers. Defining "readers" broadly as both hearers and readers, West enumerates four contributions of ordinary readers to biblical studies in Africa:

> 1) ordinary readers are by far the majority of 'readers' of the Bible on the African continent; 2) recent trends in biblical scholarship—such as postmodernism, reader-response criticism, and liberation hermeneutics—push us in the direction of the ordinary reader; 3) there are elements of ordinary readings in our own 'scholarly' reading processes; 4) [with a concern for connecting biblical studies to contextual theology,] biblical scholars will have to recognize the foundational resources that ordinary 'readers' of the Bible bring with them to the task.[52]

West explains in several articles how the combination of these ordinary readers with "socially-engaged biblical scholars" has the potential to create space for social transformation.[53] This dynamic collaboration of ordinary reader and biblical scholar begins with an ordinary reader community inviting a biblical scholar to participate in a stated thematic project. In the process the scholar who is "called to interpret the Bible with ordinary poor and marginalized communities is usually one who is already involved in forms of social struggle, reconstruction, and development, and who already has taken sides with the poor and marginalized in their struggles for survival, liberation, and life."[54] The scholar also provides resources for a critical reading of the Bible—most often from a literary criticism that leads to socio-historical input to enhance the appreciation of the text. Quite often the biblical texts studied are themselves marginalized and the interpretive community combines both

---

51. West, "On the Eve of an African Biblical Studies," 108.

52. Ibid., 105.

53. West, "Reading the Bible Differently"; West, "Mapping African Biblical Interpretation"; West, "Unpacking the Packages that is the Bible in Africa Biblical Scholarship"; West, "Indigenous Exegesis."

54. West, "Contextual Bible Study in South Africa," 599.

hermeneutics of trust and suspicion to the text. The aim in such a venture is social transformation.[55]

Another contribution that West offers in his study is the impact of the Bible in Africa not so much as a literary artifact but as a symbol of power.[56] West suggests a new line of inquiry by reading historical missionary documents against the grain.[57] He presents the re-reading of the encounter between Africans with one missionary in southern Africa in the nineteenth century. It was the first encounter between Christian missionaries and a certain ethnic group. West shows how during the exchanges of several weeks the Bible was revered by the missionaries in a way that may have easily been interpreted by the indigenous community as religio-magical. Furthermore, they argued that the Bible contained knowledge that is to be equated with power. Such power could be manipulated by the possessor of the Bible. While the missionaries were in camp, as West tells it, one of the missionaries received a letter from a colleague who was on the coast. The local community was intrigued by this notion of written communication. As they inquired through interpreters, they learned that the person who carried the letter didn't necessarily know what the letter contains. West suggests that this might describe the complex relationship of the Bible, missionaries, and Christian Africans. Just because the missionaries brought the Bible does not mean that they master all that it contains. Africans can find knowledge (and therefore power) within its pages that missionaries are unaware of. Such inquiries present fresh insights into the appropriation of the Bible in Africa. "Already we see emerging evidence from this very early encounter of a recognition that the Bible is power/knowledge, that as power/knowledge it can be manipulated by those that control it, that it is beginning to be prized from the hands of the missionaries by indigenous experience and indigenous questions, and most significantly, that the bearer, like the bearer of the letter, might not know the power/knowledge that it contains."[58]

---

55. A pertinent critique of this method comes from Dube and Maluleke who question the dichotomy of "ordinary" and "trained" readers. Dube suggests that this encourages more a theology "from above" than "from below." Dube, "Villagizing, Globalizing, and Biblical Studies."

56. West, "Unpacking the Packages that is the Bible in Africa Biblical Scholarship."

57. West acknowledges Vincent Wimbush's influence from African American history on this method. Wimbush, "The Bible and African Americans."

58. West, "Unpacking the Packages that is the Bible in Africa Biblical scholarship," 94.

FROM ORALITY TO ORALITY
Consuming the Colonial Bomb

Three biblical scholars from southern Africa have engaged in a fresh discussion of Bible Translation in regards to colonialism and contextualization. The exchanges began with a paper Musa Dube wrote in 1999 titled "Consuming the Colonial Bomb: Translating *Badimo* into Demons in the Setswana Bible."[59] In this article Dube uses Ngũgĩ Wa Thiong'o's concept of colonial bomb.[60] Dube reworks Ngũgĩ's emphasis by changing the argument from the abusive use of European languages by colonizers to colonize Africans linguistically. Rather, Dube asserts that the vernacular languages themselves have been used—co-opted—with the intent to colonize the minds of Africans. "I will examine the use of the languages of the colonized to subjugate them. I will be examining 'the colonization of local language[s].'"[61] In this regard, Dube follows the earlier research of John and Jean Comaroff.[62]

Dube shares her research on texts from Matthew's Gospel in the vernacular Setswana with women. Armed with a recent translation of the Setswana Bible, Dube began reading texts from Matthew to women. The women stopped her repeatedly and challenged her use of a modern translation as opposed to their beloved 1908 Wookey translation, "an upgraded version of Robert Moffat's Bible of 1857."[63] Dube had been unaware of this earlier translation and discovered something in the translation that became the focus of her article. Throughout Matthew's Gospel whenever demons were discussed, the Setswana word *Badimo* was used. *Badimo* is generally understood as "ancestral spirits." Dube goes on to argue that such a translation was intentional; it was planted by the missionary translators to denigrate the ancestors and to corrupt the Batswana thinking about their ancestors, to demonize them. The article goes on to show how these women had learned to consume this colonial bomb without it exploding. To counter this, they found creative ways of using the Bible in ways not intended by the missionaries and they reinterpreted texts in a way that did not demonize their ancestors.

---

59. Dube, "Consuming the Colonial Cultural Bomb."
60. Ngũgĩ, *Decolonization of the Mind*, 1986.
61. Dube, "Consuming the Colonial Cultural Bomb," 36.
62. Comaroff and Comaroff, *Of Revelation and Revolution*, vol. 1, 218–20.
63. Dube, "Consuming the Colonial Cultural Bomb," 37.

The issue of *Badimo* continued with a second paper—this time shared at a conference of the Studiorum Novi Testamenti Societas (SNTS) outside of Pretoria in 1999 by Eric Hermanson, a white South African biblical scholar who was also a translation consultant with the Bible Society of South Africa.[64] Hermanson wrote to present further information about this translation issue and to offer another way of understanding the Wookey version's use of *Badimo*. Hermanson first corrects Dube's assertion that Wookey's 1908 translation used *Badimo* in following Moffat's 1857 translation. He presents his findings that none of Moffat's translations used *Badimo*, but rather used the transliterated English word for "demon." Furthermore, other than the 1908 Wookey version, no other translation used *Badimo* in its translation of demon or unclean/evil spirit. As for this 1908 use of *Badimo*, Hermanson critiques Dube's lack of understanding of the complex issues of translation. Hermanson stated that the Setswana language does not have a rich vocabulary for demons or evil spirits. In fact there were only two options available to the translators in the early twentieth century: transliterate something from the Greek (or English) or contextualize the translation with a known word with less than exact lexical correspondence in the text. Based on the fact that most of the Matthean texts for demons had to do with illness and that the Batswana context placed some responsibility for ill health on the *Badimo*, Hermanson argues that the translators contextualized the translation with the best term that would still be understandable. Furthermore, Hermanson argues that instead of only critiquing the translation, Dube, as a biblical scholar, should have suggested some alternative translations. Hermanson insisted that translation is a complicated task that requires more than simply a native speaker. Translators must be trained by recognized institutions, Hermanson argues, in the numerous disciplines involved in modern translation activities. In the end, Hermanson concludes (as he titles his paper) by suggesting that one should "Let the Ancestors Rest in Peace."

Dube responded two years later with the words of Pilate, "What I have written, I have written."[65] Dube's response is a postcolonial analysis of Hermanson's paper. She ends with several critiques of Hermanson and his paper: 1) Hermanson does not appreciate the Roman imperial context of the New Testament in general nor its influence on Matthew 28:18–20;

64. Hermanson, "Badimo a ba robale ka kagiso."
65. Dube, "What I Have Written, I Have Written."

2) Hermanson denigrates the Setswana term of "*badimo*" (refusing to use uppercase in its reference) and in insinuating with his title that the ancestors should be left to die; 3) Hermanson limits translation training to Western-controlled institutions; he insists that any African translator be fully trained by these institutions, thus negating the contribution of the indigenous translator. Although Dube was trained in such institutions, Hermanson accuses Dube of refusing to begin her critique with a discussion of the Greek text; rather, she began with the context of the women in Botswana; 4) Hermanson refused to express his social location and admit that it affects his response and work (unlike Dube who states up front her ideological positions).[66]

In the August 2005 edition of *Missionalia*, a South African journal, Tinyiko Maluleke summarizes these exchanges and suggests that the subject of Bible Translation should be taken to the next level.[67] As stated elsewhere, Maluleke disagrees greatly with the findings of Bediako who is one of the primary African proponents of vernacular Bible Translation. He suggests that the agency of Africans in these translations sheltered Africa from the European influence of European-language theologies. Maluleke sees in the Dube-Hermanson debate the combination of New Testament studies, Biblical translation studies, Missiology, and Postcolonial studies as a fresh combination to continue the discussions of Bible Translation in Africa.[68]

I present these exchanges in detail because I consider them as representative of potential future exchanges in regard to Bible Translation in Africa.[69] In many ways Dube and Hermanson (and Maluleke) were

---

66. When Hermanson first presented his response to Dube's paper at the conference, the conference attendees were scandalized and expected Dube to respond immediately. Yet she was silent. Later, she indicated that her lack of response was to allow the conference attendees to judge for themselves the merits of Hermanson's arguments.

67. Maluleke, "The Next Phase in the Vernacular Bible Discourse." Maluleke had stated a similar challenge to Bible translation in an earlier article: "African Christianity, the Bible, and Theology."

68. Maluleke also used this debate as the basis of his plenary paper at "The Bible in Africa" conference in September 2005, where he reiterated the findings of his *Missionalia* paper. In a personal communication to me, Hermanson related how he had hoped to have his paper published as a prompt response to Dube's initial paper. He was surprised to see excerpts of his paper later used in publications by Maluleke.

69. Such exchanges are occurring as demonstrated in the 2007 SBL section in African Biblical Hermeneutics, where the first session discussed "The Politics of Bible Translation in Africa."

speaking across each other without being fully understood. Dube (and Maluleke) introduces an important subject into the area of Bible Translation: postcolonial criticism. However, Hermanson, through his response, demonstrates the complexities of translation where there is not a simple one-to-one exchange of words in translation. I suggest that both assertions are important to the future work of Bible Translation.

The critical disconnect between Dube and Hermanson seems to be their starting point: Hermanson, the New Testament Greek text; Dube, the Batswana worldview. Whereas traditional Bible Translation proponents are constantly seeking to be faithful to the New Testament Greek text, postcolonialists are seeking to be faithful to the local communities. Such a distinction has become an important development in translation studies, studies which are just now beginning to affect Bible Translation theories (see chapter 6). My proposed paradigm for Bible Translation as contextualization incorporates this postcolonial critique while not forfeiting the complexities of the translation task.

Orality

Throughout this survey of African theologians, it is clear that contextual theologies of liberation and inculturation are central to their approach to theology and biblical studies. The contexts demonstrate their varied responses to colonialism and neocolonialism. Central to those involved in inculturation is the establishment of their identity. Equally central to those seeking liberation is the recognition of oppressive social and economic structures and the search for freedom from them. Each of these theologians recognizes the predominance of oral communications in Africa. At times this orality is presented in a simplified dichotomy with literacy, or negatively as illiteracy. However, more accurately, there is an interface of literacy with the spoken word. Yet this interface is significantly different than a Euro-American print bias. The majority of Christian Africans today engages and expresses their faith in oral forms. Not only do they hear this faith proclaimed in sermons, prayers, and songs, but they themselves proclaim it in their own prayers and songs. They experience this proclamation as the "word" embodied through liturgies and rituals. "[O]ral theology is produced in the fields by masses, in African languages, through song, sermon, teaching, prayer, conversation and the like. It is theology in the open air, often unrecorded, often heard only by small groups and audiences, and is generally lost as far as libraries and seminaries are concerned."[70] Pobee pursues this assertion in his article "Oral Theology and Christian Oral Tradition: Challenge to our Traditional Archival Concept." "In Africa where history, be it mission or otherwise, is being made, the society is predominantly non-literate and lives on oral tradition and history. Africans come to the church with all their skills of oral communication inherited down the ages . . . There is a living oral tradition which gives direction to a people who do not read or write."[71]

Oduyoye and Dube likewise see the importance of orality in their work. For womanist theologians of Africa, they value the oral traditions of their societies as sources for doing theology—sources frequently competing with the Bible. It is often those members of communities without literacy skills who offer to Dube the critical clues as to how colonial bombs can be consumed without harming a community. Maluleke understands this postcolonial view of orality as only a part of Africans' involvement in theology. "There is and should therefore be at least a two-way critical relationship between literature on African Christianity and actual African Christianity. To a greater or lesser extent the one estimates and needs the other. Whilst African Christianity may generally be said to be marching ahead of theology, there are times when African theology is and should be marching ahead of African Christianity."[72] West has presented a grassroots method of biblical studies with ordinary readers. Although West is consistent in placing "readers" in quotes, thus including hearers, there is the latent assertion that communicative modes are neutral. Yet the situation is more complex. At times West questions this neutrality by citing one of his South African colleagues, Jonathan Draper: "Draper's research, however, probes more deeply and raises difficult questions. How do textually oriented readers and orally oriented 'readers' work together with the Bible? When we 'read' the Bible are we dealing with the same thing? What are the prevailing interpretive practices in these respective communities? What implications does our textual biblical and

---

70. Mbiti, *Bible and Theology in African Christianity*, 47.
71. Pobee, "Oral Theology and Christian Oral Tradition, 88.
72. Maluleke, "Black and African Theologies in the New World Order," 17.

theological training have pedagogically for preparing people to minister in predominantly oral communities?"[73]

In his article "Theology with a New Voice? The Case for an Oral Theology in the South African Context," Piet Naudé as a white South African has questioned the minimal impact that orality has made with academic African theologians. He distinguishes between first and second order oral theology: "First order oral theology refers to the varied religious expressions of an oral community based on their underlying faith experiences. And second order oral theology is the systematic reflection up on the manifold expressions of first order oral theology in the specific light of an oral hermeneutic."[74] Whereas liberation theologies have struggled in the contexts of race, gender, and class in South Africa, there has been almost a complete ignorance of issues of orality in the struggle for liberation.[75] Naudé suggests an "epistemological break" that would bring about a shift in favor of learning from an oral perspective.[76] Naudé recognizes the growing influence that orality theories have had in biblical studies throughout the world and especially in South Africa since the 1990s. He urges that second order theologies make similar progress in the application of an oral hermeneutic to first order oral theology.[77]

South Africans are responding to this call. Jonathan Draper is the editor of a two-volume collection of papers given at a conference in Pietermaritzburg, South Africa, in 2001, titled *Orality, Literacy, and Colonialism in Antiquity/South Africa*.[78] The two volumes present a wide range of essays that are divided between those subjects addressed in the context either of Mediterranean antiquity or contemporary southern Africa. The predominant assumption of these essays is that literacy as a technology has been an instrument of power for the subjugation of

---

73. West, "On the Eve of an African Biblical Studies," 106.

74. Naudé, "Theology with a New Voice?" 23.

75. "But one important aspect of the oppressive situation has hitherto been neglected, namely the strong literate-illiterate dichotomy (or rather the oral/non-oral distinction)." Ibid., 25.

76. Ibid., 28.

77. In a book review of Naudé's *The Zionist Christian Church in South Africa: A Case-Study in Oral Theology*, Maluleke gives a scathing critique where he ends the review by encouraging Naudé to "research and re-write this book." Maluleke, Review of *The Zionist Christian Church in South Africa*.

78. Draper, *Orality, Literacy, and Colonialism in Antiquity*; Draper, *Orality, Literacy, and Colonialism in Southern Africa*.

people in oral contexts. Such a presupposition illustrates recent discussions of orality that do not focus on the cognitive issues of orality but on the "socio-dynamics" of orality-literacy. "The connection between the emergence of the great empires and the emergence of written texts in the ancient world is not accidental but integral."[79] Many of the essays combine historical/anthropological research with biblical studies. Several of these essays comment on issues of Bible Translation in the African (oral) context.

Understanding literacy as inherently colonial, Draper argues that the colonially supported missionary efforts of Bible Translation were instrumental to the oppression of the oral cultures of (southern) Africa. "In colonial and postcolonial Southern Africa, the relationship between text and hegemony is particularly clear, since the subjugated peoples had an entirely oral culture."[80] A counterpoint to this thesis is that there is evidence that Africans in a role as agents subverted these colonial efforts—either by their use of literacy or by sustaining a parallel oral culture of subversion. "The process of *bricolage* meant that cultural symbols and doctrines ostensibly drawn from the missionaries and the Christian faith in Africa could change their shape and reference. They were turned back against their own proponents."[81] Such postcolonial discussions of orality and Bible Translation indicate that any proposed paradigm shift of Bible Translation must take issues of orality as central. It is this very stance that I am taking in understanding Bible Translation as contextualization. It does not assume that Bible Translation is dependent upon literacy. Rather, both in the procedures and in the resultant expressions, orality reshapes Bible Translation.

Composite of Bible Translation as Contextualization

From the discussions above I begin to put together a composite view of Bible Translation as contextualization for African contexts. Despite certain African theologians' hesitancy to recognize the Bible as predominantly beneficial to Africans, the majority of "ordinary" African

---

79. Draper, *Orality, Literacy, and Colonialism in Antiquity*, 1.
80. Ibid., 3.
81. Draper, *Orality, Literacy, and Colonialism in Southern Africa*, 5.

Bible Translation in the Contexts of Africa

Christians highly esteem the Bible.[82] They may not use the Bible as missionaries initially intended, but they demonstrate their agency by appropriating the Bible and its messages as they work out their local theologies in their specific contexts.[83] It is appropriate, therefore, to pursue reflections on the Bible in Africa and in particular Bible Translation. The following reflections incorporate several assertions of African theologians as reflected in the preceding sections of this chapter.

As stated in the introductory chapter, Bible Translation is neither a neutral nor a simple activity. The challenges and complexities of translation involve issues of power and issues of effective communication. All translation is interpretation. As a result, all translations reflect to varying degrees the social locations of those who were involved in the translation. Despite great acclamations of objectivity, this is not obtainable. Moreover, Bible Translation is ideologically motivated.[84] Bible Translation is also a very complex communicative activity. Skills are necessary in many different disciplines by many people involved in the translation task.[85] Linked to this, translation cannot be presented as a simple dichotomy of source and target/receptor languages. To present language communities as "targets" reeks of colonial agendas. To name them as "receptors" presupposes a unilateral strategy whereby local communities are viewed as objects with outsiders not benefiting from the experience. I propose that such communities be understood as "host communities."[86] These are communities who engage themselves in translations; they negotiate their relationships to translations by appropriating them—simultaneously being shaped by them and also shaping the translations. In this way, Bible Translation becomes an activity where host communities contribute to World Christianity. In theological language, diverse linguistic and cultural perceptions reflect the manifold glory of God. Bible Translation offers to World Christianity multiple understandings of Christianity. Such efforts not only symbolically represent the inherent translatability of Christianity, but in a very concrete way offer multiple understandings of the Scriptures as they are appropriated by local communities.

82. Mbiti, *Bible and Theology in African Christianity*.
83. Sanneh, *Translating the Message*.
84. Yorke, "Bible Translation in Anglophone Africa and her Diaspora."
85. Wilt, *Bible Translation: Frames of Reference*.
86. This nomenclature comes from a presentation at the section "Ideology, Culture, and Translation" of the Society of Biblical Literature in Washington, DC, 2006.

Second, a theology of language is crucial. As suggested in the previous chapter, a theology of the incarnation is directly related to Bible Translation and the myriad of ways God comes to humanity through vernacular languages. Perhaps this can be broadened out to consider Creation as a primary demonstration of diversity and communication. God speaks things into being. Beyond the Tower of Babel (often understood as God's resultant curse by diversification), we recognize not only God's approval but pursuit of the use of diverse languages at Pentecost in Acts 2. People hear the "wonders of God" in their own language. Eschatologically, we are told of a vision of "a multitude from every nation, tribe, people, and language" in the book of Revelation. Rather than seeking unanimity, the Bible portrays linguistic diversity as a divine goal.

Languages are taken seriously because languages shape our theological categories. Whether we argue this point from the Sapir-Whorf hypothesis or the Translation theologies of Bediako or the postcolonial struggles of Ngũgĩ Wa Thiong'o and Dube, to marginalize the effects of languages on theologies is harmful and irresponsible. History has demonstrated how dominant languages have determined the very questions that Christians address. In the past few centuries this theological stranglehold has been loosened by Bible Translation. Yet, it is only in recent years, in response to postcolonial critiques, that an intentional study of Bible Translation and its cultural, societal, and theological consequences have been considered. At the same time, Bible Translation has continued to be viewed predominantly as a tool of evangelism or of unilateral church edification. In order to more effectively discover the contributions and challenges of Bible Translation in response to postcolonial questions, an alternative understanding of Bible Translation is needed. Bible Translation exhibits a theology of language that permits mutual exchanges at the site of Bible Translation. Host communities utilize Bible Translation in their search for relevancy and freedom.

Thirdly, modes of communication must not be understood as neutral. There have been significant studies of the differences between orality and literacy. Unfortunate dichotomization of these modes of communication has distracted researchers from the interface of orality and literacy. In Africa, where various functional levels of literacy exist, there remains today a strong oral dominance. This oral ethos has been recognized by African theologians, anthropologists, and missionaries, but until recently its legitimacy has been marginalized. Proponents of

Bible Translation in Africa have vaunted the introduction of literacy into Africa by Bible Translation. The benefits of literacy to Africa should not be neglected. Yet, postcolonial studies question whether the oral ethos of Africans has been sacrificed in the pursuit of literacy. The situation ought not to devolve into another dichotomous discussion of literacy vs. orality. However, African theologians insist that there is a significant myopia in ignoring the riches of African oral communities and theologies. This has been particularly true with Bible Translation because it has historically set its goal as a literary conversion of the population. Whereas literacy offers significant benefits, it should not be at the expense of oral denigration. Recently Bible Translation efforts have become aware of the effectiveness of oral communications in Africa.[87] I am reluctant, however, to embrace these efforts because they reflect a paradigm of evangelism and do not engage in what I propose as an activity of contextualization. Such efforts appear to use orality as a means to an end that does not engage African communities as agents, but rather as objects.

Fourthly, the contextual approach to Bible Translation that incorporates the parameters of African theologians could greatly benefit from an adjusted inculturation hermeneutics and West's ordinary readers.[88] Such a hermeneutic addresses the tension that has been noted by numerous African theologians as they discuss the starting point of doing theology: the Bible and the local contexts. Experiencing the Bible in community, as the participants foreground their social locations, is a genuine combination of these two starting points. Furthermore, West neglects the importance of orality in the methods of ordinary "readers." Although a more complete description of the incorporation of orality into these methods will be discussed later, the point here is this: the immediate and obvious adjustment to these methods would centralize the oral reception and impact of biblical compositions. Likewise, such an adjustment would not neglect the vernacular language contribution (as argued above under theology of language). Such adjustments would not permit the trained reader or hearer to monopolize the presentation of the biblical passages. Rather, the host community would contribute to the presentation and

---

87. See http://www.chronologicalbiblestorying.com/.

88. Such an approach is supported by recent research of Loba-Mkole, "Bible Translation and Inculturation Hermeneutics"; Loba-Mkole, *Triple Heritage*; Loba-Mkole, "The New Testament and Intercultural Exegesis in Africa."

reception by means of oral performances. It is this concept of oral performances that will occupy much of the remaining chapters.

This composite sketch of components of Bible Translation can only be a beginning. Yet, its outline is necessary here to demonstrate how it is informed by the reflections of African theologians. I have applied this sketch to the preceding chapter's missiological proposition of an alternative paradigm for Bible Translation. This view seeks to express how Bible Translation can be understood as a theological activity that aims at contextualization. The Bible continues to be cherished by Africans. As it is translated into local languages, people are appropriating it according to their cultural, social, and religious locations. African methodologies of inculturation hermeneutics and ordinary "readers" promise constructive methods for assuring that activities of Bible Translation are centered in the contexts of the host communities. Oral performance criticism can provide an adaptation of these literary-biased methods. In the next two chapters I construct a framework for understanding oral performances. This involves historical research as well as anthropological investigation. Whereas Bible Translation has demonstrated its capacity for contextualization in recent centuries—despite its literary bias—I suggest that a thorough reconstitution of aims, theories, and procedures for Bible Translation as informed by oral performance studies can enhance this capacity for contextualization.

3

ORALITY, LITERACY, AND PERFORMANCE

Introduction

THE PRECEDING CHAPTERS HAVE ARGUED FOR AN UNDERstanding of Bible Translation as contextualization. This paradigm responds to African theologians' plea for relevancy in the pursuit of identity and liberation. A critical piece of a composite method that flows from this paradigm is the component of oral performance. This view challenges the assumption of earlier activities of Bible Translation on the African continent that have been intimately connected to literacy. A prejudiced focus on literacy has often marginalized the oral performance context of Africa. This chapter addresses this marginalization by presenting a review of the issues involved with orality, literacy, and performance. Whereas it would be more complete to illustrate the early debates of literacy and orality in the twentieth century,[1] I limit the presentation to a brief overview

---

1. Parry, "Studies in the Epic Technique of Oral Verse-Making, I: Homer and Homeric Style"; Parry, "Studies in the Epic Technique of Oral Verse-Making, II: The Homeric Language as the Language of Oral Poetry"; Parry, "Whole Formulaic Verses in Greek and Southslavic Heroic Songs." Lord, *The Singer of Tales*. Parry may have been inspired in this direction by Marcel Jousse, a French Jesuit scholar, who had published on issues of orality in 1924, "Études de Psychologie Linguistique: Le Style Oral, Rhythmique et Mnémotechnique chez les Verbo-Moteurs." Jousse's work on orality was part of his larger research on the Anthropology of Gestures but included a focus on orality—especially on the impact of oral composition on the New Testament. In the late 1920's this subject of orality was being hotly debated in Sorbonne, where Parry was doing graduate research on Homer. It seems quite evident that Parry was influenced by Jousse and the debates around orality at the time. The discussion of orality took on new fervor around 1960 with several publications: Ong, *Ramus*; Lévi-Strauss, *La Pensée Sauvage*; McLuhan, *The Gutenberg Galaxy*; Havelock *Preface to Plato*; Goody and Watt, "The Consequences of Literacy."

of what has become known as the great-divide debate. After this, my intention is to lift up related studies that have attracted less attention in biblical studies. These studies involve the social (ideological) functions of literacy. From a separate school of research—sociolinguistics—I summarize the technical distinctions of communicating by means of orality and literacy. Having touched on these media, I then turn to oral performance as viewed by folklorists who have developed an area of research called ethnopoetics. The chapter proceeds by following closely the work of John Miles Foley who has documented much of the history of the orality-literacy debate. His work currently moves the discussion ahead significantly and becomes a central theoretical component of my pursuit of the translation of biblical passages as oral performances. The final section explores intentionally the challenges of translating performances.

The Great Divide

The claim for a great divide states that there is a significant difference between communities who are solely oral in their communications and those communities who are literate. Such a distinction suggests a technological divide that affects people's thought processes and social organization. Walter Ong is perhaps the most recognized proponent of this distinction of oral mentality with his "psychodynamics of orality."[2] However, critics have interpreted Ong in recent years as supporting the notion of inferiority of societies that they perceive to be derogatorily named "oral cultures" by Ong.[3] Such distinctions of mentalities, according to this argument, are presented as a thinly veiled reworking of the primitive-civilized dichotomy. Ong avoids a romantic view of oral communities yet underscores how they perceive the oral word differently than either a manuscript or print-biased community.

Another general accusation made against Ong is his supposed denial of orality beyond oral cultures. It is undeniable that oral communication continues to be the predominant mode of communication throughout the world—whether or not the culture is described as oral or print. Ong does not deny this pervasive mode of orality. In fact, he helpfully offers terminology to differentiate how societies use their orality:

2. Ong, *Orality and Literacy*.
3. Furniss, *Orality*.

Orality, Literacy, and Performance

primary, secondary, residual, etc. This leads to a further critique: the absolute division of orality and literacy. I suggest that Ong and others of this period asserted a strong separation between the written and the oral due to the hegemonic understanding of communication based on literary principles. In a hyperbolic way, Ong and others needed to clarify that communication does work differently depending upon the mode used. Nonetheless, this separation has led to a substantial backlash by critics against what has become known as the "great divide."

Other opponents in orality-literacy debates include Jack Goody and Ruth Finnegan. Goody and Finnegan have created their theories based on personal field research, particularly as social anthropologists in Africa. Although most of Goody's publications have revolved around literacy and its implications, his field research in northern Ghana was in a primarily oral setting, where writing was not immediately known. Goody's starting point for writing about literacy begins with orality. Countering a cultural relativity, Goody clearly promotes the view that there is an evolution from orality to literacy whereby this process towards literacy indicates the intellectual possibilities offered by the literary mode of communication. Goody challenges a literate-bias mentality that assumes a given method of logic, memory, or categorization, naming these assumptions as ethnocentric. These various methods, Goody argues, are not available in the same way in a primarily oral setting. More than thirty years after his initial publications on literacy, Goody firmly argues against a negative assessment of his work: "the point Watt and I made is that the formal logical operations involved in the development of the Aristotelian notion of contradiction, of arguments such as the *modus tollens* or of the explicit notion of the syllogism, were critically dependent on the introduction of writing."[4]

Ruth Finnegan's early work in African orality has helped the world appreciate the wonder and intricacy of what she terms "oral literature."[5] Avoiding comments on oral style or mentalities, her research focuses on performance: the role of the performer, and his or her innovations, the cultural context in which the performance occurs, and how the audience participates in shaping the performer and performance. Finnegan has been highly critical of what she asserts as Goody's binary treatment of

---

4. Goody, *The Power of the Written Tradition*, 6.
5. Finnegan, *Oral Literature in Africa*.

orality and literacy.[6] She criticizes Goody for promoting a "technological determinism" with regard to literacy and she challenges the generalizations of the consequences of literacy with empirical studies. She states that her "central point is . . . [that the situation] is more complex than can be summed up in simple causal attributions between literacy on the one hand and specific results on the other."[7] Goody counters: "If I am interested in the general comparison of how writing can influence cultures, I am concerned with comparing the artistic and other productions of cultures that are purely oral (in the sense of not having writing) and those that utilize the written channel in various ways and in various contexts, giving rise perhaps to restricted literacy. Hence to refer to this basic schema as binary, as a great-divide theory, as is done by Finnegan, for example, seems to me a fundamental misunderstanding."[8]

Social Functions of Literacy

What is the relationship of orality to literacy? Though disputed, all sides agree that orality is the predominant mode of communication in the world and that literacy is a relatively recent technological development in human history.[9] The question might be refined as, what is the impact of literacy on individuals and on societies?[10]

> The effects of literacy on intellectual and social change are not straight-forward . . . it is misleading to think of literacy in terms of consequences. What matters is what people do with literacy, not what literacy does to people. Literacy does not cause a new mode of thought, but having a written record may permit people to do something they could not do before—such as look back, study, re-interpret, and so on. Similarly, literacy does not cause social change, modernization, or industrialization. But being able to read and write may be vital to playing certain roles in an industrial society and completely irrelevant to other roles in a traditional

---

6. Finnegan, *Literacy and orality*.
7. Ibid., 159.
8. Goody, *The Power of the Written Tradition*, 22.
9. For a helpful presentation of the chronology of media development, see Foley, *How to Read an Oral Poem*, 23–25.
10. Street, "Introduction: New Literacy Studies"; Olson, "Literacy and Objectivity: The Rise of Modern Science."

Orality, Literacy, and Performance

society. Literacy is important for what it permits people to do—to achieve their goals or to bring new goals into view.[11]

Brian Street suggests a distinction: autonomous vs. ideological. Autonomous here means viewing communication modes in isolation from the socio-political contexts. For Street, the question ought to be, how has literacy been used in various cultures? Referring to the great-divide theory as autonomous theory, Street explains an alternative: "Researchers dissatisfied with the autonomous model of literacy and with the assumptions outlined above, have come to view literacy practices as inextricably linked to cultural and power structures in society, and to recognize the variety of cultural practices associated with reading and writing in different contexts."[12] One of the strengths of such a view is that literacy is no longer presented as monolithic. Empirical research demonstrates that people from different cultures employ literacy differently. This variety of literacies parallels Ong's recognition of multiple oralities. The other major component of Street's presentation of an ideological model is that of power. Lévi-Strauss' statement on power and literacy below has been made use of in recent discussions of orality and literacy in regards to postcolonialism:

> The only phenomenon with which writing has always been concomitant is the creation of cities and empires, that is the integration of large numbers of individuals into a political system, and their grading into castes or classes . . . It seems to have favoured the exploitation of human beings rather than their enlightenment . . . My hypothesis, if correct, would oblige us to recognize the fact that the primary function of written communication is to facilitate slavery. The use of writing for disinterested pleasure is a secondary result, and more often than not it may even be turned into a means of strengthening, justifying or concealing the other.[13]

Although such a strong statement is countered by the numerous uses of literacy for liberation, the ideological model of literacy demonstrates that communication modes involve issues of power.

---

11. Olson et al., *Literacy, Language, and Learning*, 14; quoted in Olson and Torrance, "Introduction," 1.

12. Street, "Introduction," 4.

13. Lévi-Strauss, *Tristes Tropiques*, 392–93, quoted in Draper, *Orality, Literacy, and Colonialism in Antiquity*, 1.

FROM ORALITY TO ORALITY

The dichotomization of orality and literacy (great-divide theory) continues to be discussed intensely.[14] The critical concerns of cognitive processes and social implications continue to be discussed in relation to the modes of communication. Perhaps lost in this discussion is the inherent power of the spoken word.

Sociolinguistics

There is a vast diversity of emphasis in the discussion of orality and literacy, based in part on the perspective of the discipline of the researcher. Stemming from early twentieth-century anthropological studies, a certain branch of linguistics has looked at language in the context of society: sociolinguistics. Representative of studies in the 1980's on orality-literacy from a sociolinguistic perspective is the work of Michael Halliday and Deborah Tannen.[15] Important background to these studies is that English was predominantly the language of study and that the genre of language was conversational speech. Tannen along with the other articles in her edited book argue against a great-divide theory in favor of continuity. Tannen suggests understanding orality and literacy as distinct "strategies" which can be employed in either a spoken or written mode of communication. Consistent with continuity theory Tannen rejects the nomenclature of oral cultures or societies in light of the fact that all societies use oral communication. In another article, Wallace Chafe distinguishes the oral and written by its involvement or integration, respectively.[16] The integration of writing occurs by literary means of nominalization, participles, attributive adjectives, series, and sequences of prepositional phrases, complement clauses, relative clauses—each of these strategies

---

14. Olson groups them ("Literacy and Objectivity," 149) as follows: Group one (continuity theory)—Scribner and Cole, *The Psychology of literacy*; Leach, "Ritualization in Man in Relation to Conceptual and Social Development," 403–8; Douglas, *Edward Evans-Pritchard*; Eisenstein, *The Printing Press as an Agent of Change*; Street, *Literacy in Theory and Practice*; Group two (great-divide theory)—McLuhan, *The Gutenberg Galaxy*; idem *Understanding Media*; Havelock, *Preface to Plato*; Jack Goody, *The Domestication of the Savage Mind*; Greenfield, "Oral and Written Language: The Consequences for Cognitive Development in Africa, the United States and England," 169–78; Ong, *Orality and Literacy*; Stock, *The Implications of Literacy*; Olson, "From Utterance to Text," 257–81.

15. Tannen, *Spoken and Written Language: Exploring Orality and Literacy*; Halliday, *Spoken and Written Language*.

16. Chafe, "Integration and Involvement in Speaking, Writing, and Oral Literature," 35–53.

occurring more frequently in written communication than oral. Oral communication, however, has the following characteristics: it involves interaction between the speaker and the audience with the use of the first person; it refers to the speaker's mental processes; there is a monitoring of information flow; it contains emphatic particles; there is a certain fuzziness in communication; and it involves many direct quotes.

Such distinctive linguistic strategies are pursued by Halliday. Understood as different modes, Halliday asserts, "Writing and speaking are not just alternative ways of doing the same things; rather, they are ways of doing different things."[17] Oral communication differs dramatically from written by the sheer use of the voice, and the variations of prosodic features: "rhythm, intonation, degrees of loudness, variation in voice quality ('tamber'), pausing, and phrasing . . ."[18] These prosodic features—especially the intonation contours of speech—lead Halliday to a discussion of punctuation and its development in literary societies. Written communication is based on grammatical features whereas oral communication punctuation reflects phonological features.[19] Halliday notes further distinctions in these communication "registers" or modes of communication by the lexical density of the written and the clausal intricacies of the oral. Lexical density describes the use of a noun that represents an underlying event, which is often expressed by a verb in the oral—thus requiring explicit subjects and objects.[20] As for clausal intricacies, this is an interweaving from one sentence or clause to another of

17. Halliday, *Spoken and Written Language*, xv.

18. Ibid., 30.

19. These assertions are incorporated into studies for Bible translation with Sundersingh, "Toward a Media Based Translation: Communicating Biblical Scriptures to Non-Literates in Rural Tamilnadu, India." The two main areas where Halliday has influenced Sundersingh is with punctuation and information rate. Sundersingh suggests that punctuation for aural reception should be based on the phonology—most often the intonation patterns—of the host language rather than by the grammatical-lexical constraints of language. Secondly, Sundersingh suggests that a media-based translation should be less dense in its information rate. Whereas much can be compacted into a literary style for writing, the aural comprehension of such a composition is drastically reduced. However, if the information rate is lower, with less compact structures and abstract words, the aural reception can be enhanced with repetition and the use of function words to link one clause equally to another (rather than through subordination).

20. "Redemption" is lexically dense, with the underlying event of "redeem." This verb requires a subject or agent and quite often an explicit direct object: "the time of redemption draws near" might be expressed: "the time when God will redeem Israel draws near."

subjects with frequent anaphoric references, that is, references to previously mentioned items.

Halliday summarizes his distinctions of written and spoken language:

> The written language presents a synoptic view. It defines its universe as product rather than as process. Whether we are talking about a triangle, the layout of a house, or the organization of a society, the written language encodes it as a structure or, alternatively, as a chaos—but either way, as a thing that exists. In principle we can freeze it, attend to it, and take it in as a whole. The cost of this perspective may be some simplifying of the relationship among its parts, and a lesser interest in how it got the way it is, or in where it is going next.
>
> The spoken language presents a dynamic view. It defines its universe primarily as process, encoding it not as a structure but as constructing—or demolishing. In the spoken language, phenomena do not exist; they happen. They are seen as coming into being, changing, moving in and out of focus, and as interacting in a continuous onward flow. The cost of this perspective is that we may have less awareness of how things actually are, at a real or imaginary point in time; and a lessened sense of how they stay that way.[21]

Halliday and the other sociolinguists offer some helpful distinctions between orality and literacy. These distinctions, however, are not intended to be a litmus test to determine what is oral and what is written. As a reminder, these are predominantly distinctions in the English language with conversational speech as the primary genre of orality.

Discussions of orality and literacy from anthropological and sociolinguistic perspectives as mentioned above contribute to a fundamental component of understanding Bible Translation as contextualization: orality. The discussion of orality as not only a distinct way of understanding the world but a way of using language should impact how Bible Translation is conceived and implemented. More recent anthropological research—ethnopoetics—has challenged earlier studies of performances and their recordings. In fact, ethnopoetics offers to Bible Translation a model and tools that valorize oral performance in both the source (the Bible) and host contexts.

---

21. Halliday, *Spoken and Written Language*, 97.

Orality, Literacy, and Performance

Performance

Richard Bauman describes performance in this way: "performance usually suggests an aesthetically marked and heightened mode of communication, framed in a special way and put on display for an audience. The analysis of performance—indeed, the very conduct of performance—highlights the social, cultural, and aesthetic dimensions of the communicative process."[22] As stated above, Bauman accents how performance is "framed in a special way," thus distinguishing performance from other genres of verbal communication. This framing is particular to each speech community. However, there are certain generalities (universals might be too strong since they need to be understood as culture-specific), presented by Bauman as "keys to performance": special codes, figurative language, parallelism, special paralinguistic features, special formulae, appeal to tradition, disclaimer of performance.[23]

When these keys appear, this alerts the community that what follows must be understood as performance, thus moving beyond a direct transfer of information to a poetic use of language that taps into the community's culture and its identity. "Cultural performances may be primary modes of discourse in their own right, casting in sensuous images and performative action rather than in ordered sets of explicit, verbally articulated values or beliefs, people's understanding of ultimate realities and implications of those realities for action."[24] Understood in this way, performance cannot be seen simply as entertainment; it is an aesthetically appealing means of powerful social change. "The consideration of the power inherent in performance to transform social structures opens the way to a range of additional considerations concerning the role of the performer in society."[25]

In anticipation of the next chapter's presentation of the oral component of the biblical compositions and in reflection of my proposed paradigm of Bible Translation as contextualization, I suggest that Bauman's insights into performance are extremely relevant. Bauman's definition of ethnopoetics could be adapted to Bible Translation as contextualization: "concern for the aesthetic patterning of oral literary forms [in the

22. Bauman, "Performance," 41.
23. Bauman, *Verbal Art as Performance*, 16.
24. Bauman, "Performance," 47.
25. Bauman, *Verbal Art as Performance*, 45.

Bible] and the problems of translating and rendering them in print in such a way that the artistry of their oral performance is not lost." Such a goal is combined with the social impact of performances as presented by Bauman: "to transform social structures." Insights into the nuts and bolts of how to go about such a rendering of performance into print come from other folklorists as discussed below.

Ethnopoetics—Dell Hymes and Dennis Tedlock

Richard Bauman defines ethnopoetics in this way: "centrally concerned with the aesthetic patterning of oral literary forms and the problems of translating and rendering them in print in such a way that the artistry of their oral performance is not lost."[26] Whereas some sociolinguists have discussed the relationship of orality to literacy from the predominantly English language and conversational genre, others have researched non-Indo-European languages with a focus on their narrative genre. This is particularly true of Dell Hymes and Dennis Tedlock.[27] Both Hymes and Tedlock have studied in-depth Native American languages—Hymes starting from Linguistics, Tedlock from Cultural Anthropology—ultimately studying the verbal art of different ethnic groups as it functions in society. Hymes counters formal Linguistics by integrating the structure of the language with its functions in community. "In short, primacy of speech to code, function to structure, context to message, the appropriate to the arbitrary or simply possible; but the interrelations always essential, so that one cannot only generalize the particularities, but also particularize the generalities."[28] Hymes proposes an "ethnography of communication" in which "one needs to investigate directly the use of language in contexts of situation, so as to discern patterns proper to speech activity."[29] Hymes reflects the influence of his linguist mentor, Edward Sapir. Hymes problematizes Sapir's assertions of a direct relationship of language to worldview by noting that each language community uses language differently. Yet, language contributes to the ways in which reality is perceived. "[T]he

26. Bauman, "Folklore," 39.

27. Hymes, *Foundations in Sociolinguistics*; Hymes, *Now I Know Only So Far*; Tedlock, *Finding the Center*; Tedlock, *The Spoken Word and the Work of Interpretation*.

28. Hymes, *Foundations in Sociolinguistics*, 9.

29. Ibid., 4.

role of language as a device for categorizing experience and its role as an instrument of communication cannot be so separated, and indeed, the latter includes the former."[30]

Sapir's fieldwork and that of Franz Boas have also greatly affected Hymes' understanding of verbal art.[31] From his own fieldwork, Hymes recognized that traditional field notes only partially recorded verbal performances. Similarly he understood that Boas and Sapir's collections were limited by their transcriptions. Oral performance presented many other levels of communication that were not contained in notebooks that transcribed words and sentences without cues to vocal modulation, pauses, and volume, to name only a few. Hymes regretted that these earlier transcriptions understood the oral narratives as prose—dividing chunks of speech by paragraphs—with no insight into their poetic organization. Hymes asserts: "oral narratives are organized in terms of lines, of patterned sequences of lines . . . In my experience, however, paragraphs conceal or at best make it difficult to recognize what actually goes on in a narrative: how action is shaped, how emphasis is distributed, what is marked against a common background. If the nature of the work that is necessary can be summed up, it is: not paragraphs but lines."[32] This introduces what Hymes terms verse analysis: "Narratives consist, not only of lines, but of lines in patterned relation to one another. Differences in emphasis and shape and interpretation can be specified in the texts themselves."[33] This verse analysis has been a continuing investigation of the internal organization of oral narratives. Lines form verses, verses stanzas, stanzas scenes, scenes acts, and acts compose the narrative. For Hymes, the source for this research has been the transcribed notebooks of early anthropologists such as Boas and Sapir. It is too simple to summarize Hymes' research as segmenting lines by linguistic particles—although this is admittedly how he first discovered such patterning.

Hymes' earnest concern is that the vast documentation of oral narratives be reinterpreted by means of verse analysis. This would correct an ethnocentric distinction of poetry and narrative by demonstrating the internal organization of narratives. This in turn would continue the

30. Ibid., 19.

31. Boas' work is multiple. A general introduction is Stocking, *The Shaping of American Anthropology 1883–1911*.

32. Hymes, *Now I Know Only So Far*, viii.

33. Ibid., x.

agenda of people like Boas who sought to demonstrate how oral narratives shared with European languages grammatical patterning; oral narratives also demonstrate poetic patterning, not through line-internal meters, but through inter-line measured patterning. The first step in this process is to reformat the narratives by lines, verses, stanzas, etc., based on internal patterning. A critical step in this hierarchical division is the method of translation from the source language. Past translations did not respect the source-language linking of etymologically related words, but were primarily concerned with context-sensitive semantics. Hymes urges another way by recognizing the "failure to translate the same words the same way. Identity of words is often an essential part of larger organization (e.g., initial particles)."[34] Hymes' translation method does not easily separate form from meaning, but realizes that form is critical to meaning. "Suppose that part of the point of narrative is not to provide news, but satisfying form . . . The interest is not so much in what will happen as in how it will happen."[35]

Ultimately it is Hymes' commitment to previously transcribed oral narratives—narratives whose language and its speakers may no longer exist—that separates him from Tedlock's research on narrative performances. The distinction between the two researchers is presented in the following way by Hymes: "It might be a fair summary to say that Dennis is concerned most of all with the moment of performance, and I am much concerned with the competence that informs it. Dennis trusts most of all the speaking voice, I evidence of recurrent pattern. That means I run the risk of finding pattern that isn't there . . . Dennis runs the risk of missing pattern that is there."[36] The differences, however, cannot be simply stated as many summarize and as Hymes mockingly presents: "What is particularly not so is the equation Tedlock : Hymes = pause : particle."[37]

Tedlock agrees with Hymes that the fundamental contribution of ethnopoetics is the understanding of oral narratives as a form of poetry; oral narratives are best represented in print by lines and not paragraphs. Tedlock acknowledges that the segmentation of lines can be understood through syntax and overt grammatical markings. However, given Tedlock's focus on working with live performances, the critical indicator

34. Ibid., 35.
35. Ibid., 48.
36. Ibid., 36.
37. Ibid., 37.

Orality, Literacy, and Performance

of line-breaking is silence, the pauses between lines and the more lengthy pauses between verses, stanzas, and scenes. These pauses are accompanied by other prosodic features such as the narrator's vocal qualities, volume, cadence, intonation, and so on. Distant transcriptions of oral narratives where languages and speakers are extinct, therefore, are not the primary area of research for Tedlock. How can one divide into lines a narrative that was transcribed in prose in the nineteenth century? The distinction methodologically, therefore, between Hymes and Tedlock can be generalized by whether one researches a living or extinct language tradition. Tedlock's overall critique of Hymes' work is that it is literary-biased and does not demonstrate the oral dynamics of performance.

Tedlock's challenge is to re-present oral narrative performances on paper. His motivations for fixing these performances on paper include safe-guarding them for posterity. Scripting these performances also enables (literary) researchers to study the intricacies of oral performances. Given that these performances are in Native American languages, the constant accompanying challenge is translation. The format for these translations is what Tedlock calls either a script or a score. Such nomenclature communicates that more than the verbal wording is translated; stage directions, vocal qualities, intonation contours, cadence, volume, and of course the salient feature of silence are each communicated by Tedlock's scripting. According to one of Tedlock's "Guide to Reading Aloud," pauses are represented with separate lines, or longer pauses with dots (•). Higher volume is represented with capital letters whereas quieter volume with smaller font sizes. This system allows for crescendos (building up of volume). Chants are presented with words on different lines (perhaps subscript and superscript). "Glissandos" (falling/rising intonations) are presented in staircase steps of the vowel. Lengthening of vowels is with double-hyphenated lines whereas consonants are represented with repetition of consonant. Paralinguistic guides (to gestures, tones, audience responses) are italicized and placed in parentheses.[38] By scripting an oral narrative in this way, Tedlock is hoping to demonstrate how one might translate the style of the narrative as it was performed.

Tedlock offers several points of guidance for the translation into scripts of oral performances.[39] A scripted translation seeks to reproduce

---

38. Tedlock, *Finding the Center*, xlv.

39. General points extrapolated from Tedlock, *The Spoken Word and the Work of Interpretation*, 41–61.

the "original effects of formality."[40] Oral performances tend to use archaic interjections, which Tedlock suggests leaving them untranslated with explanatory notes. Similarly, onomatopoeic words generally do not need a translation, according to Tedlock, as context often permits understanding. Prosodic or paralinguistic features are understood by Tedlock to be central and not peripheral to a translation, necessitating some means of communicating them in the script. The most important of these features for Tedlock is that of silence; he follows others in this way: "according to Fieda Goldman-Eisler, as much as half the time spent in delivering spontaneous discourse is devoted to silence, and 'pausing is as much a part of the act of speaking as the vocal utterance of words itself.'"[41]

As a demonstration of Tedlock's concern for the original form, he considers the very issue of the original syllable count as potentially translatable, but with further reflection permits other ways to translate this. "Where the length of lines is concerned, it would be difficult and foolish to slavishly follow the exact Zuni syllable counts in translation, but it is possible to at least approximate the original contrasts in line length."[42] These translation guides are a response to Tedlock's experience with translations of oral performances that communicated little of the original oral dynamic. "The apparent flatness of many past translations is not a reflection but a distortion of the originals, caused by the dictation process, the notion that content and form are independent, a pervasive deafness to oral qualities, and a fixed notion of the boundary between poetry and prose."[43] After all, for Tedlock, the goal is not simply to transmit information, but to communicate the rhetorical impact of the performance. "The treatment of oral narrative as dramatic poetry has a number of analytical advantages . . . What oral narrative usually does with emotions is evoke them rather than describe them directly . . ."[44]

Whereas these principles might be accurate for the source performance, it seems that Tedlock is not as concerned with the host language tradition and its potential difference of function of some of these styles. That is, does raised volume in the Zuni language function rhetorically

---

40. Ibid., 41.
41. Ibid., 48.
42. Ibid., 50.
43. Ibid., 54.
44. Ibid., 51.

in the same way as English, for example? Do longer pauses communicate the same thing in French as they might in Xhosa? The strength of Tedlock's translation is its accuracy in form to the source language. The weaknesses may be in how such forms are understood in a host language.[45] This discussion of the tension between accuracy to the original language style and rhetorical impact in the host language tradition is a critical subject that will be discussed in chapter 5.

Elizabeth Fine

A principal challenge for folklorists is how to present in print what has been orally performed. This concern is addressed by Elizabeth Fine in her book, *The Folklore Text: From Performance to Print*.[46] Fine renders an important service by presenting the developing history of folklorists and their treatment of performance. Beginning with Boas and his contemporaries, she presents an evolution of theories and field research up through Hymes, Tedlock, and Bauman. Even more important is her incorporation of other disciplines to her principal thesis: how do you transfer a live oral performance to a print medium? In addressing this question Fine is respectful of the treatment of recent ethnopoetics, but insists that textmaking must go beyond verbal recording and even performance notation to a theoretical foundation for intersemiotic translation.[47] Along the way to developing this theory, Fine differentiates various genres of communication with oral performance—mainly in that such verbal art involves an aesthetic transaction. That is, oral performance is not simply a transfer of information, but it demonstrates an epistemological shift whereby knowledge is acquired through an aesthetic experience. It is a transaction in which the audience is not passive, but participates with the

---

45. In Tedlock's later work, it seems this weakness is addressed. Fine summarizes the change: "Tedlock has changed his practice of leaving Zuni onomatopoeic words untranslated: 'In *Finding the Center*, I left Zuni onomatopoeia untranslated wherever I preferred its sound to that of the English alternative, but I have since come to the view that an onomatopoeic word helps give a story immediacy, an immediacy that would be lessened by the sudden intrusion of a foreign word in the translation.'" Tedlock, "Translator's Introduction," Sanchez, "The Girl and the Protector," a story translated from the Zuni by Tedlock, 111, quoted in Fine, *The Folklore Text*, 158.

46. Fine, *The Folklore Text*.

47. The term "intersemiotic translation" as a translation from one medium to another follows Jakobson, "Closing Statement: Linguistics and Poetics," 350–77.

performer in the development of the performance. Fine attempts to demarcate what makes a live performance so different from other means of knowledge; live performance is: active-receptive, sensuous, immediate, intuitive, preanalytic, integral, unique, and intrinsic.[48] These descriptions differentiate live performance from silent, individual reading.

Another contribution that Fine makes in developing her methodology is the distinction between a performance report and a performance record. The report is a synopsis of the performance that permits the reader an appreciation of the performance context, event, and notational devices used within the actual performance record. This report, suggests Fine, should follow Hymes' categories for an ethnography of speaking: setting and scene; participants; ends—that is, goals—and Act Sequence; key and instrumentalities (gestures); key (guide) to projections (notation); norms and genre.[49] The need for this report is twofold: in order for the new audience to appreciate the original performance this information is needed; an attempt to include this information into the actual performance record overloads it and makes interpretation of the performance too complicated. As for the actual performance record, Fine combines the work of several anthropologists—including Tedlock—in a three-part record. The left margin is for paralinguistic information, e.g., the quality of the voice in speaking; the right margin presents the kinetic information, that is, the body language, gestures, and facial expressions of the performer. The text proper includes similar notation as Tedlock for intonation contours, syllable stress, and volume. Fine recognizes that each performance situation may require varied notation, depending on cultural and linguistic patterns. There is also notation of audience participation.

This task of transferring an oral performance to print requires translation—both intersemiotic and often interlingual. Fine uses primarily Eugene Nida's theory of translation to guide her aims of translation. According to Nida, an adequate translation must: 1) make sense; 2) convey the spirit and manner of the performance; 3) be natural and easy to read, and 4) produce a similar response.[50] Fine sets up a translation theory that is in tension on four poles: formal—dynamic; analytical—

---

48. Fine borrows heavily from Berleant, *The Aesthetic Field*, 78–86.

49. Hymes, "Models of the Interaction of Language and Social Life."

50. Fine, *The Folklore Text*, 111, following Nida, *Toward a Science of Translating*, 162–63.

perceptual. She decides that the ultimate tension for performance scripting is formal—perceptual.[51] Fine, therefore, wants to adhere to the formal style of the source yet permit the same rhetorical impact on the host community. Procedurally, she presents the following two steps: 1) translate the formal style of original into host language; 2) find functionally equivalent forms for the host community. This second step will require performance of the formal script to see where things need to change. Fine has contributed greatly to both a theoretical and practical approach to performance and its representation in print. Her dated understanding of communication theory—especially as reflected in her adherence to Nida's theory of translation—will be challenged later in discussions on other communication models. Nevertheless, she attempts to hold in tension the formal features of the source performance and the necessity for the host community to experience the performance according to its own cultural and linguistic sensitivities.

Annekie Joubert

A great deal of field research and theoretical discussion has occurred since the beginnings of ethnopoetics in the 1970s and 1980s. The availability of audio and video equipment to researchers has permitted the audio-visual recording of live performances, supplementing written scripts. Yet, the challenge continues as to how most effectively to communicate to others outside the original live performance what is the communicative and social impact of the performance. The geographical area of study of folklore has also broadened beyond the Americas to places such as Africa. Representative of the contemporary research of performance is the work of Annekie Joubert, an African folklorist textmaker. Joubert builds on the previous ethnographic research of Hymes, Tedlock, Bauman, and Fine. Her social location and the site of her field research in South Africa—both prior to and after Apartheid—become important components of Joubert's methodology. She appreciates the ideological elements of an outsider, white, South African woman working with indigenous, black communities—communities which she describes

---

51. "In order for a text to record verbal art as performance, then, and not some other mode of communication, the textmaker must strive for formal and perceptual equivalence." Fine, *The Folklore Text*, 158. I understand her use of "perceptual" as similar to Nida's use of "functional." De Waard and Nida, *From One Language to Another*.

as "primary and semi-oral cultures."[52] Joubert demonstrates, both in her book and in the accompanying DVD, her fluency in one of the languages of performance. Each of these is significant to what Joubert treats within her broader goal of discussing how to record—through print and video—live performances.

Joubert follows closely the sociolinguistic understanding of language in that where "social function gives shape to linguistic form, language has social as well as referential meaning."[53] This understanding supports her view of performance: "Performance event [is] a mode of communication."[54] Earlier discussions have well distinguished the written mode from orality. Yet orality only partially describes performance. Besides the oral/aural channel, Joubert follows Fine's distinctions of other channels: visual (including kinesthetic, artifactual, proxemics), tactile, and olfactory.[55] Performance therefore encompasses much more than simply oratory. Beyond these performative channels are the societal contexts in which performance occurs. Performance combines both a community's traditions and the performance event itself: "The term *performance* refers, according to Hymes, to two aspects: recognition of known traditional material as situated in a context, and the character of a social event with emergent properties unfolding within that context."[56]

The challenge first discussed by Tedlock and then extended by Fine is central to Joubert's task: how does one record live performances? Taking advantage of affordable and portable audio-visual technologies, Joubert insists that a written record needs to be supplemented by audio-visual recordings. These multimedia recordings become a part of Joubert's "performance-directed text." Joubert augments Fine's two-part representation of a live performance (performance report and record) by suggesting a four-part performance-directed text:

1. Pre-text which refers to a preface, or background information regarding the performance event, for example setting and scene in which the performance is taking place, the participants involved in

---

52. Joubert, "Defining and Working in an Oral Culture," 4.

53. Bauman, *Folklore, Cultural Performances, and Popular Entertainments*, 43; quoted in Joubert, *The Power of Performance*, 60.

54. Joubert, *The Power of Performance*, 3.

55. Ibid., 110–19.

56. Hymes, "Breakthrough into Performance," 13; quoted in Joubert, *The Power of Performance*, 60.

Orality, Literacy, and Performance

the performance, the uniqueness of every performance regarding cultural specificity and variability, the message form and content, the historical, cultural and social context in which the performance takes place and the genre of the performance event;

2. transcribed text, which refers to the transcription in an alphabetic notation system of the verbal utterances of performance event;

3. sub-text, which can be regarded as the performance directions, because it contains inherent visual and auditory codes which are operative in a performance event;

4. an interpretive text, which refers to the interpretation and emergence (concretization) of the performance event.[57]

Perhaps the most striking point that can be made about Joubert's performance-directed text is just how limited the transcribed text is to describe the actual performance. Clearly a study of this text will permit only a limited understanding of the performance. That is, its aesthetic values and its social impact will only partially be understood from a transcribed text; a full-fledged performance-directed text is necessary to attempt a more complete appreciation of the performance event.

Current Issues in Performance—John Miles Foley

It is impossible to discuss issues of orality, literacy, and performance today without referencing the work of John Miles Foley. Foley's work not only connects to the early classical work of oral-formulaic theory, but he has also engaged in sociolinguistic and anthropological research—theoretical and in the field—in regards to performance.[58] Foley's insights permit a fresh and clear way of understanding the interface of orality and literacy and the significant social roles that performance plays. He is a leader in the area of oral traditions as demonstrated by his prolific writing on the subject. Foley helps other researchers by offering a venue for publishing their works. As well, he is instrumental in educational

---

57. Joubert, "Defining and Working in an Oral Culture," 10; Joubert, *The Power of Performance*, 131.

58. Foley, *The Theory of Oral Composition*; Foley, *Immanent Art*; Foley, *The Singer of Tales in Performance*; Foley, *How to Read an Oral Poem*.

programs for future researchers in oral traditions.[59] Foley is an important bridge for my own study as he himself has discussed frequently issues of oral traditions and performance in the context of biblical studies.

One of Foley's greatest contributions is to provide a taxonomy of the oral-written spectrum. Avoiding a binary categorization, Foley acknowledges the interface of orality and writing in what he calls "oral poetry."[60] Such a taxonomy is not myopic in looking only at issues of composition but also that of reception. Four points on this spectrum are shown in the table below:[61]

TABLE 1
Foley's Oral-Written Spectrum

	Composition	Performance	Reception	Example
Oral performance	Oral	Oral	Aural	South Slavic Epic; Hananwa or Xhosa praise poetry; South Sothon migrant songs; folk sermons from North America
Voiced text	Written	Oral	Aural	Slam poetry
Voices from the past	Oral/Written	Oral/Written	Aural/Written	Homer's *Odyssey*; Gospel tradition
Written oral poems	Written	Written	Written	Bishop Njegoš

The taxonomy refuses to limit oral poetry to some purist view of oral performance, where the composition, performance, and reception take place without the written medium. "Oral poetry cannot be reduced to a single pristine form that arises strictly in letterless societies and out of the mouths of certifiably preliterate speakers."[62] Foley understands oral

---

59. The journal *Oral Tradition* has been published since 1986 and can be found online at: http://journal.oraltradition.org/. Foley is also involved in teaching courses in an MA program in Oral Traditions at *The Graduate Institute*; the website can be accessed at: http://www.learn.edu/.

60. Foley admits that "oral poetry" has its difficulties. Poetry is modified by "oral" to permit people to quickly understand that the phrase is used in a special way, not assuming a Euro-American literary bias. See Foley, *How to Read an Oral Poem*, 29–30.

61. Joubert, "Defining and Working in an Oral Culture," 3; Foley, *How to Read an Oral Poem*, 39; Foley, "Indigenous Poems, Colonialist Texts," 14.

62. Foley, *How to Read an Oral Poem*, 26.

Orality, Literacy, and Performance

performances recorded in writing—often from antiquity—also as oral poetry—whether or not they were composed and/or received with the aid of writing. Oral poetry demonstrates how it defies binary categorization with poems composed in writing and either performed and received by means of writing or orality. This taxonomy provides space for an "oral poem" that only occurs in writing, but has a clearly distinct oral style. Another important corrective Foley makes with this taxonomy comes from ethnopoetic studies. Early on, the oral-formulaic theory dominated orality studies to the point that researchers were looking for oral features that were similar (or even identical) to what Parry and Lord had found in Homeric and Slavic epics. Foley underscores that each oral tradition needs to be researched on its own terms and not forced into predetermined categories of genres and features.

Foley's contributions continue as he incorporates Bauman's study of performance. Combining his earlier work of the oral-formulaic theory with performance studies, Foley suggests the notion of word-power in his continuing discussion of tradition. "In the present context *word-power* will name that particular mode of meaning possible only by virtue of the enabling event of performance and the enabling referent of tradition."[63] This word-power occurs in performances that permit a special comprehension, understood by Foley as a framed context. This notion comes from Bauman: "performance sets up, or represents, an interpretive frame within which the messages being communicated are to be understood, and that this frame contrasts with at least one other frame, the literal."[64] This context of performance is "keyed" by specific features, but they take on new significance when understood as indicators that a performance is occurring and the performer and audience are "keyed" to the meanings of performance as accessed by tradition.[65] Foley has captured what performance studies have been alluding to: the study of performances should not be limited to an attempt to replicate the live performance as

---

63. Foley, The Singer of Tales in Performance, xiv.

64. Bauman, *Verbal Art as Performance*, 9; quoted in Foley, *The Singer of Tales in Performance*, 8.

65. As noted above, examples of these keys—though in no way understood as prescriptive or universal—are listed by Bauman: "special codes, figurative language, parallelism, special paralinguistic features, special formulae, appeal to tradition, and disclaimer of performance." Bauman, *Verbal Art as Performance*, 22; quoted in Foley, *The Singer of Tales in Performance*, 11.

a written document. This structural study must be combined with the tradition to see how performance functions in society, how performance creates meaning.

A third important contribution that Foley brings to the discussion is how tradition is central to the social function of performance. Foley prefers to discuss oral traditions that immediately connect any verbal art to a culturally-specific set of traditions. More is being said and done than simply the words of a performance. The performer works within a cultural context where one assumes many important cultural connections with one's audience. The audience actively participates in the performance and interprets the performance from a context of that specific cultural tradition. This is what Foley describes as "Immanent Art," as explained in the subtitle: "From Structure to Meaning in Traditional Oral Epic."[66] Foley refuses to limit his research of oral poetry to the structural features of the verbal art. "[W]e have yet to appreciate in any thoroughgoing way how these features affect or influence the meaning embodied in the works in question."[67]

Foley understands that meaning is created between the performer and the audience by the use of cultural references in the performance. Given that the performer and audience share much of the cultural traditions, references to them do not need to be full-fledged, but can be coded "metonymically," with a part standing for the whole.[68] In this way, a word, phrase, gesture, expression can metonymically communicate an entire narrative that is not fully expressed in the performance, but nonetheless is fully accessible to both performer and audience. Foley uses the Internet as an appropriate demonstration of his use of metonym in Immanent Art: "Immanent Art contends that this and other non-epithet formulas are keys or switches—not unlike links on a Web page—that summon a larger context via a specialized code."[69]

Foley makes use of Receptionalism from literary studies and applies it to oral poetry.[70] The receptionalist distinction shifts attention away from the author to the reader, thus empowering the reader to bring

---

66. Foley, *Immanent Art*.
67. Ibid., 2.
68. Ibid., 7.
69. Foley, *How to Read an Oral Poem*, 113.
70. Iser, *The Act of Reading*.

meaning to a text. Shifting from a context of reading to performance, more is communicated in a performance than the words (or other channels of communication). There is an active role of the audience to participate in creating meaning from the performance. "The key idea to keep in mind as we further refine this retooled Receptionalist model is the immanence of tradition: it is the ever-impinging presence of the extratextual, summoned into the process of interpretation under the rules of the traditional contract, that rationalizes the textless environment of oral tradition as well as enriches the understanding of oral-derived texts."[71] This understanding of meaning does not permit an objective, monovalent meaning. Meaning is negotiated between performer and the audience. Performers have intentions in what they want to communicate, but once the performance begins the gaps of indeterminacies are filled by the plural audience. If meaning then becomes a negotiation between the performer and the audience, is every interpretation appropriate? Foley responds negatively to this question because of what is presumed above: tradition. Oral poetry depends upon oral traditions; it is the traditions of the community that set up a parameter of acceptable interpretations. "The tradition in effect makes each performance an authoritative 'document,' each textual structure a unique signal, by stipulating its significance, by institutionalizing its invariable, inherent meaning in the face of the ever-shifting superficial designs of performance, version and so on."[72] In this way, tradition is the decisive authority—just as a written text can be authoritative.

Social Memory

The subject of tradition in the discussion of performance leads to another contemporary issue: social or collective memory.[73] Performance engages oral tradition in its mode of communication. Tradition is connected to social memory. In fact, some constructionists hold that tradition is the invention of present-day hegemonic elites. This is in reaction to the earlier notion of tradition as an objective view of historical events. Most researchers today reject both of these extremes and suggest more of an

---

71. Foley, *Immanent Art*, 45.

72. Ibid., 44.

73. The understandings of social (collective) memory are taken from Kirk, "Social and Cultural Memory," 1–24.

interplay between the present and the past. "Collective memory is this negotiation, rather than pure constraint by, or contemporary strategic manipulation of, the past. . . . The relationship between remembered pasts and constructed presents is one of the perpetual but differentiated constraint and renegotiation over time, rather than pure strategic invention in the present or fidelity to (or inability to escape from) a monolithic legacy."[74]

Social memory depends on an ever-evolving master narrative as it establishes, negotiates, and confirms a community's identity. Performance of narratives that support this master narrative become the primary way to reinforce this identity, while still adjusting to present experiences. Memory in performance therefore is not static, but dynamic as a community works through its current situations in relation to its salient past. "The goal of memory is not retrieving data but rather re-creating and re-living an experience."[75] The special features that key performance are often mnemonic in a double sense: they aid the performer in the remembrance of what to perform, but they are also the metonymic references that engage an audience in their tradition. These special features act (metonymically) as a gateway for the audience to access their traditions by hearing a few brief words or phrases in a performance. One of the foremost researchers on social memory, Jan Assmann, connects the elements in this way: "But memory remains always the main carrier of the central stock of cultural knowledge, and ritual performance remains the dominant form of reproducing the cultural texts."[76]

This close connection of performance to social memory underscores the importance of treating performance with translation as contextualization—specifically how inculturation responds to issues of identity. Performance is understood as more than simply an aesthetic correction to a literary-bias view of narrative; it is an epistemological shift as a mode of communication, intricately involved in a community's identity through its social memory.

---

74. Olick and Levy, "Collective Memory and Cultural Constraint," 934; quoted in Kirk, "Social and Cultural Memory," 21.

75. Foley, "Memory in Oral Tradition," 92.

76. Assmann, "Form as a Mnemonic Device," 78. Assmann explains his use of "text": "In my terminology, formalization is what turns an utterance into a text . . . Text is speech in the status of a mnemonic mark" (ibid., 72).

Orality, Literacy, and Performance

Performance and Translation

This section is intended to introduce some of the theoretical issues of translation—especially in terms of performance. My intent here is to introduce briefly commonalities between Foley's Immanent Art and Relevance theory, the communication model adapted to translation; such a connection is not made by Foley himself. Each of the earlier discussions above on performance presupposed a certain methodology of translation: Nida's dynamic-functional equivalence. Fine comes the closest to challenging this presupposition by attempting to juxtapose a respect of the form with the functional impact of the performance. Dynamic equivalence and its subsequent articulations have been appropriated by many translators to separate form from meaning. It has been acknowledged that Nida based his theory of translation on a communication model for machine communications, whereby "the meaning" can be separated by the linguistic form and transferred to a second linguistic form.[77] This model of communication and its ensuing theory of translation have been increasingly critiqued over the years.[78] These critiques, however, are not mentioned in early or recent discussions of performance and its accompanying task of translation. However, other work has begun not only to question this theory and its assumptions about communication but to propose other theories that are based on other communication models.

Nida's translation theory has been described as linguistically-based. Relevance theory utilizes a communication model, based on cognitive studies. The difference between a linguistic and communication basis becomes immediately noticeable with the figurative use of irony. An ironic statement is made, where the literal meaning of the words is not the intended sense; rather it is often the opposite of the literal meaning that is intended. This distinction of literal and figurative meaning coincides with performance studies' distinction of referential and effective meaning. Secondly, both Relevance theory and Foley's revamping of Receptionalism for performance are audience-oriented. The audience plays a critical role in the determination of meaning. This is illustrated by what Foley introduced as metonymy and later explicates as "communicative economy."[79] More meaning occurs than simply the words

77. Fine, *The Folklore Text*, 104.
78. Mojola and Wendland, "Scripture Translation in the Era of Translation Studies."
79. Foley, *The Singer of Tales in Performance*, 53–56.

spoken. In fact, according to this model of communication, gaps of indeterminacies are critical to avoid boredom and to promote audience participation. A similar understanding of communicative economy is expressed by one of Relevance theory's practitioners: "Terms are like addresses for concepts. Using a term evokes all the information stored at that address, both the dictionary meaning of the concept as well as a range of encyclopaedic information."[80] It seems appropriate to me to investigate the possible benefits by looking at the translation of performance from the perspective of Relevance theory. Ethnography of speaking, ethnopoetics and performance studies have concluded that a transcription of the words alone in performance is insufficient. Foley's Immanent Art has employed these earlier methods to reinforce the role of tradition in performance. The translation of oral poetry must include aspects of this tradition as it was metonymically communicated in performance if the translation is to communicate even the partial social and rhetorical impact of oral poetry.

Voices from the Past

An important point for this study in Foley's spectrum of oral poetry is his "voices from the past." These "voices" were initially orally performed but have since been fixed in written text. Foley includes the gospel tradition and several other sections of the Bible in this category. Having examined the leading issues of orality, literacy, and performance, I approach the narrower field of research in New Testament studies. This chapter's examination of the issues becomes a backdrop for appreciating the literary bias that has marked biblical studies in a parallel way as it has shaped broader issues of orality and literacy. In many ways the relatively recent introduction of orality issues into New Testament studies has followed the course of the classicists and folklorists: an initial great-divide approach that has since become more nuanced. It has been only in the very recent past that this discussion has begun to be articulated in terms of performance. Much of the work by folklorists and the work of Foley have yet to be incorporated into New Testament studies. An assumed subject within this study is that of translation: how does one translate voices from the past? Almost all previous responses to this question have begun from a literary bias. A persistent motivating question for this study

---

80. Hill, *The Bible at Cultural Crossroads*, 126.

is: what are the implications of performance studies for New Testament translation? Yet, even broader, given the overwhelming prominence of performance throughout the world, how might a performance-oriented approach contribute to Bible Translation as an expression of contextualization? Orality, performance, and New Testament studies become the subjects of the next two chapters.

4

LITERACY AND ORALITY IN RELATION TO THE NEW TESTAMENT

Introduction

GIVEN THE OVERARCHING THEME OF TRANSLATION IN this book, it is important to discuss in depth the New Testament as the source of such translation. This chapter includes discussions of the New Testament and how numerous scholars have understood issues of literacy and orality in relation to the New Testament. In a similar fashion to the rise of discussions of orality in classical and anthropological circles in the 1960s, biblical scholars found a renewed interest in the importance of orality in their work in the 1980s. Beyond earlier twentieth-century hypotheses of form and source critics in regard to the oral environment of the first-century, researchers are approaching issues of media with a more sophisticated appreciation of orality's role in the composition, transmission, and reception of the New Testament. Paralleling the pattern of classicists and anthropologists, early studies sought to dichotomize communication by opposing the written to the oral word, following the great-divide theory. In time, such binary categorization became less helpful in describing a more complex communication environment: an interplay of literacy and orality more appropriately describes the history of the New Testament.

For the past two-and-a-half decades, New Testament scholars have begun to reexamine the genres of the New Testament with an ear to hearing the acoustic values of the compositions. Certain researchers remain satisfied with the structural insights of the texts whereas others seek to

Literacy and Orality in Relation to the New Testament

understand the social functions of these texts in relation to their media. It is clear that Biblical Studies has rediscovered important insights into the New Testament as a result of these pursuits. However, there remain many questions and further need of clarity in terms of media in not only the historical context of these compositions but also their rhetorical and social functions in the first century. An important correlative question is: how might such an awakening to orality enliven discussions for twenty-first century audiences? This chapter looks at the historical development of research in the past twenty-five years in regard to the issues of media in the New Testament. The insights of various researchers in regard to the value of New Testament orality studies in general and the more narrow studies of particular New Testament texts are explored below. This exploration is foundational to Bible Translation and the paradigmatic shift towards translation as contextualization.

Beyond Form Criticism

The topic of orality has been discussed in Form, Source, and Redaction criticisms in the last century. The concern of these discussions has been the composition of the New Testament texts. Researchers recognized the existence of orality and understood how oral traditions influenced the eventual written composition of New Testament texts. The following discussion presents only a narrow path in this broad area of studies. Werner Kelber's *The Oral and the Written Word* marks an important point in discussions of orality in relation to the composition of the Gospel of Mark.[1]

Kelber's view of the synoptic transmission is that there is a stark difference between the oral and written word, a difference that leads to distinct hermeneutics. An oral hermeneutic is exemplified by the historical Jesus, argues Kelber. "If Jesus was a charismatic speaker, he risked his message on the oral medium and did not speak with a conscious regard for literary retention. As oral performer he had neither need nor use for textual aids, nor did he speak with an eye toward textual preservation."[2] Kelber asserts that Mark's Gospel is the beginning of something new. Clearly there was oral tradition prior to the writing of the Gospel, but

---

1. Kelber, *The Oral and the Written Gospel*. Twenty-five years later, a collection of reflections on this seminal book has been published: Thatcher, ed., *Jesus, the Voice, and the Text*.

2. Kelber, *The Oral and the Written Gospel*, 19.

once it was written a new hermeneutic was introduced. This is clearly stated in his new introduction of his book: "Mark's gospel became a written document less from an extension of the antecedent oral traditions than in resistance to oral norms, drives, and authorities."[3]

Kelber finds support for such dichotomous understandings of these issues in the classical studies of Parry and Lord. "Together with the model of synoptic evolution we must forego the one closely connected with it, that of original form. The form-critical search for the archetypal composition, and the compulsion to honor it as a first rung in the evolutionary ladder betray the bias of textuality and ignorance of oral behavior. The works of Milman Parry and Albert B. Lord have made it incontrovertibly plain that each oral performance is an irreducibly unique creation."[4] Even more influential to Kelber is the work of Walter Ong and his psychodynamics of orality. Kelber places the Apostle Paul's use of the oral word in opposition to the written Mark. The support for these assertions echoes Ong's proposals.[5] Despite this hyperbolic talk of the separation of the oral from the written, Kelber reintroduced the issue of orality in fresh ways into biblical studies.[6] His research laid bare the literary bias of researchers. His later work brings greater nuance to the relationship of the oral and written word. Nonetheless, he remains firm on how Mark's Gospel introduces the new hermeneutic of the written word in the synoptic tradition. Kelber's contribution extends beyond the debate of synoptic transmission. His insights into the vitality of oral communication in the first century have engendered fresh looks at New Testament texts in regards to orality.

James Dunn brings a fresh perspective to many oft-debated topics in the New Testament. Dunn's work with issues of orality and the Jesus tradition are no exception as he incorporates the work of Kenneth Bailey on the transmission of oral tradition as applied to the synoptic tradition.[7] The title of his recent book, *Jesus Remembered*, reflects Dunn's

---

3. Kelber, "Introduction," xix.
4. Ibid., 30.
5. Ong, *Orality and Literacy*.
6. A collection of responses to Kelber's book indicate how some of his claims may need to be tempered. See especially Boomershine, "Peter's Denial as Polemic or Confession," 47–68.
7. Dunn, *Jesus Remembered*; Dunn, "Altering the Default Setting: Re-envisaging the Early Transmission of the Jesus Tradition"; Bailey, "Informal Controlled Oral Tradition

understanding of the crucial importance of the remembered impact of Jesus on the life of the early followers of Jesus. This impact was expressed through the stories and teachings of and about Jesus. Core elements and key themes were retold with a level of flexibility (following Bailey) held in check by the community who already possessed a knowledge of these traditions. "The hypothesis which Bailey offers on the basis of his reflections on these experiences is that informal, controlled oral tradition is the best explanation for the oral transmission of the Jesus tradition."[8] Dunn asserts that early form-critical quests for discovering the buried literary treasures of Jesus' words is "wrong-headed" in that it understands the synoptic tradition as a literary process rather than as an oral tradition process. The Gospels we have now in written form reveal a glimpse of one specific oral performance frozen in writing. "The point is that we should not assume that such compositional procedures came into the process only at a later stage of the process or only when the tradition was written down."[9] The written tradition, however, has in no way impeded the continued oral performances in the many decades following their transcription. Dunn's view permits the written and oral word to coexist and does not perceive them (as Kelber does) as antithetical. The way in which these performances occurred, according to Dunn, demonstrates a middle ground: "Rather it points a clear middle way between a model of memorization by rote on the one hand and any impression of oral transmission as a series of evanescent reminiscences of some or several retellings on the other."[10]

Several other issues of Form Criticism could be discussed.[11] However, this quick overview is intended as a backdrop to discussions of

---

and the Synoptic Gospels"; Bailey, "Middle Eastern Oral Tradition and the Synoptic Gospels."

8. Dunn, *Jesus Remembered*, 209. Dunn includes three assertions of Bailey in this regard: "(1) a community would be concerned enough to exercise some control over its traditions; (2) the degree of control exercised would vary both in regard to form and in regard to the relative importance of the tradition for its own identity; (3) the element in the story regarded as its core key to its meaning would be its most firmly fixed element" (Dunn, *Jesus Remembered*, 209).

9. Ibid., 248.

10. Ibid., 249.

11. Byrskog. "A New Perspective on the Jesus Tradition"; Derrenbacker, *Ancient Compositional Practices and the Synoptic Problem*; Botha, "Mark's Story as Oral Traditional Literature"; Henderson, "Didache and Orality in Synoptic Comparison";

orality and the New Testament. Whereas the earlier form critics focused on the composition of these New Testament texts, my interest is more in the transmission and reception of these compositions. This is a significant shift in emphasis and will permit me to examine several biblical scholars' contributions to the evidence for an intentional primary oral-aural transmission and reception of New Testament texts. Such a shift in emphasis resonates with my general thesis of Bible Translation and the oral nature of the New Testament and contemporary oral societies. Prior to the more specific examination of individual texts, it is important first to look at the general communication environment of the first-century Mediterranean world.

Communication in Antiquity

As indicated in the previous chapter, the spoken word is as predominant in communication today throughout the world as it was in antiquity. However, technological development in communications has changed dramatically over the centuries.[12] Prior to the invention of the printing press in the fifteenth century in the West, technological development beyond the spoken word consisted of handwriting, for the most part with manuscripts. Leaving the study of the development of the alphabet to others, my primary focus here is the communication context of the first-century Mediterranean world.[13] Important resources to view this context are William Harris' *Ancient Literacy* and Rosalind Thomas' *Literacy and Orality in Ancient Greece*, supplemented by Harry Gamble's *Books and Readers in the Early Church*.[14] Evident throughout these sources is the

---

Derico, "Upgrade and Reboot"; Hollander, "The Words of Jesus: From Oral Traditions to Written Record in Paul and Q"; Lord, "The Gospels as Oral Traditional Literature"; Horsley and Draper, *Whoever Hears You Hears Me*. For an unconvincing argument against the oral connection to the gospels, see Henaut, *Oral Traditions and the Gospels*.

12. Eisenstein, *The Printing Press as an Agent of Change*.

13. Histories of this development can be found in Havelock, *The Muse Learns to Write: Reflections on Orality and Literacy from Antiquity to the Present*; Goody, *The Interface Between the Written and the Oral*.

14. Harris, *Ancient Literacy*; Thomas, *Key Themes in Ancient History*; Gamble, *Books and Readers in the Early Church*; Hezser, *Jewish Literacy in Roman Palestine*; Carr, *Writing on the Tablet of the Heart*. These secondary sources make use of the primary sources of antiquity. It is beyond the scope of this chapter to cite these primary sources.

fact that generally speaking, researchers have anachronistically projected today's print-biased presuppositions of communication on antiquity.

Evidence of written literature has led people to assume that the majority of the population was able to read and write. The falsities of this presupposition become immediately clear by what is often the first supposedly simple question of the period: what was the literacy rate in antiquity? Several underlying issues must first be addressed prior to responding to this question. First, what is literacy? Does it mean both reading and writing? What is the object of these activities, that is, what is being read or written? And more insightfully, how are things being read and written? Who is doing these activities? And finally, why does one write (or not write) in antiquity? There are other significant questions to ask on this subject, but these should suffice to indicate the complexity involved in discussing communication in antiquity. Responses to these questions will give large brush strokes to the setting in which the area of study is narrowed to the New Testament.

Both Harris and Thomas demonstrate that literacy throughout Greek and Roman history is neither uniform in its appearance nor stable in its growth. Social contexts influence how literacy functions. This understanding undermines a view of technological determinism with literacy.[15] Furthermore, as pockets of literacy are described in ancient Greece, the development of literacy does not resemble a steady, evolutionary growth. Rather, it is more of an ebb and flow as certain city-states demonstrate evidence of more abundant literary remains in earlier periods than later. Such an unsteady progression underscores the social conditioning of literacy as well as the non-evolutionary pace of literacy, thus calling into question a modern view that equates literacy with civilization and the lack of literacy with what is primitive. Harris suggests that an overall literacy rate (problematic in its generalizations) "is not likely to have risen much above 10–15%."[16] Whatever the levels of literacy in antiquity, it could never be described as mass literacy. Harris points to certain social components being necessary for such a movement: primarily the printing press's capability to produce inexpensive large quantities and a

---

15. Brian Street and Ruth Finnegan accuse Jack Goody, Walter Ong, and Eric Havelock of such an autonomous view of literacy in which literacy is presented as the sole determinate for social and cognitive change. Street, *Cross-cultural approaches to literacy*; Finnegan, *Literacy and orality: studies in the technology of communication*.

16. Harris, *Literacy and Orality in Ancient Greece*, 328.

philanthropic spirit to invest in an extensive education system. "The following chapters will show that some of the vital preconditions for wide diffusion of literacy were always absent in the Graeco-Roman world, and that no positive force ever existed to bring about mass literacy."[17]

An accurate description of communication in antiquity must reflect the interplay of literacy with orality. A dichotomous view is either anachronistic (print-bias) or insupportable due to the considerable evidence of writing. Throughout ancient Greece and Rome there are abundant artifacts—both literary and archeological—of writing. These could be divided into portable and non-portable media. Five portable materials are: papyrus, parchment, wax tablets, wooden tablets and potsherds. Durability becomes an issue that divides these materials into two groups, with papyrus and parchment more durable. Wax and wooden tablets along with potsherds are argued to function well in note-taking and as an equivalent to modern scratch paper, respectively. The reusable tablets were less expensive than parchment and papyrus. The format of these more expensive materials can be divided into the roll and codex. Either material could be used for either medium, although parchment was more durable and expensive.[18]

A significant distinction with these two materials is the manner in which access to the text occurs: a scroll is one continuous text, whereas the pages of a codex allow for more random perusal.[19] We might make a modern comparison between an audiocassette and a compact disc. Other than delineating the materials for writing, it is necessary to underscore the economic considerations for writing. Personal libraries and multiple copies of scrolls and codices demonstrate that certain people were able to own their personal "books." However, given economic priorities as well as their inability to read, the majority of the population would not possess their own written material.[20] As for the non-portable writing materials,

---

17. Ibid., 12.

18. Discussions of materials for writing in antiquity can be found in both Harris and Thomas as well as Gamble's chapter on "The Early Christian Book," 42–81. Discussions of how this information relates to the way Paul communicated by means of epistles are found in Richards, *Paul and First-Century Letter Writing*.

19. Width of columns of text was determined by the width of a thigh, on which one steadied the scroll or codex. See Derrenbacker, *Ancient Compositional Practices and the Synoptic Problem*, 37–39, for a discussion on this.

20. Harris, Thomas, and Gamble all discuss the monetary issues of written materials. Gamble, given his thesis, corrects previous social views of early Christians by

Literacy and Orality in Relation to the New Testament

these include inscriptions on stone, metals, frescos—all of which were intended for public viewing by the population. Issues of authority are involved in both portable and non-portable writing. The decrees of the governments, written for public consumption, were not simply literature; they were displays of power. Inscriptions were not direct indications of literacy of the general population. Inscriptions could be iconic in value, read by some, indirectly interpreted by all.[21]

In terms of the act of writing with scrolls and codices, the practice of writing involved primarily dictation in antiquity. This is important for several reasons. First, the composition and sending of a written document does not presuppose that the author was literate. Scribes were used for this task. Oftentimes a literate slave-owner would use a literate slave to transcribe his dictation. For these reasons, first-century writing is often described as scribal. A class of scribes was employed by people to write and send letters and other written messages. Scribes were also employed for reproduction of written materials.[22] A second important element to dictation is the centrality of the spoken word. Dictation required vocal composition. Crucial to this method is that words were not judged only for their referential meaning but also their aesthetic value. This artistic concern went beyond the level of the word to the entire discourse. A compelling communication must be appealing to the ear. A third element of writing by dictation in antiquity involves the actual placement of letters on the parchment or papyrus. The general practice was *scriptio continua*, "continuous script."[23] Partially due to economic reasons, entire "pages" of documents were filled with letters, without spaces between words, without punctuation. The end of a line required the continuation on the next line, whether or not there was a syllable or word break. Eventual word breaks and punctuation were included, but very few first-century manuscripts benefited from them. Such continuous script does imitate the stream of speech of the spoken word, but

---

acknowledging that it was more wealthy Christians who owned writing materials. Nevertheless, the majority of the population had more basic needs for their money. See also Derrenbacker, *Ancient Compositional Practices and the Synoptic Problem*, 30–37.

21. Harris argues these points throughout his book with particular mention on pages 265–67. Issues of power are addressed in Draper, *Orality, Literacy, and Colonialism in Antiquity*.

22. Harris, *Literacy and Orality in Ancient Greece*, 231.

23. Gamble, *Books and Readers in the Early Church*, 203–4.

it does not indicate the pauses and extended silence that typographic features can partially indicate in modern print. This posed no problems for the scribe or the composer of the document. However, it did create challenges for the reader.

Scriptio continua and the aural component of dictation lead to a discussion of reception of the message. The default setting for twenty-first century recipients is silent, individual reading. However, throughout antiquity reading was generally communal and aural, that is, reading aloud. Whether *scriptio continua* was as difficult to an ancient reader as it is for a modern is still being discussed, but there are several expectations of ancient reading that suggest that the reader must be quite familiar with the composition in order to read it publicly. The author may be the reader of the document, but more often it would be another person. Familiarity with the text—either by oral communication with the author or preparatory study of the text—was essential for public reading aloud. Rhetorical expectations demanded that the reading be smooth, emotional, and effective. To describe the delivery of the composition as reading can be misleading. Perhaps recitation or oral performance is more accurate. This indicates that memory is involved in the public presentation of the composition. Of Aristotle's five components of rhetoric—invention, arrangement, style, memory, and delivery—discussions of memory are often overlooked.[24] Memory was integral to public presentation.[25] As a result, documents were composed not only for the aesthetic appreciation of the spoken word, but for retention. The compositions were structured to facilitate the retention for the oral performer as well as for the hearing audience. Written texts can be understood as memory aids.

A helpful presentation of the complexity of writing and reading in antiquity is presented by Lucretia Yaghjian.[26] She suggests six points on a continuum: auraliterate, oraliterate, oculiterate, scribaliterate, illiterate, literate.[27] "Auraliterate reading is the practice of hearing something read . . . [while] oraliterate reading is oral recitation or recall of a memorized text . . . Oculiterate reading is linguistic decoding (by eye) from a written

---

24. This was also recognized by Botha, "Letter Writing and Oral Communication in Antiquity," 26.

25. Yates, *The Art of Memory*; Carruthers, *The Book of Memory*.

26. Yaghjian, "Ancient Reading."

27. Ibid., 208–9.

Literacy and Orality in Relation to the New Testament

text, performed by readers who can decode written letters . . . [while] scribaliterate reading is reading for technical, professional or religious purposes on behalf of a particular interpretive community." "Illiterate" technically denotes "lack of ability to decode written communication." However, it is commonly used today pejoratively to connote uncivilized. "Literate [is used] in a technical sense to denote the ability to decode written communication, their definition applies to oculiterate and scribaliterate readers only." Such a continuum is helpful in several ways. First, it corrects a bias where being illiterate is understood as primitive. Furthermore, being illiterate does not limit access to either the reception or performance of written texts (as indicated by auraliterate and oraliterate reading). If the majority of the population in antiquity was illiterate, this did not preclude other types of literacy. Nevertheless Yaghjian's continuum is biased to literacy by its very use of "literate" in its nomenclature. This unfortunately supports the use of literate as the default, with varied modified types of literacy. More accurate is taking oral as default. Why not begin with people as aural recipients and oral presenters? Nonetheless, Yaghjian presentation helps us understand the situation of communication in antiquity as more complex than a literate—oral dichotomy. Rather than discussing these media monolithically, it would be more appropriate to discuss them in the plural: literacies and oralities.

Communication and the New Testament

The New Testament is a subset of this larger communication context of antiquity. Its setting is not dramatically different from what is described above although distance from Rome and Greece in conjunction with the rural context suggests an even lower literacy rate.[28] Richard Horsley suggests, "Outside of a few aristocrats and scribes in ancient Greece, Rome, and Israel, however, virtually no one could read and write . . . The vast majority of people, the Galilean, Judean, and other villagers, were largely illiterate. One recent study places the literacy rate in Roman Palestine as low as 3 percent."[29] This indicates that the communication setting was predominantly oral. Yet as we have noted above, predominantly oral does not

---

28. This lower rate is argued for by Bar-Ilan, "Illiteracy in the Land of Israel in the First Centuries C. E."; Hezser, *Jewish Literacy in Roman Palestine*.

29. Horsley, "Mark as Oral," 53–55.

exclude literacy. Written manuscripts circulated and were communicated in community settings. Written inscriptions were present and symbolized authority. Nevertheless, the implications for the ubiquitous role of orality has been neglected in biblical studies. Kelber sought to enliven the discussion with a hyperbolic claim to Mark's written Gospel as distinctive from the oral context. However, most New Testament scholars today recognize a more nuanced interaction of writing and orality. Vernon Robbins suggests that this interplay be understood in regards to the setting for the New Testament as a "rhetorical culture" rather than an oral culture.[30] J. A. (Bobby) Loubser also presents his continuum of orality-literacy based on the core issue of a manuscript culture so that pre-first century would be understood as a low manuscript culture and by the second century it would be described as high manuscript culture. The first century of Mark's context is described by Loubser as intermediate manuscript culture.[31] Despite the potential misunderstanding of the term "oral," it seems appropriate to me to counteract the print-bias assumptions of modernity by asserting the clear oral bias of the first century.[32]

---

30. Robbins, "Progymnastic Rhetorical Composition and Pre-Gospel Traditions, 116; Robbins, *Exploring the Texture of Texts*; Robbins, "Oral, Rhetorical, Literary Cultures"; Robbins, "Interfaces of Orality and Literature in the Gospel of Mark." In these last two references, Robbins presents a spectrum in which "rhetorical culture" is placed: He presents a spectrum of this interface: 1) oral, 2) scribal, 3) rhetorical, 4) reading, 5) literary, 6) print, 7) hypertext—affirming rhetorical as the most appropriate understanding of Mark's context. Several other New Testament scholars opt for this terminology: Harvey, "Orality and Its Implications for Biblical Studies," 99–109; Hearon, "The Implications of Orality for Studies of the Biblical Text," 3–20; Shiner, "Memory Technology and the Composition of Mark."

31. Loubser, "What is Biblical Media Criticism?"; Loubser, *Orality and Manuscript Culture in the Bible*.

32. Holly Hearon acknowledges the interplay of the written and oral and thus accepts in part the term "rhetorical culture." However, she also acknowledges a distinction of the two media by noting the evanescence of the oral and the fixidity of the written in *The Mary Magdalene Tradition*, 14–15.

Literacy and Orality in Relation to the New Testament

TABLE 2
Literacy-Orality Continua[33]

	Havelock (Literacy)	Boomershine (Media)	Ong (Orality)	Loubser (Culture)	Robbins (Culture)
	Pre-literate	Oral	Oral	Oral	Oral
3300 BCE				Scribal culture	
600 BCE	Craft-literate		Radically Oral		
500 BCE	Recitation-literate			Primary manuscript culture	
400 BCE	Script-literate			Intermediate manuscript culture	Scribal
			Largely Oral		
100 CE		Manuscript			Rhetorical*
					Reading
150 CE				High manuscript	Literary
			Residually Oral		
1400 CE	Type-literate	Print			Print
1700 CE		Silent Print	Minimally Oral		
2000 CE		Electronic	Secondarily Oral		Hypertext

* Vernon K. Robbins suggests a continuum within a rhetorical culture in terms of intertextuality: reference, recitation, recontextualization, reconfiguration, and echo ("Oral, Rhetorical, and Literary Cultures," 82–88).

An early influential biblical scholar in relation to issues of orality is Pieter J. J. Botha. Botha has done a great service by condensing Harris' general study of ancient literacy as well as contributing his own insights in his approach to New Testament studies.[34] An important assertion by

---

33. Adapted from Harvey, *Listening to the Text*, 38. Loubser addition from Loubser, "Reconciling Rhetorical Criticism with its Oral Roots," 99. Robbins addition from "Oral, Rhetorical, Literary Cultures," 77; Robbins, "Interfaces of Orality and Literature in the Gospel of Mark."

34. Botha, "Mute Manuscripts"; Botha, "Letter Writing and Oral Communication in Antiquity; Botha, "Greco-Roman Literacy as Setting for New Testament Writings"; Botha, "Living Voice and Lifeless Letters"; Botha, "The Verbal Art of the Pauline Letters: Rhetoric, Performance and Presence."

Botha is that the media—orality and literacy—are not neutral. The media shape the message. "Communication media not only *reflect* culture but also *influence* it fundamentally."[35] Botha confronts recent biblical studies and accuses scholars of assuming a print bias in their research. "The thesis of this paper is that an unrecognized assumption underlies most exegetical activities, namely that writing implies a constant role and/or function in communication."[36] While admitting that every society uses oral strategies in communication, Botha pushes to recognize a distinction in societies where oral communication is highly valued. "Orality refers to the experience of words (and speech) in the habitat of sound."[37] Botha is not seeking to establish a great-divide theory, but recognizes that communication media are culture specific. For the first-century setting, a fusion of written and oral was used, a fusion that made use of the oral bias of the society. "Particularly, it is the insight that writing and speech are culturally embedded phenomena, similar to other social conventions, that we need to facilitate in a comprehensive approach to our texts."[38] Noting the predominance of orality, yet appreciating the gradation of literacy in antiquity, Botha understands literacy's role in the service of orality. However, Botha notes an important point that will be discussed in greater detail below: the relationship of bureaucratic power with literacy. This aspect of power is linked to religion: "But more significantly, the written word itself exercised religious power . . . But the use of the written word to convey religious messages remained connected to the oral (this is so even for Paul)."[39]

Besides the link of political and religious authority to literacy, Botha pursues the function of literacy in letter writing. This is especially helpful in order to imagine the use of literacy in the New Testament epistles—especially Paul.[40] Beginning more broadly, Botha corrects some potential anachronistic assumptions about first-century literacy. Education does not equal literacy: "In Greco-Roman societies one could be educated

---

35. Botha, "Mute Manuscripts," 35.
36. Ibid., 39.
37. Ibid., 40.
38. Ibid., 45.
39. Botha, "Greco-Roman Literacy as Setting for New Testament Writings," 209.
40. Although the quotations in this paragraph are from a different article, Botha has articulated the same claims for Paul's letter writing in "The Verbal Art of the Pauline Letters."

without having the ability to read and write."[41] "To describe the Hellenistic age as an oral world does not mean that the people were not familiar with writing and did not employ writing during their lives . . . Writing was a product and a commodity to be sold, not an intellectual process . . . Whatever we make of ancient letters, orality was part and parcel of the whole process . . . The point to see is that they are texts that originated as and were designed for oral presentations."[42] The critical point about letter writing in an oral setting—specifically of the first century—is the communal and auditory components. Botha suggests a "co-authorship" in New Testament letters. "The true import of the issue [of amanuenses] . . . is that communication was not experienced as a message from one mind to another. It was a communal event . . ."[43] "Receiving a letter meant hearing both a message conveyed on behalf of the sender and a written document."[44] Botha anticipates the centrality of performance in the reception of these letters.

> While many scholars turned to Greco-Roman rhetoric for help in interpreting Paul's letter (with worthwhile results), the oral, performative aspect of ancient communication, and specifically ancient rhetoric have been neglected . . . Speech and rhetoric cannot be separated as Hellenistic culture basically was an oral culture . . . We gather a distinct sense of how thoroughly a reader must have been acquainted with his text, and must have worked to internalize its performative values . . . The point that the oral reader was the instrument for embodying the contents of the text being performed, has become clear . . . Paul's dictation of his letter was, in all probability, also a coaching of the letter carrier.[45]

Botha contributes the findings of his own research on the Greco-Roman context in terms of communication media.[46] He examines several (written) texts of Plato (and Socrates), Papias, Seneca, Clement. Botha asserts that it is the elite few who are using writing. However, even these elites have a view towards writing that in many cases favors the "living voice" of orality. Botha refutes the interface of these two media as a relationship

41. Botha, "Letter Writing and Oral Communication in Antiquity," 18.
42. Ibid., 21.
43. Ibid., 23.
44. Ibid., 24.
45. Ibid., 26–27.
46. Botha, "Living Voice and Lifeless Letters."

of symbiosis or dichotomy in the context of communication in antiquity. Rather, the written medium is subsumed in the oral context. Writing is a way of communicating speech. Very little of these findings of Botha are directly applied by Botha to the New Testament, but one can imagine some important clarifications. Botha names two: re-evaluation of the concept of an "original" version; a change away from a doctrine of Scripture to a theology of tradition (in terms of authority and its loci). These assertions are supported by both classical and anthropological research.

A final scholar in this survey who appreciated early on the oral aspect of the New Testament is Joanna Dewey. Her primary focus has been Mark's Gospel, although she has made some important contributions to Pauline studies, as indicated in the next section. Dewey responds to Kelber's assertion of a disconnect between pre-Markan orality and the written Gospel. "Yet, in a manuscript culture with high residual orality, there is considerable overlap between orality and textuality . . . Thus oral techniques of composition are to be expected in the Gospel even if it was composed in writing."[47] Dewey is a primary example of applying Classical Studies' orality studies to research oral features found in biblical texts. In this early study, Dewey makes assertions, based on Havelock's orality studies, of the oral components of Mark's Gospel: connecting teaching to events; the use of visible imagery; the aggregative, episodic development (rather than linear, chronological progression).[48] Furthermore, Dewey argues for an oral method of narrative development of Mark as it demonstrates oral features: variation within the same; acoustic principle of echo; ring composition (*inclusio*)—Marcan "sandwiches"; balanced patterns ("acoustic responsions"); and chaining method.[49] Dewey concludes, "Mark certainly seems to have followed the oral method analyzed by Havelock for the tale as a whole . . . It is made up of happenings which are easily visualized and which are not arranged in a logical order. Rather the happenings appear in an endless chain of association, based on the echo principle."[50] The evidence within Mark of these oral features is sufficient proof against Kelber's claims: "it seems more likely that Mark is building on an existing oral narrative tradition of some sort—not connecting the

47. Dewey, "Oral Methods of Structuring Narrative in Mark," 33.

48. Ibid., 35–38. The non-linear character of Mark is furthered argued in Dewey, "Mark as Interwoven Tapestry."

49. Dewey, "Oral Methods of Structuring Narrative in Mark," 38–40.

50. Ibid., 42.

Literacy and Orality in Relation to the New Testament

disparate episodes of the synoptic tradition for the first time."[51] Dewey clarifies that she is not arguing for an oral composition of Mark or that Mark lacks dramatic development. Rather, she is suggesting that Mark be studied with an oral hermeneutic whereby Mark's composition is analyzed with an ear to its strategy of interwoven development, a strategy distinct from a purely modern literary approach.[52]

Structure and Social Functions of Orality in the New Testament

Although the appreciation of issues of oralities in the New Testament is relatively recent, numerous studies in the past fifteen years demonstrate the potential insights for historical, literary, and postmodern interests. As with all new methodologies, clarity in the midst of this research can be challenging as new terminology, revised categorizations, and fresh implications are suggested. Insights from related fields of study can be drawn to help negotiate these challenges. Borrowing from Brian Street's categorization of orality-literacy studies, I adopt the terminology of autonomous and ideological.[53] By autonomous, I mean research of oralities and literacies that are separate from societal influences. I use the autonomous category here to demarcate the studies of New Testament orality that limit themselves to the structural characteristics.[54] As for ideological, I would like to emphasize that my understanding of ideological here is related to the social functions of orality (and/or literacy) in the New Testament contexts.

A second potential categorization is that of genre. The New Testament is traditionally understood as consisting of three main genres: narrative, epistolary, and apocalyptic. It promises to be helpful to look at these different genres to determine if orality is used differently with each. Clearly there are some differences in composition and transmission—especially between narratives and epistles. It can be argued that the

---

51. Ibid., 44.
52. Dewey, "Mark as Interwoven Tapestry," 234–36.
53. Street, *Cross-cultural Approaches to Literacy*.
54. This is different from Street's use of autonomous where he places such studies as proponents of a great-divide theory whereby literacy becomes an example of technological determinism.

narratives were composed orally and later written down. Whether this is the case or not does not dispute the fact that oral features are exemplified in written form. With epistles, I argued above that these written documents were first composed by the method of dictation. Whether one is looking at narratives or epistles, the written form reflects the oral features. In terms of reception, whether narrative, epistolary, or apocalyptic, these writings were composed to be heard. The aural aesthetic is an important goal of each of these genres.

Oral Structures

Numerous biblical scholars have presented oral features within New Testament compositions.[55] Margaret Dean states clearly the potential for orality studies: "The systematic analysis of sound in texts can indicate how literary compositions are structured and how they make meaning."[56] The point argued in orality studies of the New Testament is that a silent reading makes use of neither the oral nature of these compositions nor the intended aural effect on the hearers. "If New Testament literature in its first-century rhetorical context was publicly spoken and heard rather than privately written and silently read, each composition's public, oral delivery and auditory reception is essential to its full and faithful interpretation."[57]

An earlier study by Dean and Bernard Brandon Scott presents a thorough example of how such sound studies of New Testament passages can be done.[58] Their careful analysis of the Sermon on the Mount delineates sections according to phonetic recursions as a hierarchical structure. These subdivisions are discovered by means of aural structures and often conflict with traditional literary subdivisions. Dean and Scott envision a sound map as the initial step towards a full exegetical study of a passage: "If the analysis of sound is the first step, what should be the

---

55. Besides those discussed here, other orality studies include: Aitken, *Jesus' Death in Early Christian Memory*; Upton, *Hearing Mark's Endings*; Borgman, *The Way according to Luke*; Winger, "Orality as the Key to Understanding Apostolic Proclamation in the Epistles."

56. Dean, "Textured Criticism," 90.

57. Ibid., 81.

58. Scott and Dean, "A Sound Map of the Sermon on the Mount." Another article that begins to implement these issues of orality with translation is: Scott, "A New Voice in the Amphitheater."

Literacy and Orality in Relation to the New Testament

second? We would suggest that a comprehensive methodology would involve theoretically four steps: sound analysis, rhetorical analysis, literary analysis, and ideological analysis."[59] Dean and Scott limit their expansive study in the article to the issue of sound. As they reason, "For too long New Testament studies have ignored the most basic level of textual reception, the sound of the language. It is time we began to pay it serious attention."[60]

Bobby Loubser presents such an analysis from one of Luke's pericopes, 9:51–56.[61] Loubser seeks to discover oral features on two levels with this pericope: first, how Luke communicates a story to his audience; second, how characters within this story demonstrate these oral features in their interactions with other characters within the story. Loubser compares the Greek text with the ancient Latin Vulgate and modern English translations to bring into relief the oral features of the Greek. The modern English translations, in attempts to make the passage more literary, remove many of these oral features, thus underscoring the oral components lost in many modern translations.[62] Loubser begins with the paratactic style of the Greek, where eight phrases begin with a coordinate conjunction: *de* (three times) or *kai* (five times). Loubser identifies a formulaic use of words within this pericope for "face" and "village." Whether formulaic or simple repetition, such repetition is not followed in the translations because it is deemed to be dully repetitive. Loubser argues that the pace of the text quickens at verse 54 with the use of a participle at the beginning of the phrase.[63] The change of pace or rhythm contributes to the overall rhetorical impact upon the hearers. Within the story itself, the characters exhibit their oral ethos. The pericope tells us

---

59. Scott and Dean, A Sound Map of the Sermon on the Mount," 717.

60. Ibid., 718.

61. Loubser, "What is Biblical Media Criticism?" Similar argumentation in Loubser, "How Do You Report Something That Was Said With a Smile?" Loubser is interacting in a translation workshop in South Africa in 1984. Papers from this conference are found in Louw, *Sociolinguistics and Communication*.

62. "It is clear that the modern translators, reconstructing the text in terms of a new medium—i.e., that of prose—transformed the oral conventions of the Greek text, whereas the Vulgate sought to maintain it" (Loubser, "How Do You Report Something That Was Said with a Smile?" 309). These features included: conjunctive particle, formulaic expressions, repetitions, rhythm of text, etc.

63. This participle is translated as a finite verb in the English, a choice that forces the verb towards the end of the sentence.

that Jesus, a wandering teacher, sends his disciples ahead with an oral message. The disciples' plea to call down "fire from heaven" would evoke, within the hearers, oral traditions of God's judgment on people (for example Sodom) or the reference to fire as associated with God's Spirit and purification. In other words, the phrase is metonymic (following Foley) whereby it evokes a larger oral tradition immanently accessible to the audience. Finally, the closing scene of the pericope is Jesus' rebuke of the disciples. Within an oral ethos, words do not just transmit information; they are active, affecting change (following Speech Act theory). When Jesus turns to rebuke the disciples, his words (reinforced by his bodily turning) point to the disciples' diametrically opposed position to Jesus setting his face towards Jerusalem.

Whitney Shiner (as well as Loubser) treats the prologue to Mark's Gospel in terms of oral composition.[64] Shiner suggests that this prologue be considered the equivalent of a rhetorical *exordium*, serving "to put one's listeners in the right frame of mind to receive the speech."[65] Understood as including the audience, Mark's use of the pronoun "you" is not limited to those personages within the textual world, but reaches out to the listening audience. The beginning composite citation from Isaiah announces the arrival of a messenger "who will prepare *your* way." Shiner avers that this citation not be restricted to its historical context, but that the audience be included in this announcement. Loubser studies the implications of how the prologue is composed for auditory impact. This is not limited to emphatic enunciations of key terms but is reflected in the syllabic rhythm of the passage. Loubser notes the short and long syllables and how the alternation of these two types builds a pattern that is both pleasing to the ear and also supportive of the meaning of the text. This is particularly clear in Mark's citations of Exodus 23:20 and Isaiah 40:3 in verses 2–3. Noting how the Greek translation of the original Hebrew text differs from Mark's citations, Loubser asserts that "one has to conclude that unity of rhythm and sound was the guiding principle for the seamless conflation of texts into a new unit."[66]

In terms of epistolary genre, numerous recent studies present oral structuring. A few selected examples should suffice. John Harvey has

---

64. Shiner, *Proclaiming the Gospel*; Loubser, "New Possibilities for Understanding Ancient Gospel Performances."

65. Shiner, *Proclaiming the Gospel*, 184.

66. Loubser, "New Possibilities for Understanding Ancient Gospel Performances," 12.

put together an entire book that presents "oral patterning of Paul's letters": chiasmus, inversion, alternation, inclusion, ring-composition, word-chain, refrain, concentric symmetry.[67] Harvey notes a descending frequency in oral patterning, based upon the length of Paul's epistles, but yet a significant percentage of the text is affected by oral patterning. According to Harvey, Paul's use of these patterns reflects both an influence of experience with the Hebrew Scriptures and to a lesser degree the Greco-Roman rhetorical strategies of the day. An important question for Orality Criticism is how such a method offers more insight into the New Testament than a strictly literary study. Harvey suggests five contributions, that it:

1. offers further information on issues of integrity;
2. clarifies Paul's argument;
3. delimits the extent of certain passages;
4. gives clues to Paul's intended focus; and
5. clarifies relation of focus in regard to the surrounding context.

"In sum, it may be said that oral patterning offers an additional body of 'formal' evidence that can be used in conjunction with other exegetical methods to help 'fine-tune' the interpretation of Paul's letters."[68]

Casey Wayne Davis presents an eclectic methodology that he names "oral biblical criticism." Such an approach begins with the communication setting of the first century as an interplay of the written and oral word. Davis brings together Rhetorical Criticism and modern linguistics—specifically discourse analysis—in his focus on the auditory values of the epistle of Philippians. He argues that an understanding both of oral communication as relational and of the concentric structure are crucial to understanding the integrity of Philippians.[69] The relational aspect of the communication is evident especially in the beginning and ending of the letter as specific addressees are named, but it can also be recognized throughout by means of grammatical structures, such as the use of vocatives and imperatives. The oral nature of communication

---

67. Harvey, *Listening to the Text*, 283–84.
68. Ibid., 300.
69. "What is referred to here as 'concentric structure' is also alluded to in scholarly literature as chiasm, *inclusio*, responsion, parallelism and ring composition" (Davis, *Oral Biblical Criticism*, 99).

is also demonstrated through the concretization of ethics that are not abstractly philosophical but fleshed out by the description of good and bad behavior of individuals. The concentric structures of Philippians are exemplified with repetition of words and themes in both chiastic and chaining strategies. Davis argues throughout that the contribution of Oral Biblical Criticism is how such structures can be recognized by means of sound. "Oral biblical critics look for *aural* thematic and structural markers and mnemonic pegs which have been used by the composer not mainly because a large amount of analytical thought has been given to the material but because such markers are a sub-conscious tool which is used in all forms of communication in an oral society."[70]

My own study of Paul's epistle to Philemon brings out several oral features of this brief communication.[71] Despite Harvey's dismissal of Philemon as lacking these features, I find Philemon to be a powerful example of the dynamic of composing a message to be heard in community.[72] A discourse structure of Philemon follows generally the epistolary conventions of the first century. Constructions of *inclusio* demarcate the opening greeting with *Christou Iēsou—Iēsou Christou* (Christ Jesus—Jesus Christ) with verses one and three, respectively. There are numerous examples of homoioptoton, the repetition of sounds at the end of words due to grammatical categories and suffixes. This can be recognized with the long 'u' sound (sound indicated with underlining) in the benediction at verse twenty-five: *Hē charis tou kuriou Ieēsou Christou meta tou pneumatos humōn* (May the grace of the Lord Jesus Christ be with your spirit). An example of paronomasia—word play—demonstrates the acoustic dexterity and intentionality of Paul with a play on the proper name Onesimus (meaning 'useful'). Paul recognizes Onesimus' usefulness rather than his uselessness. A further acoustic variation might be *achrēstoñ euchrēston* ('useless/useful') could have been pronounced *achrīston/euchrīston*, giving the sense of 'christless' and 'christfull.' One final insight whose perception is enhanced when the epistle of Philemon is heard rather than silently read is the repetition of the word *splanchna* (bowels/mercies/heart). Paul uses this word in a logical series of three:

70. Davis, *Oral Biblical Criticism*, 60.

71. Maxey, "New Testament and African Orality."

72. Harvey does include a brief chapter on Philemon, but excludes it in his summary of exegetical insights. Harvey, *Listening to the Text*, 277–82, 292. This section is a summary of a longer paper of mine: "Translating Philemon."

Literacy and Orality in Relation to the New Testament

1) Paul praises Philemon for refreshing the hearts of the saints; 2) Paul names Onesimus as Paul's heart; 3) Paul invites Philemon to refresh his heart, thus asking Philemon to refresh Onesimus by receiving him well.

Numerous other oral characteristics can be heard in relation to Philemon and the other New Testament compositions. Such features function like hearing aids to the listening audiences. To receive these messages in silent reading reduces the effects intended when they were composed. That is, there is a high degree of intentional aesthetic qualities to the New Testament that are neglected when not acoustically received. However, such artistic oral features function beyond the structure to the social.

Social Functions

A consistent theme throughout this book is the description not only of structures and events but also of the description of their functions in society. In the case of the subject of this chapter, I take a tremendous step by recognizing that the New Testament was composed in a predominantly oral culture and was created to be heard by a communal audience. With this presupposition, a justification for the study of the oral structures becomes readily apparent. Nevertheless, an additional step is required in order to appreciate the communicative goals of the New Testament. Central to this step is asking the question: what is the intended sociorhetorical impact of these oral structures? This moves the study beyond philology to pragmatics.

I am not the first to employ Street's taxonomy with biblical studies. Richard Horsley recognizes the two distinct approaches to orality-literacy studies.[73] Horsley laments the lack of ideological analysis of the issues: "Even these studies generally lack analysis of the social location of orality and the uses of literacy and the power relations involved, which is necessary to accomplish anything more than an appreciation of particular literary documents of relatively high culture."[74] Horsley understands that the very low literacy rate of first-century Palestine, nevertheless, only served the uppermost strata of society. "In late second-temple Judea and Galilee, like the rest of the Roman Empire, literacy was concentrated in the political and cultural elite. The scribes and Pharisees and other teachers constituted the professional literate stratum of the Jerusalem

---

73. Horsley, "The Oral Communication Environment of Q."
74. Ibid., 124–25.

temple-state."[75] Horsley continues by laying out the social functions of writing at that time in Palestine along with the interaction of orality with literacy in these functions. The first-century populations continued to view writing in a magical way with the words empowered to bring about curses for misbehavior. Writing was symbolic with epitaphs on monuments and tombstones, whereby the passerby could "hear" the words of the one memorialized in the words of stone. The state's use of writing was primarily symbolic as well. Engraved laws were displayed "to cultivate authority and to intimidate their citizens."[76] Record-keeping was used by the military for taxes and tracking debts.

In terms of the religious documents of the period, Horsley asserts that the Hebrew Scriptures functioned in many ways as the Greek and Roman law inscriptions: "to legitimate and authorize the centralization of political-religious power."[77] Horsley demonstrates through research of both the Qumran community as well as Josephus' account of Pharisees the oral bias of these communities who nonetheless possessed written texts. One recognizes how these written texts were revised with a frequency and fluidity that belies the oral ethos of the communities. This interplay of orality and textuality is also demonstrated in the synoptic Gospels. Horsley understands that scriptural references in the Gospels are at times anachronistic projections (for example, Luke 4) or developed scribal skills (Matthew's fulfillment references) with Mark not demonstrating evidence of referencing a written text.[78] Even when such literary phrases as "it is written" and direct reference to "Scripture" are made, it is not necessary to understand these references as a citation. Rather, Horsley argues that these are references to the general authority of Scripture. In Mark, references to scripture are used either against the Pharisees' system of authority or in explanation of the passion narrative. "Throughout, the terms *gegraptai* ('it is written') and *graphe* ('scripture')

---

75. Ibid., 125.
76. Ibid., 130.
77. Ibid., 135.
78. References to scripture follow a variety of relations to the actual written text. Vernon Robbins suggests a continuum within a rhetorical culture: reference, recitation, recontextualization, reconfiguration, and echo. (Robbins, "Oral, Rhetorical, and Literary Cultures," 82–88).

Literacy and Orality in Relation to the New Testament

are not so much citation formulas or references to a particular written text as references to the authority of the scripture."[79]

Jonathan Draper is also keenly interested in the social function of the oral structure of biblical texts. Like Horsley, he uses the findings of folklorists like Dell Hymes as well as the insights of John Miles Foley as he restructures the text in order to more clearly determine the metonymic references within the oral-derived text.[80] In his research on Q Draper shows how the structure of a discourse can be presented with the use of lines, verses, and stanzas. Such typographical restructuring aligns elements of the text in a more perceptible way than the traditional paragraph style of prose. The result of this first step is a presentation of the oral patterning of the biblical composition. However, this initial step is strengthened by determining the metonymic references contained within these patterns. Following Foley, Draper asserts that a close study of the traditions of the first century as portrayed in the Hebrew Scriptures and other extra-canonical resources permits a greater appreciation for the social meanings of the texts. His example from Q 12:49–59, where Jesus speaks of his casting fire on the earth, is helpful. Rather than understanding this as an apocalyptic proclamation, Draper interprets the image of fire as a metonymic sign within the Hebrew Scriptures of God's judgment to those who break his covenant. Draper further extrapolates that the breaking of God's covenant in this case is the exploitation by Jerusalem's leaders of the marginalized peasants. The two-step method of reconstructing the oral patterning in preparation for interpreting the metonymic reference is a significant contribution to Oral Biblical Criticism.

As seen above, Joanna Dewey has significantly contributed to a better understanding of the oral structure of the New Testament, particularly Mark. Her insights are not limited to the oral structural patterns but include the ideological insights of orality and literacy in first-century Mediterranean cultures.[81] Leaning heavily upon Harris and Botha, she depicts a setting where oral communication was ubiquitous—even when the written word was present. Nevertheless, Dewey demonstrates how literacy was predominantly an elite medium of power. Dewey refutes

---

79. Horsley, "The Oral Communication Environment of Q," 144.

80. Draper, "Recovering Oral Performance from Written Text in Q." Draper also demonstrates this approach to discovering the "hidden transcripts" of biblical passages in "Practicing the Presence of God in John."

81. Dewey, "Textuality in Oral Culture."

an early literary hermeneutic of Christianity and argues on the basis of Paul's epistles that the first-century Christian movement functioned with an oral hermeneutic, not looking to the written scripture for authority. Throughout history, according to Dewey, a literary bias reshaped our interpretation of the early Christian period. This is especially the case in Protestantism after the printing press. Dewey seeks to reclaim the earlier understanding of authority associated with an oral hermeneutic. "The shift from oral hermeneutics and authority to manuscript hermeneutics and authority is *not* a neutral matter."[82] The oral hermeneutic benefited from oral communication, whether as aural reception of written communications or more expansively through storytelling. Street entertainers and religious storytellers would communicate the news of the dominant elite. However, the communication was altered, at times by inaccuracy, but more often it was the subversive turning of stories to express the experiences of the marginalized. This is similar to Horsley's use of the little tradition and the hidden transcripts.[83] Oftentimes it was women who were storytellers; they were influential in their families and thus by extension in the lives of community.[84]

Besides the numerous articles that Bobby Loubser has written on oral hermeneutics in regards to the New Testament,[85] he has also demonstrated an awareness of how orality functions in societies, both in African cultures and those of the first-century New Testament world.[86] Loubser does not confuse the historical distinctions of the first century with the contemporary African cultures, but he does find considerable similarities that aid in appreciating the overwhelming influence of orality.[87] In

---

82. Ibid., 56.

83. See, for example, Horsley and Draper, *Whoever Hears You Hears Me*, 98–104; Horsley, *Oral Performance, Popular Tradition, and Hidden Transcript in Q*.

84. This function of storytellers is also pursued by Scobie, "Storytellers, Storytelling, and the Novel in Greco-Roman Antiquity"; Wire, *Holy Lives, Holy Deaths*; Hearon, *The Mary Magdalene Tradition*.

85. Besides those already mentioned above, Loubser, "Orality and Pauline 'Christology'"; Loubser, "Orality and Literacy in the Pauline Corpus."

86. Loubser, "The Oral Christ of Shembe"; Loubser, "Possession and Sacrifice in the NT and African Traditional Religion"; Loubser, "Moving Beyond Colonialist Discourse"; Loubser, "Invoking the Ancestors".

87. Jonathan Draper also uses contemporary African experiences of orality in his study of first-century orality issues of the New Testament: "Many Voices, One Script," 44–63.

a discussion of the function of the genealogies in Matthew's and Luke's Gospels, Loubser understands these lists as central mythological references that enable the hearers to place the ensuing Gospels in the context of the Hebrew oral traditions of the ancestors. Borrowing from Foley's metonymic reference, Loubser demonstrates the value of understanding these genealogies as part of the oral performance of the Gospels, not only evoking through the spoken word the remembered stories but in a speech-act sense of illocution, "invoking the ancestors." Loubser recognizes the structuring of Matthew's genealogy of three sets of fourteen as a mnemonic aid to both the performer and the audience. He also notes the rhythmic phrasing of Matthew 1:1–17. He suggests that this rhythmic cradling of the genealogy permitted an "altered mind state." This allows for audience participation in the narrative: "They become immediate participators in the multiplicity of stories that supply meaning and purpose to their lives."[88]

Throughout this section on the functions of media in New Testament studies, references have been made to Foley's work with oral tradition and metonymic references. Behind such research is the instrumentality of social memory. In a recent informal *Festschrift* to Werner Kelber, three areas of Kelber's contributions are celebrated: narrative studies, ancient media, and social memory.[89] Following the work of Jan Assmann and other researchers, Kelber recognizes the social function of orality and literacy in the construction of history: "In remembering the past we reconstruct it."[90] For Kelber, memory should not be limited to a verbatim memorization (as with early Form Critics) but a creative presentation of the past as it relates to a community's present situation in terms of their identity.[91] Kelber argues for how the destruction of the Temple in 70 C.E. created a context for the "remembering" of Jesus traditions in creative ways in the light of the ensuing instabilities. He discusses the "gospels'

---

88. Loubser, "Invoking the Ancestors," 137.

89. Horsley et al., *Performing the Gospel*. The three areas were presented by Kelber himself in "The Case of the Gospels," 55–86. Further reflections on the subject of memory are in Kelber, "The Works of Memory."

90. Kelber, "The Case of the Gospels," 55. See chapter three's section on social memory for a discussion of Assmann's contributions as presented in Kirk and Thatcher, *Memory, Tradition, and Text*.

91. Kelber sees the medium of writing as more conducive to creative remembering in that the writer can avoid the immediacy of the community's corrective response to past events in an oral performance setting; "The Case of the Gospels," 57–58.

agility in critically and creatively molding their narratives as they appropriate and respond to issues that are live concerns both in their respective communal settings and in the larger Greco-Roman-Jewish historical environment."[92] Kelber's approach to the Gospels is not limited to the oral structuring of the compositions. "But what matters most in the literary-memorial composition of the gospels, I would insist, is not the preservation of tradition per se, but rather the maintenance of tradition for the purpose of shaping and preserving group identity."[93] This assertion aligns itself well with my overall thesis in regard to Bible Translation: Bible Translation as contextualization is an expression of shaping and reinforcing a community's identity.

My own studies of Philemon and the first eleven verses of 1 Corinthians 15 indicate several social functions of the oral arrangement. Paul's epistle to Philemon is a magisterial exhibit of using the social milieu as an effective rhetorical device in persuading Philemon to respond positively to Paul's request for leniency with Onesimus. Paul's use of kinship, flattery, community peer pressure, and his evocation of Philemon's indebtedness to Paul are each enhanced by the oral structuring of the communication. To imagine the reception of this epistle in Colossae by Philemon and his family in the public sphere of a community presentation underscores how the weight of the argument would be lessened if we project a silent individual reading of the letter. The aesthetic beauty of the composition combines with the social function of the communication to have an effective result. In 1 Corinthians 15:3-7 the social function of the creedal tradition demonstrates Foley's use of metonymic reference with the four staccato references of Jesus' death, burial, resurrection, and appearance. These events are evoked in the hearing of the audience in a way that the community can immediately access the Passion narrative in their recently created oral tradition of Jesus. The rhythmic balance of syllables in this section demonstrates the careful auditory intentions and expectations.[94] Each of these examples above illustrates how the oral

---

92. Ibid., 78.

93. Ibid., 80.

94. Sibinga, "1 Cor 15:8/9 and Other Divisions in 1 Cor 15:1–11," 54–59. This article argues for a series of balanced sections of thirty-eight syllables in the creedal tradition section. This careful composition is incorporated into the broader issues of the passage in my paper: Maxey, "Oral Evocations of the Kerygma."

patterning of the New Testament compositions reinforces the broader social aims of these communications.

Conclusion

This chapter has narrowed orality-literacy studies to the domain of the New Testament. We have seen how both the written and oral word were functioning in a social context dominated by the spoken word. The minimal capacity of the general populations to read and write is accentuated by the logistic difficulties involved in the scripting and deciphering of written communications. Such written means are subservient to the oral word and are oftentimes symbolic of ruling authorities. Although this predominant oral nature of the first century was recognized to a degree by early form critics, they perceived its influence as minimal in the composition, transmission, and reception of the New Testament. Twentieth-century orality studies have contributed to a new appreciation of media in antiquity. By recognizing the oral features of New Testament texts numerous scholars have begun to appreciate the auditory quality and acoustic patterns of these compositions. Others have pushed to understand these oral qualities as they function pragmatically in societies. Great strides have been taken in the past twenty-five years in these regards. However, an appreciation of the oral features along with their social functions demonstrates scholars' penchant to disembodying communication. We see in the next chapter that a renewed interest in the auditory is a helpful step forward. Nonetheless, I have found it helpful to move beyond the aural sense to the total kinetics of performance. The emerging discipline of Biblical Performance Criticism addresses this eclipse of communication. Such an approach not only challenges biblical studies but also requires Bible translators to respond to a host of new questions in regard to what is translated and the communicative theories necessary to guide methodologies that seek to translate New Testament oral performances. It is this recognition of the centrality of oral performance in the task of Bible Translation that offers to the hermeneutical circle a way for translation to participate in contextualization.

5

BIBLICAL PERFORMANCE CRITICISM AND BIBLE TRANSLATION

Introduction

THE PREVIOUS CHAPTERS HAVE ARGUED FOR THE CENTRALity of translation in Christianity and how translation is a demonstration of contextualization, a contextualization that expresses inculturation as well as liberation. Furthermore, I have argued that translation's literary bias in the past few centuries has obscured the historical reality and powerful capacity of performance. Performance emanates from an ethos of orality, even when this orality interfaces with literacy. Performance challenges earlier models of communication and requires new methods for appreciating the epistemological shift involved in this mode of communication. This paradigmatic change disputes the way one approaches the New Testament and its translation. New tools are needed to deal with these challenges. An emerging new discipline in New Testament studies that builds upon yet goes beyond orality studies is Biblical Performance Criticism (BPC). BPC reconfigures many established biblical methodologies—including translation—as it recognizes the existing value communities place on performance, a value that promises to reinvigorate the appropriation of the Bible by these communities. This chapter seeks to present BPC, examine potential reconfigurations of certain existing biblical criticisms, and then discuss the implications of this method for translation. Such a discussion requires a treatment of translation theories where past theories need to be revised and more recent theories incorporated in order to respond to the challenges of BPC.

Biblical Performance Criticism

The term Performance Criticism is not unique to biblical studies, but has been adapted from several disciplines: cultural anthropology, theater studies, literary theory, and others to express an original approach to the Bible.[1] The roots of this emerging discipline come from the experience of performing biblical compositions. New Testament scholar David Rhoads is recognized as the one who has articulated his experience of performing New Testament compositions as well as the resulting insights and propositions for methods of such an approach.[2] More than three decades of performance have enriched Rhoads' research and teaching of the New Testament. Recently he has presented his understanding of BPC in a two-part article entitled, "Performance Criticism: An Emerging Methodology in Second Testament Studies."[3] These introductory articles establish the motivation, elements, and potentialities of BPC. What follow are a basic introduction to this emerging discipline as presented by Rhoads along with supplemental insights from other scholars as well as my own interaction with its development.

Following a newly created website for BPC, the following responses are made to the question, "What is Performance Criticism?"[4]

- Embraces many methods, including Historical Criticism, Narrative Criticism, Form and Genre Criticism, Reader-Response Criticism, Rhetorical Criticism, Textual Criticism, Orality Criticism, Speech Act Theory, Social-Science Criticism, Linguistic Criticism, The Art of Translation, Ideological Criticism, Theater Studies, and Oral Interpretation Studies.

---

1. Approaches to the Hebrew Scriptures from Performance Criticism perspective include: Levy, *The Bible as Theatre*; Giles and Doan, *Twice Used Songs*.

2. Rhoads wrote an early exposé on issues of performance and the New Testament that has since been republished in a recent book. Rhoads, "Performing the Gospel of Mark."

3. Rhoads, "Performance Criticism: An Emerging Methodology in Second Testament Studies—Part I"; Rhoads, "Performance Criticism: An Emerging Methodology in Second Testament Studies—Part II." This two-part article articulates many important facets of Performance Criticism that cannot be fully explored here. Rather the major components and contributions of Performance Criticism as I understand them are discussed—especially those that may have consequences for translation. A revision of these articles is scheduled for publication: Rhoads, *Biblical Performance Criticism*.

4. www.biblicalperformancecriticism.org, accessed December 11, 2008.

- Reframes the biblical materials in the context of oral/scribal cultures of the early church, aspects of which include the performance event, performer, audience, context, and text.
- Constructs scenarios of ancient performances.
- Learns from contemporary performances of these materials through the translation, preparation, and performance of a text for group discussion of the performance event.
- Reinterprets biblical materials accordingly.

Performance Event

The previous chapter has presented a historical setting of the media used in the first-century Mediterranean world; it was a context predominantly oral. Furthermore, this communicative context was communal in that such communications as the New Testament narratives and letters were not received individually but communally. These are essential points with a reconstruction of first-century performance scenarios. This fundamental background, although acknowledged in other biblical criticisms, has been consistently under-emphasized as the result of an established literary bias in previous studies of the New Testament. This lacuna promotes anachronistic analyses of these New Testament compositions and their reception.[5] Moreover, this literary bias is prevalent in the imagination of how people are to engage in the Bible today. In other words, the neglect of the predominant oral ethos of both the first-century Mediterranean world and the modern world—whether in the secondary orality of the electronic age or the cultures where literacy plays a minor part in daily life—has inhibited reflection of the Bible as a collection of performance-oriented compositions. BPC addresses this bias and the resulting gaps in both the first and twenty-first century contexts. Central to BPC is the performance event, including: the act of performing, composition for performance, performer, audience, material context, social-historical circumstances, and rhetorical impact.

---

5. Boomershine, "Peter's Denial as Polemic or Confession," 48.

Biblical Performance Criticism and Bible Translation

Act of Performing

The recently established Oral Biblical Criticism parallels much of BPC's concern with the predominantly oral ethos of the first-century Mediterranean world. Yet even a close study of the written words of biblical compositions does not fully perceive the paralinguistic features of the human voice: rhythm, intonation, degrees of loudness, variation in voice quality, pausing, and phrasing.[6] However, BPC extends the communicative mode beyond simply that of oral-aural, beyond a disembodied voice. Performances of these biblical compositions were not only heard, but also visualized; they were embodied by a performer. Performance goes beyond hearing the sounds to seeing the performer's posture, gestures, facial expressions and the performer's proximity to the audience. The performer becomes the medium for the performance event.

Composition for Performance

The challenge for BPC is to imagine what a first-century performance was like, even though all that remains of the performance is a limited text. However limited, the written text still contains hints of the performance. These hints can be overt when it comes to certain lexical themes and phonological alliterations. The text may also include stage directions that indicate the movement, vocal quality or emotional state of the performer —as well as the expected state of the audience. Nonetheless, the biblical texts that we have were not transcribed with all the details of a scripted performance that we might hope for. As can be recalled from chapter three, this is the same predicament that folklorists find themselves in with earlier transcribed narratives. This challenge became the impetus for the development of ethnopoetics whereby attempts are made to discover via the remnants of transcriptions the performance-directed text.[7]

Performer

The performance event places the performer as the medium of the message. As recognized years ago, "the medium is the message."[8] Moreover, the performer is an interpreter of the message. Objectivity is not possible;

---

6. Halliday, *Spoken and Written Language*, 30.
7. Joubert, *The Power of Performance*, 131.
8. McLuhan and Fiore, *The Medium is the Massage*.

denial of this is unhelpful and can be interpreted as an attempt to obscure a latent agenda. When one attempts to reconstruct the New Testament performance settings, there is an appreciation of the relationship that the composer of the message has with the one who performs it. Besides the actual text transcribed, we can understand the first-century performer being coached as to how to place emphasis, how to appreciate the audience's responses, how to elaborate sections of the message if needed, etc.[9] The composer would strategically choose the person who would perform the communication. Speech-act theory appreciates this strategy in order for the performance to have its intended effects. As J. L. Austin notes, "There must exist an accepted conventional procedure having a certain conventional effect, that procedure to include the uttering of certain words by certain persons in certain circumstances, and . . . the particular persons and circumstances in a given case must be appropriate for the invocation of the particular procedure invoked."[10] The performer would need to be a "certain person," selected by the composer in order to have the intended impact.[11]

Audience

The performance is experienced by the audience—communally not individually. This is not a passive reception, but an active participation. Audiences are actively participating in the performance, influencing the performer, responding to the performer—verbally and nonverbally—at times joining in the role of performer themselves. It is often the response of the audience that marks the effectiveness of the performer. This audience orientation of performance is addressed below with the reconfiguration of Reader-Response Criticism. As is the case with the performer, the social location(s) of the audience is determinative of the performance. Issues of gender, race, religion, nationality, class, and so on are not abstract concepts in performance. They are embodied in the performers and audiences and play considerable roles in the content and manner in which something is performed and interpreted.

---

9. Botha, "Letter Writing and Oral Communication in Antiquity."

10. Austin, *How to Do Things with Words*.

11. This parallels the rhetorical function of *ethos*. Kennedy, *New Testament Interpretation through Rhetorical Criticism*.

Biblical Performance Criticism and Bible Translation

Setting

The physical locale or setting of the performance affects the performance. Whether this is temporal, spatial, or relational, the environment in which the performance takes place participates in the performance. A first-century house community shapes the performance differently than a public forum. In modern performances, a cramped classroom changes the dynamics of performance when compared to a spacious auditorium. The lighting, the acoustics, the distractions—each contributes to the performance event. Speech-act theory informs the contribution of context as well. Words spoken in different contexts have different effects. A judge's sentencing or a clergy's pronouncement not only depends on "certain persons" but also on the appropriate place for the activity. BPC understands that first-century performances (as well as modern ones) do not occur in a vacuum; the physical surroundings of a performance contribute to the performance.

Social-Historical Circumstances

Broadening the notion of context beyond the material, BPC recognizes the social context's critical role in performance. The oppressive context of the Roman Empire has been significantly ignored until recent years. The Greco-Roman religious influences offer important insights into New Testament conflicts and assertions. These social and historical realities were the presupposed backdrops of performers and their audiences. Foley has encouraged us to go beyond structural issues of a performance to issues of the significance beyond the words, kinetics, and paralinguistic features of the performance.[12] The worlds of meaning can only be discovered through socio-cultural research. In the case of biblical performances, historical studies and Social-Science Criticism are crucial to understanding the dynamics at play in the first century. Without such research, projections of other dynamics—often our own—will disfigure these socio-historical realities. This has clearly been the case when biblical research has assumed that communication in the first century was similar to the literary, print communication of today.

---

12. Foley, *Immanent Art*.

Rhetorical Impact

The point of the performance is transformation.[13] This may result in a confirmed identity of the community. Or, the performance may seek change by evoking within the audience the desire and capacity to change. With such transformation in mind, performance is not limited to what it might mean, but what it does.[14] As Rhoads states, "Put another way, what does a story or a letter lead the audience to *become*—such that they are different people in the course of and as a result of experiencing the performance?"[15] This experience was often due to the emotional force of performances. Whitney Shiner places critical stress on the value of emotion in first-century performances: "The success of verbal art was often judged by the way it affected the emotions of the listeners."[16]

Biblical Performance Criticism's Interaction with Other Disciplines

BPC is admittedly eclectic in its composition. It is informed by several well-established biblical criticisms as well as some recent contributions to biblical research. BPC does not attempt to eclipse these important methodologies but it does hope to contribute to a reconfiguration of them. Arguing against a subordination of BPC under an already established field, Rhoads states, "However, precisely because performance criticism is an eclectic discipline bringing together many different methods already employed in Second Testament studies, it would be advantageous to treat performance criticism as a discrete discipline."[17]

The reconfiguration of these other disciplines is yet to be fully imagined. Rhoads himself presents several suggestions to the following methodologies: Historical, Narrative, Form and Genre, Reader-Response, Rhetorical, Textual, Orality, Social-Science, Linguistic, Translation, Ideological, and Speech-Act Theory.[18] Rhoads introduces two other extra-biblical disciplines that could contribute significantly to BPC: Theater

13. Although understood more broadly, Barton discusses transformation in conjunction with performance in "New Testament Interpretation as Performance."
14. Rhoads, "Performance Criticism—Part I," 13.
15. Ibid., 14.
16. Shiner, *Proclaiming the Gospel*, 57.
17. Rhoads, "Performance Criticism—Part II," 165.
18. Ibid., 165–73.

Biblical Performance Criticism and Bible Translation

Studies and Oral Interpretation Studies. I have already indicated above some potential ways that BPC might reconfigure Orality, Historical, and Social-Science criticisms. Following the lead of Foley and his reconfiguration of Iser's Receptionalism, I discuss more closely below how BPC might reconfigure Reader-Response Criticism. In a similar reworking, I look at how BPC might reconfigure West's work with Inculturation Hermeneutics and Ordinary Readers, a reconfiguration that addresses issues of Ideological Criticism. Following Foley and other performance researchers, I close this section with a discussion of how Ethnopoetics can inform BPC.

Audience-Response Criticism

BPC's understanding of the active participation by an audience suggests incorporating a type of Receptionalism that understands that meaning is not unilaterally determined by the text or performer's intent, but that the understanding of a performance, its significance, is at least partially determined by the audience.[19] Following Iser, Foley differentiates the static text from the dynamic "work." In a reader-oriented receptionalism, the reader actively participates in the work as she or he co-creates the work, negotiating the gaps of indeterminacy. These gaps are "unlabeled regions on the textual map, that are as much and as important a part of the text as the explicit directions of construing its meaning."[20] The task of the reader in relation to these gaps is "consistency building, filling the gaps of indeterminacy only with interpretations that harmonize with the rest of the work."[21] Thus, Receptionalism presupposes the necessity of affective meaning, "for meaning arises only from the interplay of the text and the individual reader's imagination."[22] Foley recognizes the usefulness of this theory for oral performance: "the oral performance or oral-derived text also consists of a 'map' made up of explicit signals and gaps of indeterminacy that must be bridged in accordance with certain rules and predispositions."[23] Thus the primary contribution of audience-response

---

19. Iser, *The Act of Reading*; Fowler, *Let the Reader Understand*; Daar, *On Character Building*.
20. Foley, *Immanent Art*, 41.
21. Ibid.
22. Ibid., 42.
23. Ibid., 43. Foley cites Bauman in footnote seven: "the focus is on the role of the reader, no longer as a passive receiver of the meaning inherent in the text, but as an

criticism is the claim that a listening audience participates in the making of meaning. More is communicated than simply what is said. An audience infers meaning at important gaps of indeterminacies. Nonetheless, Iser's Receptionalism presupposes an individual, silent reader. This differs significantly in two ways from performance: the "text" in performance is neither singular nor fixed, but multi-form and fluid; second, the audience is communal (not individual).

It would seem with such pluralized performances and audiences that any notion of authority in deciding acceptable interpretations would be difficult, given that there is not a static, authoritative text. Foley asserts that the tradition of the community becomes the authority in determining the appropriate meanings of a performance. "The key idea to keep in mind as we further refine this retooled Receptionalist model is the immanence of tradition: it is the ever-impinging presence of the extra-textual, summoned into the process of interpretation under the rules of the traditional contract, that rationalizes the textless environment of oral tradition as well as enriches the understanding of oral-derived texts."[24] Foley insists that it is this immanence within the oral tradition that differentiates performance from reading, a difference described as *inherent* meaning in oral performance versus *conferred* meaning.[25] This inherent meaning is in the very structure of what is performed: "the 'reader' must be aware of the most fundamental rhetoric of the document—the inherent meaning encoded in its very form."[26]

I begin the task of transposing these notions of Receptionalism and Immanent Art to BPC with Reader-Response Criticism as described by biblical scholar Robert Fowler. He states the commonalities of a wide variety of approaches subsumed under Reader-Response Criticism: "a critical model of the reading experience which itself has two major aspects: (1) an understanding of reading as a dynamic, concrete, temporal

---

active participant in the actualization—indeed, the production—of textual meaning as an interpretive accomplishment, much like the members of an oral storytelling audience" (Bauman, *Story, Performance, and Event*, 113.)

24. Ibid., 45.

25. Foley acknowledges that this distinction diminishes as performance becomes textualized: "Of course, as one proceeds from unambiguously oral to oral-derived texts, the 'author' begins to emerge, the individual audience member or reader gains significance, and the gaps of indeterminacy call increasingly for solutions unavailable in the immanent world of the poetic tradition" (Foley, *Immanent Art*, 48 n. 16.)

26. Ibid., 56.

experience, instead of the abstract perception of a spatial form; and (b) an emphasis on meaning as event instead of meaning as content."[27] These aspects lead Fowler to express the act of reading in terms that are very similar to the experiential, temporal, and event-oriented nature of performance: "In arguing for a temporal model of reading rather than a spatial one, we are adopting an understanding of language that has significant affinities with the language of oral culture."[28] Fowler's discussions of meaning as event utilize the disciplines of Speech-Act theory and Orality studies; he echoes many of the early assertions made about the active power of language in oral settings. Given that Fowler's object of study is Mark's Gospel, he resonates with the oral nature of Mark: "Mark is an audience-oriented narrative, from an era in which audience-oriented language prevailed, and an audience-oriented approach to the narrative and its meaning is at least appropriate and perhaps unavoidable."[29]

Throughout Fowler's work there is a clear articulation of the oral environment of first-century Mediterranean world. He also accepts that Mark's Gospel was initially orally performed and experienced. Many important insights are presented once one grasps that Mark's Gospel aims to impact the reader rhetorically. Nevertheless, these insights become more understandable—and more powerful—in the context of performance. As acknowledged by Rhoads, Fowler's work with figurative language or in his words the "rhetoric of indirection" is helpful.[30] If we understand that irony or paradox is spoken or dramatically portrayed for the benefit of the reader, we are not distracted by a historical or cultural search for an explanation. However, this rhetoric of indirection becomes even more powerful when words take on the intonation of irony or a performance demonstrates certain rhetorical incongruities. In other words, a reconfiguration of the method to audience-oriented criticism, presupposing performance, permits a greater appreciation for the rhetorical effects of Mark's story in both the first and twenty-first centuries.[31]

---

27. Fowler, *Let the Reader Understand*, 25.
28. Ibid., 45.
29. Ibid., 52.
30. Rhoads, "Performance Criticism—Part II," 167.
31. Recent presentations by Fowler indicate his support of a performance-based understanding: Fowler, "Why Everything We Know About the Bible is Wrong."

FROM ORALITY TO ORALITY

Ideological Criticism

Ideological Criticism encompasses several discussions of inequalities of power and dominance and therefore is critical to my thesis of translation as liberation. Colonialism's equating of orality with primitiveness or illiteracy demonstrates the power issues involved in Bible Translation.[32] For the past several centuries Bible Translation has been a literary enterprise. BPC questions this dominance. Oral performance is central to all cultures as it interfaces in different ways with literacy. The authoritative text in literacy becomes the authoritative tradition in oral performance. The (translated) Bible as authoritative then must be re-examined to consider the sources of authority beyond a written text.[33]

It is this profound difference of performer-text-audience participation that leads me to understand that the act of translation and the performance of a performance-oriented translation are sites of interpretation. Whereas postcolonial views interpret Bible Translation as a text-bound tool of dominance, I understand that BPC presents biblical translation as an act of liberation and inculturation.[34] It is a liberation that underscores the agency of the audience and the performer, along with the biblical text, thus being communal. BPC's contribution to biblical translation also offers fresh insights into inculturation that invigorates local theologies according to the linguistic-cultural categories of the local context. I suggest that these possibilities could be greatly enhanced with an intentional application of BPC to both biblical exegesis and translation.

As introduced at the end of chapter two, African theologians have clearly articulated potential responses to various forms of oppression and colonialism. Gerald West has responded with similar approaches to the incorporation of Ordinary Readers into biblical reflections.[35] He has

---

32. Draper, *Orality, Literacy, and Colonialism in Antiquity*; idem, *Orality, Literacy, and Colonialism in Southern Africa*.

33. This point has already been made in chapter four with reference to the work of Joanna Dewey and Pieter Botha; it is also discussed in Barton, "New Testament Interpretation as Performance."

34. Comaroff and Comaroff, *Revelation and Revolution: Christianity, Colonialism, and Consciousness in South Africa*; idem, *Of Revelation and Revolution: The Dialectics of Modernity on a South African Frontier*; Bailey and Pippen, "Race, Class, and the Politics of Biblical Translation"; Sugirtharajah, *Postcolonial Criticism and Biblical Interpretation*.

35. West, "Reading the Bible Differently; idem, "Indigenous Exegesis: Exploring the Interface Between Missionary Methods and the Rhetorical Rhythms of Africa; Locating Local Reading Resources in the Academy; Ukpong, "Inculturation Hermeneutics";

overtly made issues of social location a crucial site for interpretation. Although West admits that "reader" should be understood to encompass non-literates, it is this lack of acknowledging the continued value of orality—and specifically oral performance—that motivates me to suggest how BPC could be incorporated into his existing methodologies and research. Whereas the procedure for working with Ordinary Readers involves a trained biblical scholar and at least one person capable of reading the biblical text, I suggest that a communal encounter of the biblical composition through performance would be more effective.

Such an exercise would involve a group of people who double as performer and the audience for other performers. The biblical text would be initially studied—discussing the social-historical issues of that particular text. Elements of the orality of the text and the various performance issues would likewise be discussed. Whereas the historical performance would initiate the conversation, the group would discuss the local context's own performance styles. As performers memorize and perform this composition, adjusting it to their contexts, there would be time after each performance to discuss the rhetorical effects, the insights gained, and the communication challenges of the performance. These discussions would inform other performances as the original group performed these compositions in other settings. Issues of the local context, driven by concerns about inculturation and liberation, would be informing this process throughout.

Ethnopoetics

Ethnopoetics developed due to the ethnocentrism of researchers from North America and Europe who narrowly defined poetry in literary terms. Even when the study of oral performances began to increase, following the work of Parry and Lord and their study of Homeric and South Slavic epics, researchers ethnocentrically attempted to force other epics and oral performance genres into the Slavic epic model. This double-ethnocentrism was challenged with the work of Dell Hymes, Dennis Tedlock, Richard Bauman, and most recently John Miles Foley. The first discovery was that narratives in verbal art can be marked by oral char-

---

Ukpong, "Bible Reading with a Community of Ordinary Readers"; Ukpong, "The Parable of the Shrewd Manager (Lk 16:1–13)"; Ukpong, "Developments in Biblical Interpretation in Africa," 3–18; Ukpong, *Reading the Bible in the Global Village*.

acteristics different from the metric line. Folklorists questioned the transcription and grouping of Native American verbal art into paragraphs and suggested rather a line presentation that unveiled the oral poetry. This re-presentation in writing of oral performance was not limited to lines; soon numerous methods of notation of paralinguistic features and gestures were introduced.

How does this development of ethnopoetics inform BPC? Whereas Hymes and Tedlock seek to represent justly oral performances with a written script, biblical studies begin with a limited transcript of biblical performances. Hymes' approach to reworking nineteenth-century performance transcripts of Native American folklore parallels the challenge that performance critics face. Responses to this challenge come from two methods: the historical study of documented performances that were contemporary with New Testament compositions; and the internal research of the biblical compositions for clues within the text of how these performances were made. The research of two biblical scholars, Whitney Shiner and William Shiell, has furthered our understanding of first-century biblical performances.[36]

Both Shiner and Shiell demonstrate the historical research of Greco-Roman communication in the first centuries of Christianity. A wide continuum of performances were presented: private readings (mostly in wealthy contexts); public readings (Olympic games, Hippodrome); storytelling (women allowed to participate; for general audiences and perceived by wealthy as potentially crude); novels (whole books read by wealthy, but a question as to whether popular literature ever existed at this time); drama (theater was attended by common folks, banned by later Christian theologians, but probably still attended); pantomime (included a masked dancer, and a storyteller); poetry (often accompanied by lyre music, performance more notable than composition); epics (emotional portrayals at Olympic games of Homer's works). Mark's Gospel, according to Shiner, was more than likely dramatically performed in a house setting, or perhaps outdoors at a religious ceremony.[37]

The gestures and paralinguistic features of the performance are inferred from the rhetorical schools of the day. Shiner and Shiell's research of Quintilian's *Institutio Oratoria*, Pseudo-Cicero (*Ad Herenium*), Cicero,

---

36. Shiner, *Proclaiming the Gospel*; Shiell, *Reading Acts*.
37. Shiner, *Proclaiming the Gospel*, 37–56.

Biblical Performance Criticism and Bible Translation

Pliny, sculptures, paintings, and illustrations—specifically those found with Terence's comedies—orient us to how a performer was expected to follow certain social guidelines for performance. As Shiell summarizes,

> This chapter has identified the Greco-Roman conventions under three main categories: gestures, facial expression, and vocal inflection. These elements were combined when an orator imitated another character using the conventions of *prosōpopoiia*. Just as an artist visualized a sculpture before he fashioned the piece, so a performer in the Greco-Roman world visualized the appropriate places where he employed gestures, facial expression, and vocal inflection. An audience heard the text performed and saw these conventions enacted, reinforcing the meaning of the work.[38]

The comparative historical research of first-century verbal art is critical to our understanding of how biblical compositions might have been performed.

Shiner and Shiell also provide evidence for the internal clues for performance. Shiner does a brief study of the opening verses of Mark. He recognizes the appealing use of alliterations and assonances in these opening lines that are intended to prepare the audience to be receptive to the story by means of subtle rhythms and lexical harmonies. Shiner suggests that Mark includes "applause lines" that indicate when a first-century audience was expected to applaud in response to the performance: "substance of a speech; florid verbal style; extravagant delivery."[39] Applause is expected in Mark: when Jesus triumphs over enemies (or when the enemies' behavior is publicly exhibited); epigrams of Jesus as he closes off sections; pauses (with multiple performances, these places are negotiated with the audience); Mark could be the result of several performance negotiations of where pauses are placed most effectively. The episodic style of Mark enhances these places for applause as there are short sections with possible breaks and the closings of many sections end with an epigram.[40] Shiell recognizes how gestures within the book of Acts are an indication to how the performer was to gesture. "The six passages in Acts (12:17; 13:16; 19:33; 21:40; 24:10; 26:1) use four different kinds of gestures: to silence a crowd, to signal the beginning of a

---

38. Shiell, *Reading Acts*, 100.
39. Shiner, *Proclaiming the Gospel*, 154.
40. Ibid., 156–58.

speech, to begin an exordium in judicial speech, and to signal permission for someone else to speak."[41] Both Orality and Linguistic criticism offer contributions to decipher ways in which these biblical compositions were performed.[42]

Performance as Method

Alongside these two established methods of researching biblical performance, a third novel approach is central to BPC: the translation, preparation, and performance of these compositions. Rhoads suggests that BPC is not only the objective study of performance, but that the actual performance of biblical texts is a justified method of interpretation. He makes the comparison of a musicologist who limits himself to the study of scores without ever hearing a performance of the score.[43] Throughout Rhoads' work on BPC are multiple anecdotes of personal experiences with the performance of biblical compositions in a variety of settings. I discuss these insights along with my own personal experience with biblical performance in this section. Two important preliminary points need to be made: whereas others (e.g., Shiner) attempt to imitate first-century performances in their own performance, the style of performance discussed here is modern, twenty-first century performance of the ancient text. Although some performers are professionally trained for contemporary performance, this is not the norm for biblical critics.[44] Secondly, the language of performance is generally not the biblical language. The reasoning for both of these points is that the sensibilities of an audience today are different than those in the first century. Shiner talks about a "bombastic" style of antiquity, a style that would tend to alarm or distance a modern audience (rather than build community). A major thread throughout this book is the centrality of the use of the vernacular language in Bible Translation. Therefore, it is consistent that a vernacular language generally be used for modern performances.

---

41. Shiell, *Reading Acts*, 139.

42. Further demonstration of these criticisms is discussed in the section below under the Bible Societies' sub-section.

43. In a similar way, some Shakespearean experts note, "Shakespeare wrote for the stage not for the page."

44. It should be noted, however, that the Network of Bible Storytellers (www.nobsseminar.org) does involve professional storytellers.

Biblical Performance Criticism and Bible Translation

This being said, I have nevertheless experienced biblical performance in the Greek language of the New Testament. Earlier in my research, I memorized for performance Paul's letter to Philemon and the pericope of 1 Corinthians 15:1–11. Given the language restrictions, the audiences for such performances were limited to biblical scholars.[45] The experience of exegetical study, memorization, performance, and discussion with audiences about the experience was a very positive confirmation that these compositions were intentionally composed to be heard. Alliterations, phonetic word-plays, syllabic rhythms, and other oral features would be obscured with a silent, individual reading. Each of the many other methods that were used in the study of these passages was enhanced by their preparation and performance: narrative, linguistic, rhetorical, orality, and social-science. The performance pushed me as critic to ask questions that would not have come to me had I been studying the text silently, through reading. Furthermore, what was I to do with my hands, my posture, my facial expressions, my proximity to the audience? Could these all remain neutral throughout? And so the very performance of these Greek compositions urged me to ask more questions about the composition—its history and its rhetorical potential.

Within the passage of 1 Corinthians is the commonly acknowledged creedal tradition (3b–5, possibly 6–7 as well). In my earlier research on the performance of this passage with the embedded creedal tradition I assumed that the allusion to Jesus' death, burial, resurrection and ascension may have been a short-cut to the longer passion narrative. I proposed initially that a performer of the Corinthian correspondence could recount in full at this point the passion narrative. However, following Foley's metonymic reference to tradition, there would be no need for the performer to perform all these passion events, since they were already part of the social memory of the audience, a social memory of Jesus that shaped their identity. This hypothesis came about through the preparation and performance of the passage—an insight that may not have

---

45. Other than my performance for several seminary classes at the Lutheran School of Theology at Chicago, I presented a paper and performed Philemon in Greek for three Academic gatherings: the SBL section in 2005 Bible in Ancient and Modern Media; the New Testament Discipline Group of the Association of Chicago Theological Schools; Biblical Interpretation and Translation in Africa: An Interdisciplinary Dialogue, Pietermaritzburg, South Africa. The two papers are: "New Testament and African Orality: Implications for Exegesis and Orality"; "Oral Evocations of the Kerygma: An Orality-Performance Study of 1 Corinthians 15:1–11."

been available without such exercises. Despite all these insights from the performance of the Greek passages, the performance in Greek did not evoke much emotion in me or in the audiences. Without emotion there would be minimal engagement, and as a result, minimal transformation. In order to find emotion I would need to turn to my native language, and the language of the audience.

Another project of mine is the preparation and performance of Mark's Gospel. Several reasons can be stated for this choice: critics recognize the oral roots of this Gospel; several other critics have researched the orality features of Mark. As well, I was familiar with translating the Greek of Mark. Perhaps the most basic reason was that Mark has always presented itself to me as a story that invites transformation. It is particularly interesting to me from my experience of living in Cameroon where issues of purity and conflict with spirits is a conscious, common experience. As a way to speed up the preparation for performance, I began with Rhoads' translation, knowing that his style of translation already considered performance.[46] However, I have revised this translation as I gained experience in performance. My consideration of the effect of words upon an American audience has led me to change certain phrases. For example, at the beginning of Mark's story, Jesus appears and announces the arrival of the "kingdom of God," or "rule of God," or "imperial rule of God." The selection has depended to some degree on the audience and my intentions to politicize Jesus' ministry. Later on, when Jesus drives out demons, some performances have him saying to the demon, "Shut up!" while others have, "Be quiet!"—depending upon the sensitivities of the audience's (parents) ears. This dynamic nature of translation demonstrates the participation by the audience in performance—both in preparation for the performance and during the performance.

The sheer number of hours spent in memorization permits a depth of knowledge of the story that might not occur with multiple readings of the Gospel.[47] It soon became apparent that there was an overlap of subject matter from one episode to the next. Themes were forecast and later echoed in entirely different pericopes. I was no longer thinking about the

---

46. Rhoads et al., *Mark as Story*, 8–38.

47. As is described in the next chapter, issues of memorization are culturally conditioned. My modern, literary-biased, American-educated manner of memorization is significantly different from my colleagues in Cameroon, Africa. Narrow dependence on written materials may be related to an atrophy of my capacity to memorize.

separation of passages by spatial distance—one paragraph or one or more pages separating parts of the story. I was thinking temporally: how much time elapses between connecting themes? The composition with these forecasts and echoes facilitated my memory of the successive episodes. After the memorization of the words was accomplished, interpretations were furthered as I considered the use of silence. Where did the pauses occur? Their placement drastically changes the potential interpretations. As mentioned above, I was faced with a myriad of questions on what to do with my hands, posture, facial expressions and my placement on the stage. Sometimes these gestures are predictable from the text, as when Jesus "stretched out his hand" to the leper. Facial expressions and tone of voice can be predicted from phrases such as "looking around at them with anger, grieved at the hardening of their minds." The first eight chapters of Mark are divided between Jesus near the sea and Jesus away from the sea. Performing these scenes required me to choose a side of the stage for the sea and the other side for events occurring in synagogues, villages, or deserted places. This became a mnemonic device not only for me as the performer but also for the audience. Rhoads has indicated that there are over fifty different characters in Mark's Gospel. Some of these characters are to have distinctive speaking styles: demons who are screaming out, a synagogue leader who is pleading urgently for the healing of his daughter, a woman who cleverly challenges Jesus' proverb. Each of these requires a certain tone of voice, a cadence of speech, accompanied by supporting gestures and postures.

With the emergence of BPC, Rhoads and others look to the development of how this methodology will challenge and reconfigure established and recent approaches to the Bible. Such reconfiguration has been outlined above for some of these criticisms; below I look more closely at translation.

Implications of Biblical Performance Criticism for Bible Translation

The majority of research on translation in regard to oral performance focuses on issues of orality.[48] These contributions are foundational but

48. Several others involved in biblical translation have recognized the value of orality studies: Yorke, "Grace and Peace in the Pauline Corpus and the Portuguese Bible";

preliminary for performance. Many of these studies on orality presuppose electronic media for recording and transmission in a twenty-first century setting.[49] Whereas BPC might contribute to translation involving such multimedia, the primary scenario in view for BPC is the live performer in the presence of a participatory audience. As has been recognized by translation agencies, the assumed medium can no longer be print, but often involves non-print media.[50] Yet this most noticeable change of medium presupposes several other reconfigurations: the methods and theories for translation must be reexamined.

This section begins with a review of the considerable contribution of several biblical scholars and translators who address issues related to oral performance. These insights are supplemented by Rhoads' own insights into translation. Finally, I suggest some theoretical challenges and practical applications that come from my own experience with Bible Translation and performance.

Bartsch, "Oral Style, Written Style, and Bible Translation"; Elliott, "'The Word' in Text, Sound, and Image"; Fry, "An Oral Approach to Translation"; Hope, "A Text-Linguistic Model for Media Scriptures"; Sterk, "Translation and Media: How Different Can We Be and Still Be Equivalent (or at Least Similar)?"; de Vries, "Bible Translation and Primary Orality." Franklin, "Oral Societies and our Textual Bias." The Studiorum Novi Testamenti Societas (SNTS) began in 2005 a section entitled "New Testament, Orality and Bible Translation," co-chaired by Philip Towner and Gosnell Yorke with advisory co-chair, James Dunn. Papers are presented to address issues of orality and New Testament translation. Several of these papers have been cited throughout this book. An additional paper is Ellingworth, "Orality and Bible Translation." The 2007 session in Sibiu, Romania contained the following presentations: Maxey, "Performance Criticism and Its Implications for Bible Translation"; Botha, "Pragmatic Models of Text Interpretation and Bible Translation"; Wendland, "The Drama of James."

49. Three recent contributions to multimedia translations are: Muken et al., *Cultural Readings of the Bible in Africa*; Wendland and Loba-Mkole, *Biblical Texts and African Audiences*; Loba-Mkole and Wendland, *Interacting with Scriptures in Africa*.

50. As stated in chapter three, my focus on issues of orality and Bible translation differ significantly from that of the recent trend of "Bible storying" (www.chronologicalbiblestorying.com). This is evident from the survey article by SIL's International Coordinator for Oral Bible translation and Chronological Bible Storying, David Payne: "Storying is thus a reproducible evangelist and church planting approach . . ." Payne, "Oral Bible Translation and Chronological Bible Storying." My interest in issues of orality and translation originate from sensitivities to both the first-century biblical and the twenty-first century oral settings. My proposed paradigm sees translation as contextualization and not as an evangelistic tool. Furthermore, the bible storying movement has not presented many insights into the exegesis for determining orality features in biblical compositions.

Bible Societies

Thomas Boomershine

Tom Boomershine has been concerned about the translation of the oral quality of New Testament compositions throughout his scholarly career.[51] Beginning with his dissertation he utilized the method of listening to his own recitation of Mark's story of Jesus' passion in the Greek as a means to appreciate the oral features of the narrative. In his pursuit to understand the challenges of translation from one medium to another, Boomershine coined the phrase "transmediatization" when he served as a consultant to the American Bible Society Multimedia project.[52] Boomershine recognizes the dramatic changes of media from those during antiquity to the print era. He suggests that the post-Gutenberg focus on mass print and distribution became an impetus for the beginning of the Bible society movement. Such a movement differed significantly from the New Testament's original cultural and communicative setting: communal, aural reception was slowly eclipsed by silent, individual reading. Such a shift, Boomershine continues, changed the understanding of the location of meaning and authority. Whereas these were located in the communal oral proclamation, the mass distribution of Bibles supported an individualized interpretation of the printed words, thus suggesting that meaning and authority emanate from the printed word.

Boomershine's proposal, based on these assertions, is that another phase of transmediatization, into the electronic age should not be restricted by a print-bias mentality, a mentality not even original to the mentality of antiquity when these texts were first composed. In looking for theoretical support, Boomershine suggests that the semiotic communication model, on which Nida's Dynamic Equivalence is based, is limiting to the communication process.[53] He suggests that Relevance

---

51. Boomershine, "Mark the Storyteller; Boomershine, "Peter's Denial as Polemic or Confession; Boomershine, "Biblical Megatrends"; Boomershine, "Biblical Translation and Communication Technology." Boomershine's commitment to issues of oral performance and biblical studies is recognized by the inaugural publication in his honor of the series of Biblical Performance Criticism: Hearon and Ruge-Jones, eds., *The Bible in Ancient and Modern Media*.

52. Boomershine, "A Transmediatization Theory of Biblical Translation," 49–57. These multi-media projects are discussed in: Hodgson and Soukup, *From One Medium to Another*; Soukup and Hodgson, *Fidelity and Translation*.

53. Nida and Taber, *The Theory and Practice of Translation*.

Theory better describes communication theory and more broadly the various phases of Bible Translation through the millennia.[54] "Thus, relevance theory clarifies the reason why the significance of translations in particular communications systems changes in the course of time. The meaning of manuscript bibles, printed bibles, and silent study bibles changes as their relevance changes in different cultural contexts. That is, a literal definition of correspondence to the original medium will inevitably result in changes in the contextual effects of that medium and the growing irrelevance of the forms of the Scriptures in that communications system."[55] Given that the communicative context has changed, Boomershine asserts, to a multimedia environment, there is a need to revamp completely how translation is done. "To put it simply, if communication is related to receivers making inferences and that process is shaped by the calculation of relevance, print translations will have a declining communicative capacity in the future in comparison with audio, video, and multimedia translations."[56]

Ernst R. Wendland

Beyond the North American, English context other translators with the Bible Societies have struggled with current translation theories and the issue of orality. Ernst Wendland has worked for several decades in Zambia, where he has been involved in theological training and consultant work with translation projects in southern Africa. A prolific writer, Wendland has treated several aspects of issues of orality that have eventually been encompassed in a general translation theory: Literary Functional Equivalence.[57] Wendland's theoretical base is broad and eclectic as he incorporates elements of semiotics, relevance theory, and functionalism. He is quick to assure his audience that his use of "literary" incorporates the use of orality: "While the term *literary* unfortunately may imply a written text, my aim is to encourage a translated text that can not only be read, but one that also *sounds* natural to the ears of the

---

54. Discussion of Relevance Theory is in the following sub-section.
55. Boomershine, "A Transmediatization Theory of Biblical Translation," 55.
56. Ibid., 56.
57. Wendland, "A Literary Approach to Biblical Text Analysis and Translation"; Wendland, *Translating the Literature of Scripture*; idem, *LiFE-Style Translating*.

Biblical Performance Criticism and Bible Translation

primary target-language audience."[58] Wendland pushes this even further in his use of "oratorical" with the rhetorical question: "Why should vibrant phonic 'life' not characterize the words of our vernacular translations of the dynamic Book of Life, which more often than not are aurally perceived and interpreted?"[59] Discussing such issues under "phonicity,"[60] Wendland eventually describes such oral features as the "Artistry of the Scriptures."[61] He concludes his description of biblical artistry with the implications for translation: "Obviously, the detailed and sustained artistry of the S[ource] L[anguage] document contributes a great deal to the progressive and cumulative meaning (conceptual plus emotive, hence also *affective* impression) that the original text ultimately conveys. It must also be admitted that this is an aspect of meaning that has not often been either fully considered or adequately responded to during the translation process."

Wendland has presented extensive biblical research of the application of his methods for exegesis and translation. In work on John's Gospel, Jesus' high priestly prayer (chapter 17), Wendland notes the oral-elocutionary structure of the Greek: short clausal segments (expressing familiar concepts); longer clauses that are used for contrastive effect; vocatives that interrupt the rhythmic flow; contrastive and complementary sound sequences that give a distinctive lyric progression; phonological play of vowels; subtle rhyming patterns (utterance-final bilabial nasals); reiteration of word, phrase, or clause; parallel and chiastic patterns; redundant personal pronouns; word order variations; polysyndeton (use of small set of conjunctions to maintain a terse rhythmic flow).[62] These features demonstrate how the form contributes to meaning. Translation theories that separate the two and marginalize the form in translation have not translated the rhetorical effects. "Rhetoric involves linguistic form—actually, a complex structure of diverse, but integrated, forms which inevitably transmit an essential part of the original meaning."[63]

---

58. Wendland, *LiFE-Style Translating*, x.

59. Ibid., xi.

60. Wendland, "A Literary Approach to Biblical Text Analysis and Translation," 220.

61. Wendland, *Translating the Literature of Scripture*, 139–63.

62. Wendland, "Oral-aural Dynamics of the Word, with Special Reference to John 17," 19–43.

63. Ibid., 23.

The question remains, however, about how one incorporates these rhetorical features into a translation. For Wendland, he holds two models of translation in tension: functional and relevance.

> The notion of "function" is viewed as being crucial to meaning—applied meaning—in all its diversity and fullness, including those aspects of pragmatic significance that relate to the participants involved in the communication event, its situational significance that relate to the participants involved in the communication event, its situational setting, and the particular medium of message transmission employed . . . When applying the results of this hermeneutical method to Scripture translation, interlingual communicators seek to reproduce the most "relevant" aspects of the essential "meaning" intended by the biblical text, including its functional dynamics, by means of the resources of the receptor language . . . In short, is it necessary, desirable, or even possible to reproduce a 'poetic' composition in one language by means of a corresponding poetic text in another?[64]

Wendland is suggesting that the biblical literary values—including orality features—be studied to determine how they functioned in the communication. This functional purpose is pursued in a translation with the aim of utilizing recognized rhetorical strategies of the host culture and language. When Wendland experimented with this procedure with two African languages, he recognized a richness of rhetorical strategies: vocatives, intensifiers, alliterative concordial system, doublets, demonstrative/pronominal usage, idiomatic expressions, rhetorical questions, unusual syntax, borrowed words to give an aura of authority, ideophones, graphic figures of speech, inversion of normal syntactic arrangements, etc.[65] In the words of Richard Bauman, these features are a means to "key a performance."[66]

Recognizing that many of these features have been obscured in the biblical text, Wendland is eager to demonstrate the performative charac-

---

64. Ibid., 25.

65. Ibid., 24–27.

66. "In empirical terms, this means that each speech community will make use of a structured set of distinctive communicative means from among its resources in culturally conventionalized and culture-specific ways to key the performance frame, such that all communication that takes place within that frame is to be understood as performance within that community" (Bauman, *Verbal Art as Performance*, 16).

Biblical Performance Criticism and Bible Translation

ter of translations. His approach involves typographical representation.[67] Wendland understands that the original New Testament compositions were composed to be read aloud. He also recognizes that the majority of people in the southern African context in which he works will hear rather than read silently the translations produced. Even if a translation exhibits functionally and relevantly translated performance features, someone who was not involved in the translation who attempts to read the translation for communal hearing needs visual aids that direct the lector in emphasizing these features. Wendland notes that there are three literary mechanisms that help with this: "typography (for example, underlining, boldface print, capital letters, etc.), format (indention, spacing, paragraphing), and punctuation."[68] Each of these contributes to the goal: "Thus, the fundamental signals—comma, period, question mark, exclamation point, and quotation marks—are employed along with spacing, lineation, indention, type style, and so forth to indicate the structural dynamics of a message. The goal of the one who is preparing the text is to reveal the design of the discourse and thus assist the reader in enunciating as well as interpreting it, either for himself or for those to whom he is reading."[69]

Wendland presents several practical guides to how scriptures might be orally interpreted and typographically represented.[70] After an exegetical study that focuses on the rhetorical strategies of the biblical composition is completed, a search for an appropriate host genre is needed.[71] The presentation of this translation is based on the "rhythmic speech unit" which can be identified by intonation patterns and pauses (generally marked by commas).[72] One or more rhythmic speech units make up a sentence. Each new sentence begins at the left margin with subordinate units indented. New scenes or paragraphs are marked with additional white interlineal space. The right margin is non-justified in format, thus allowing for a ragged right margin which assists eye movement down the

---

67. Wendland and Louw, *Graphic Design and Bible Reading*; Wendland, "Duplicating the Dynamics of Oral Discourse in Print," 26–44.

68. Wendland, "Duplicating the Dynamics of Oral Discourse in Print," 29–30.

69. Ibid., 30.

70. Ibid., 35–38.

71. Finding a compatible host genre can be a challenge as demonstrated by Noss, "The Oral Story and Bible Translation."

72. Wendland, "Duplicating the Dynamics of Oral Discourse in Print," 35.

page. Any emphatic constructions (e.g. the culminating point of chiastic structures) are marked with boldface print. Wendland suggests that such a presentation could be used for performance:

> One might even go so far as to claim that such a translation would lend itself to "dramatic interpretation." In other words, the trained or experienced lector, especially one who had studied the pericope beforehand, would be in a position to provide an overlay of intonation and emphasis to his or her reading which would make it come alive for the listening audience. The dramatic vigor and interpersonal dynamics that are already there in the original text, but so often hidden, obscured, or mutilated by an insensitive oral rendition, would again live.[73]

Kenneth Thomas

Kenneth Thomas, as senior consultant of the United Bible Societies, has been involved with issues of orality and translation for many years. His recent monograph, *Structure and Orality in 1 Peter: A Guide for Translators*, is the culmination of many years of research.[74] Thomas states in the introduction: "This study offers an analysis of a short written text, 1 Peter, that we can assume was read aloud to listeners who were accustomed to hearing devices that assisted memory and appreciation. It is time for today's translators to experiment with what can be done to translate the text of 1 Peter with attention to its form as well as its content—to recover some of its oral features both for the listener and for the reader. In so doing, we will discover that exploring structure and sound assist in discovering the main ideas of the letter, as well."[75]

Thomas' premise is that many oral features are universal: lexical repetition, rhythm, phonological resonance, volume, line length, aphoristic speech, and grammatical parallelism and repetition. At times these features can be translated directly into a host language, but in other situations one needs to research the functional equivalents in a host language. Thomas presents the epistle of 1 Peter in a way to demonstrate its rhetorical structure—both macro and micro—and its use of oral features that enhance its message. Perhaps one feature that Thomas lifts up that has

---

73. Ibid., 38.
74. Thomas and Thomas, *Structure and Orality in 1 Peter*.
75. Ibid., 2–3.

Biblical Performance Criticism and Bible Translation

not been overtly discussed by many others is that of lexical consistency.[76] Thomas asserts that the New Testament composers purposefully used consistent key words to make cognitive connections with the audience as well as mnemonic aid to the performer. The challenge, of course, is that context often changes the range of meaning for a word.[77] Furthermore each language semantically structures words differently. Thomas urges translators to attempt to maintain lexical consistency or perhaps a compromise in which a common root of the word is consistently used.

Thomas also recognizes that the biblical composition's orality does not preclude the use of visual aids for the proper public reading of the text. He presents his version of visual helps (similar to Wendland) for a reader who is following the oral characteristics, emphases, and contributions to the biblical composition. Central to his proposal is lineation—not only for recognized poetic sections but even throughout the epistle of 1 Peter. By presenting the translation in lines, instead of paragraphs, the relationships of one line to another or one group of lines ("batch") to another is more easily visualized with lines. The dominant determiner in how these lines are presented in a print layout is the internal (discourse) structure of the text and not the traditional chapter breaks and versification.

Translation for Performance: Challenges in Theory and Practice

Despite certain allusions to dramatic readings and the acknowledgment of how these New Testament compositions were initially orally performed, Bible translation principles and methods have not addressed directly the performative nature of biblical compositions. BPC responds to the fact that many societies today continue to exhibit a predominantly oral communicative setting. Rhoads begins his comments on translation with his subtitle: "The Art of Translation." Such nomenclature refutes a mechanical process of translation and acknowledges the human aesthetic choices and qualities of translation. The introduction of oral performance into the discussion of translation supersedes the goal of translating a fixed text. The goal becomes the translation of a fluid experience. The chal-

---

76. Rhoads urges such a tactic in translation so that key themes can be recognized lexically. Rhoads, "Performance Criticism—Part II," 171. This is also an important principle for literal translation as exemplified by Fox, *The Five Books of Moses*.

77. In the New Testament the same word (*sarx*) is used to connote: meat, humanity, carnal desire, etc. Can the principle of lexical consistency be maintained with such diverse connotations?

lenge can be posed in this way: "[I]f the [New] Testament texts are scripts of live performances, are we then translating the texts or are we translating the texts-as-performances—insofar as we are able to reconstruct and re-experience them!"[78]

In order to address this question, some fundamental presuppositions of translation need to be reexamined. Many biblical scholars present their understanding of translation theory in binary terms: literal and dynamic equivalence.[79] However, this by no means exhausts the possibilities.[80] Biblical scholars need to gain further sophistication in issues of translation. Two important theoretical developments with translation are the Functionalist approach and Relevance Theory.[81] Certain points of conflict with the literalist-dynamic equivalence schema can be lifted up as they pertain to a performance-oriented translation.[82] The most fundamental notion that performance counters is the presupposition of a model of communication that separates form from meaning. I have attempted to demonstrate above that it is not merely the form of individual words, but the structural patterns, paralinguistic and extralinguistic features that contribute to the communication process.

Related to this issue of form and meaning is the location of meaning. Reader and Audience-Response criticisms challenge the notion that meaning is solely located in the written text. The audience participates in the negotiation of meaning. Such negotiation occurs in what Reader-Response criticism has named as the gaps of indeterminacy.[83] Relevance Theory also understands communication as a matter of indeterminacies

---

78. Rhoads, "Performance Criticism—Part II," 171.

79. Nida and Taber, *The Theory and Practice of Translation*. Nida later suggests the term "functional equivalence" as a synonym for dynamic. De Waard and Nida, *From One Language to Another*.

80. Mojola and Wendland present several alternatives: functionalist, descriptive, text-linguistic, relevance theory, post-colonial, literalist, foreignization v. domestication. Mojola and Wendland, "Scripture Translation in the Era of Translation Studies"; Baker, *Routledge Encyclopedia of Translation Studies*.

81. Representative (but surely not exhaustive) for the functionalist approach is Nord, *Translating as a Purposeful Activity*. Representative of Bible translators use of Relevance Theory are: Gutt, *Translation and Relevance*; Sim, *Retelling Translation*; Hill, *The Bible at Cultural Crossroads*.

82. Stine in his biography of Nida argues that these conflicts are not as stark as purported by other translation theorists. Stine, *Let the Words be Written*.

83. Fowler, *Let the Reader Understand*, 34; Foley, *Immanent Art*, 41.

Biblical Performance Criticism and Bible Translation

that are negotiated by premises and inferences. These indeterminacies contribute to potentially multiple meanings, thus calling into question an understanding of a uniquely singular meaning. Once the audience is admitted into the negotiation of meaning, it is more helpful to speak of a range of meanings or meaning potentialities. The monovalence of meaning supports a singular intention of meaning of the communicator. In the context of Bible Translation it becomes a precarious assertion to present the author's singular intent. We must admit that we are asserting our interpretation of the author's intent(s).[84]

Whereas both a literal and dynamic-equivalence approach to translation attempt to protect the source language under the notion of fidelity, other (functional) theories support the audience with the notion of loyalty. This becomes an important distinction in performance, whether one wants to reconstruct faithfully a first-century performance or present a performance that takes into consideration the audience's context as a demonstration of being loyal to their needs. Such loyalty permits the audience to contribute both to the interpretation of the performance and also to the performance itself. Nevertheless, the question arises as to the limits of a faithful performance. When do oral interpretations become unfaithful? Rhoads suggests BPC's role: "Nevertheless, performance may be one way to test the limits of viable interpretations."[85] Rather than cause more skepticism as to acceptable interpretations, BPC offers a concrete method for testing interpretations as scenes are acted out or lines are spoken. This capacity of performance to vet acceptable interpretations coincides with Foley's assertion where he understands acceptable interpretations as those that "harmonize with the rest of the work."[86]

The theoretical distinctions noted above should inform the methods of translation for performance. These methods extend beyond the implications of orality to those of performance. How do these implications affect Bible Translation? Rhoads notes some of his observations: the historical present can often be maintained in performance (as it alternates with past tenses) more freely than in print form; word order can be more varied in performance, e.g. fronting for emphasis; replication of onomatopoetic words and sounds; length of sentences; issues of

---

84. Cosgrove, *The Meanings We Choose*.
85. Rhoads, "Performance Criticism—Part II," 179.
86. Foley, *Immanent Art*, 41.

punctuation in relation to pauses and stops; contractions and elisions; lexical consistency functions to maintain echoes of events and motifs; the use of parallelism and chiastic patterns shape the rhythm and pace of performance; presentation of translation for performance on a page that reflects rhythms, pauses and pace of performance; adopting the notation of musical scores for translations to indicate pitch, tempo, and volume; footnotes for suggestions for performance.[87] Rhoads acknowledges that these are just topical suggestions that need to be fleshed out.

Within this list we recognize topics that have been addressed by others involved in translation. Admittedly, these suggestions are somewhat biased to the source biblical language with perhaps the assumption of English as the host language. The maintaining of historical presents, word orders and onomatopoetic sounds demonstrates a commitment to recognizing how form participates in the communication process. However, such a commitment to the source language may abuse the host language—even when it is intended for performance. Following Wendland and Thomas, the function of these source forms needs to be deciphered, and research of the host language is required to find appropriate forms for compatible functions. Such a principle was eventually recognized by Tedlock who initially kept onomatopoetic words in their source language in his translations but in time saw that such transliteration did not function with the same effects upon the new audience. Therefore, he sought out in the host language appropriate onomatopoetic expressions to achieve a compatible aesthetic response from the host audience.[88]

Ethnopoetics addresses many of the suggestions on how a translation can be presented in print as a script for performance. Wendland's suggestions of presentation echo Hymes and Tedlock on the use of lineation to enhance recognition of the structural patterning of parallelism and chiastic structures. Punctuation as reflective of pauses and stops reverberates the findings of Tedlock and Sundersingh (following

---

87. Rhoads, "Performance Criticism—Part II," 171.

88. In Tedlock's later work, it seems this weakness is addressed. Fine summarizes the change: "Tedlock has changed his practice of leaving Zuni onomatopoeic words untranslated: 'In *Finding the Center*, I left Zuni onomatopoeia untranslated wherever I preferred its sound to that of the English alternative, but I have since come to the view that an onomatopoeic word helps give a story immediacy, an immediacy that would be lessened by the sudden intrusion of a foreign word in the translation.'" Tedlock, "Translator's Introduction"; Walter Sanchez, "The Girl and the Protector," a story translated from the Zuni by Tedlock, *Alcheringa*, 111 quoted in Fine, *The Folklore Text*, 158.

Biblical Performance Criticism and Bible Translation

Halliday). Instead of footnotes it seems more appropriate to use margins for further guidance to a performer. I suggest that a combination of Annekie Joubert and Elizabeth Fine's proposals would be helpful here.[89] As noted in chapter three, the performance record (or transcribed and sub-text) should be differentiated from the report (or pre-text). This report would be especially helpful in biblical performance as there is such cultural, temporal, and linguistic distance from the early performances of the first century and twenty-first century performances. This report can summarize the original issues or conflicts between the composer and the audience. Below is an example of a portion of such a report that I have given audiences prior to a performance of Philemon.

> Paul's goal in writing the epistle of Philemon is to bring reconciliation between Philemon and his runaway slave, Onesimus—that he would no longer see him as his slave but as his brother in Christ. Such a view may even lead Philemon to release Onesimus from his yoke of slavery. The epistle of Philemon is to be understood as a public, oral communication. Paul takes advantage of the public arena in conjunction with the honor-shame culture in which Philemon and Paul live. Paul refuses a heavy-handed approach to resolve the problem of a runaway slave. Rather, from a posture of vulnerability and an appeal to kinship through Christ, Paul asks Philemon to be consistent with his past acts of love and faithfulness. By doing so, Philemon's honor in the Christian community is preserved. Nevertheless, Paul is aware of the wider social implications of asking Philemon to receive Onesimus as a Christian brother. Paul offers repayment for the wrongs committed, thus giving Philemon an opportunity to retain his honor. The epistle of Philemon is an example of an artful use of sounds, verbal themes, and rhetoric that provides a window into the social milieu of the first-century Mediterranean world of slavery, honor-shame, kinship, patron-client, and the early Christian movement.[90]

Accompanying the report is the record, or what could be called the script. Below is an excerpt of a script from a pericope of Mark that follows Joubert and Fine's suggestions.

---

89. Joubert, *The Power of Performance*; Fine, "Principles of Translating Performance," in *The Folklore Text*, 149–65.

90. Maxey, "New Testament and African Orality."

TABLE 3
English Script of Vuté Performance for Mark 1:40–45[91]

Paralinguistic	Text	Extralinguistic
	Now there comes to him a leper,	Performer looks up and sees someone approaching
	pleading with him,	Performer can choose to dramatize actions of leper
	falling on his knees,	
	and saying to him,	
Voice is humble, supplicating, perhaps even fearful	"If you want to,	
	you can make me clean."	
	And moved by compassion,	Facial features demonstrate compassion
	stretching out his hand,	Performer stretches out hand firmly, but gently
	he touched him	Demonstrate laying on of hands
Voice is full of compassion	and he says to him,	
Phrases said slowly and clearly	"I want to,	
Tone of authority	be cleansed."	
Pace of speech increases	And immediately the leprosy went from him	
	and he was made clean.	Lift the hands from imagined leper in demonstrative fashion
	And becoming harsh with him,	Change of expression from compassion to sternness
	immediately Jesus drove him out	Hand gesture indicating separation of leper from center stage

91. Maxey, "Performance Criticism and its Impact on Translation and Theology."

Biblical Performance Criticism and Bible Translation

Paralinguistic	Text	Extralinguistic
	and says to him,	
Tone of sternness	"See that to nobody	
	you say nothing	
	but go,	Point off stage
	show yourself to the priest,	
	and make for your cleansing the offering	
	that Moses prescribed,	
	as testimony to them.	Hand gesture of reference to unseen group (priests?); performer looks to the audience with this last word to indicate the reference to the Jerusalem authorities
Tone of surprise at disobedience of leper	But going out	Performer indicates with gestures and expressions the contradictory action of the leper
	he began to proclaim freely	
	and to spread the word	Expansive gesture to demonstrate grandeur of action
Slowing of speech with an intonation that notes the irony of the reversal	so that Jesus was no longer able	
	to enter openly into a city,	Performer steps back, creating distance from the audience
	but was outside	Look of irony
	in deserted places	
Change of inflection that indicates the incessant pursuit of the needy, and the surprise of the narrator in the crowd's persistence	and they kept coming to him	Look of astonishment
Longer pauses between phrases	from everywhere.	Outstretched arms

The script above underscores that translation is an interpretive action. The personal involvement of the translator accentuates his or her social location. It should be remembered, however, that performance is communal. The actual performance of this script will be influenced by the audience, the setting, and so forth—all the particularities mentioned above in relation to the performance event. Both during the performance and as a result of the performance the script might be changed significantly. The words of the translation might be revised along with the paralinguistic and extralinguistic features. Such revision highlights the cyclical, multiform rhythm of performance-oriented translations.

It may seem ironic that a discussion of oral performance includes the subject of a written script. In my thinking this confirms the interface of writing and orality in most societies. It should not be understood, however, that a written script is essential to oral performance. My experiences in rural Africa have assured me that the most effective method of teaching in that setting is the apprenticeship model. This hands-on approach would involve potential performers participating as an audience in the performance of a mentor. In turn, the apprentice would replicate the performance as she or he perceived it from the audience. In other words, the handing on of of oral tradition in biblical performances would replicate the already established process of learning and the passing on of traditions. An intermediate, modern insertion might be the multimedia recording and review of these performances by potential performers. In this way, the written medium is circumvented.[92] I would add that performance is not limited to a theatrical genre of performance. Performance through song, musical instruments, and other indigenous genres can be equally effective in the reanimation of biblical performance.

In the midst of discussing biblical performance and translation with its distinctions from other biblical criticisms and translation theories, it is possible to be distracted from the primary assertion of performance: biblical performance can be an expression of contextualization. Fundamental to biblical performance is the translation of the biblical compositions in a way that brings into relief the performative features of the New Testament and then presents these translations in a script format for performance. Presupposed in this translation is the use of

---

92. As Joubert notes, even a multimedia presentation is a frozen recording, lacking the participation and fluidity of a live performance. Joubert, *The Power of Performance*.

the vernacular language in a communal setting. Each of these elements brings together a force for transformation.

One final element of performance that enhances this proposal is social memory. I find many similarities in the discussions of vernacular Bible translation, Relevance Theory, Audience-Response Criticism, and Foley's Immanent Art. The similarities are twofold: oral performance relies upon communal categories of understanding the world; these categories serve to assert and maintain a community's identity.[93] Vernacular Bible translation that makes use of BPC presents a means for a community to interweave its communal narratives with the biblical narratives. The community's participation in the performance—negotiating its meanings for their context—creates interplay of how they see themselves through their tradition and how the biblical narrative casts them in the biblical tradition. Beyond the potential transformation of the community, their performances offer to the broader global community glimpses of the biblical narrative that could not be perceived without the local community's contribution. Performance-oriented vernacular translation is presented as integral to contextualization.

One final subject to be treated briefly is that of authority. Such questions of authority are not new in biblical translation.[94] We have noted above how Boomershine has challenged the Bible Societies to think beyond a text-based authority. "[T]he presupposition that the Church only recognizes a written text as authoritative is historically inaccurate."[95] William Graham has researched the authoritative use of scriptures by an oral medium in several religions—including Christianity. In response to the Reformation theme of *sola scriptura* Graham reminds us:

> The great Protestant reformers themselves evidenced a profoundly aural sensibility to the scriptural word that they raised up, under the banner of *sola scriptura*, as their ultimate authority. The biblical word to which their theology and piety gave pride of place over church tradition and papal authority was emphatically not

---

93. Foley states, "traditional structures are not only metonymic signals but also cognitive categories." Foley, *Immanent Art*, 59. Elizabeth Fine asserts, "The principle of performance, particularly narrative performance, is identification, the sharing of identity, rather than rhetorical deliberation." Fine and Speer, *Performance, Culture, and Identity*, 9.

94. Brenner and van Henten, eds., *Bible Translation on the Threshold of the Twenty-First Century*.

95. Boomershine, "A Transmediatization Theory of Biblical Translation," 53.

the "dead letter" of the written text. For all of the reformational emphasis on the need for better texts of the scriptures and closer adherence to scriptural authority, scripture was less a document than a lively vocal presence in their lives and thought.[96]

Foley discusses the issue of authority in regard to oral tradition. It is the community who authorizes certain traditions to be authoritative. This authority is placed on the oral performances that propagate the chosen oral traditions. "The tradition in effect makes each performance an authoritative 'document,' each textual structure a unique signal, by stipulating its significance, by institutionalizing its invariable, inherent meaning in the face of the ever-shifting superficial designs of performance, version, and so on."[97] BPC challenges us to consider authority beyond the written text.[98]

Conclusion

This chapter has sought to present in summary form the insights that BPC can bring not only to biblical studies but especially to the art of translation. The performance event involves the embodiment of the biblical composition by a performer who responds to the participation of the active, communal audience. The translation and transmission of these biblical compositions challenges many presuppositions of translation theory and practice. Such an approach requires imagination and interpretation, based upon social, historical, and textual evidence, as it seeks to translate not a skeletal text but a composition for performance. Such endeavors serve the broader theological discussion of contextualization. In the next chapter the reconfigurations that BPC proposes are applied to a translation project in Cameroon, Africa.

---

96. Graham, *Beyond the Written Word*, 143.

97. Foley, *Immanent Art*, 44. There could be some important correlations of this authoritative use of tradition in Christian history. Robert Schreiter gives some provocative understandings of tradition and scripture in relation to authority from a contextualization perspective. Schreiter, "Tradition and Christian Identity," 95–121.

98. This relocation of authority in relation to the Bible has been discussed in such works as Birch and Rasmussen, "The Nature and Role of Biblical Authority," 141–58.

6

BIBLE TRANSLATION FOR PERFORMANCE

A Case Study with the Vuté People of Cameroon

Introduction

THE PRECEDING CHAPTERS HAVE LOOKED AT THE ISSUES involved in Bible translation from several disciplines. Although there has been reference to experiential research—especially with performance—most of the assertions made come from textual research. This has shaped the way in which information is presented, arguments are made, and conclusions offered. In this final chapter, on the other hand, I write primarily from the vantage point of lived experiences. I present information, arguments, and conclusions here as well but oftentimes in different formats. I consider this as beneficial as I offer alternative ways of understanding the topic of Bible Translation.

This current chapter is highly personal in that it involves my experiences in Cameroon. I acknowledge the subjectivity of the discussions and in no way am suggesting my position is objective. Nonetheless, I am in a peculiar position as insider-outsider to describe some initial forays into what oral performance in conjunction with Bible Translation might look like.[1] The subjective nature of this chapter should not be understood as my manipulation of the experience. I am the first to admit that much of what I have experienced in Cameroon has been well beyond my control. The Vuté community continues to be an agent in the endeavors of

---

1. Such a role is similar to what is being asserted in the article by Thomas, "The Outsider's Role in Socially Engaged Scholarship on African Religion."

FROM ORALITY TO ORALITY

Bible Translation. Their participation, in fact, models my fundamental argument of Bible Translation as contextualization: the local community contributes to contextual theologizing through Bible Translation. Such theologizing is enhanced when an established means of communication of oral performance is recognized and infused in the theories, methods, and goals of Bible Translation.

A second preliminary comment might be helpful for this chapter. As presented in the introductory chapter, the terminology of "performance" can be misleading. At no point in this book is performance intended to be understood as a simple entertainment distraction. Performance is presented as a central means of communication in all cultures. Aesthetic enhancements of performances are intended to add to the attractiveness of the performance for the audience with the ultimate goal of transformation. When performance is linked to Bible Translation, the centrality of this social act remains in view. It is true that humor and other talents of skilled performers might be exhibited. However, the goal is that such skills are used to enhance the inherent power of performance for social maintenance and reform. In the case of Bible Translation, I have articulated such social functions of performance throughout this book as inculturation and liberation. It is true that performers may not have such abstract goals in mind with their performances. Nevertheless, the Vuté people know intimately the quest for identity and the struggle from oppression.

One further preliminary comment on oral performance and Bible Translation: I do not argue that oral performance should be the only method of Bible Translation. Moreover the general topic of performance can be further divided into several types of performances. Such methodological and performance varieties are supported by the general translation theory of *Skopostheorie*.[2] *Skopostheorie* understands that the aim of the translation as determined by the intended audience informs what type of translation is done. The theory extends beyond communication theory to the organizational planning that results in a translation brief. It is the translation brief that guides those involved in translation in terms of the host audience and the function of the translation. In many contexts throughout Africa, I can see translations for performance to be a central *skopos* (purpose) of a translation brief. Yet even with this

---

2. Nord, "Basic Concepts of *Skopostheorie*," 27–38.

narrower choice of type of translation made, there will be the need for further refining of types of performances. Following *Skopostheorie*, the host audience is determinative of the style of performance. For example, in a church building during a worship service or Mass a more formal type of performance might be expected and planned. Such formality might change if the context is a neighborhood setting in a house or in the open air. The formality of the performance is perhaps another way of talking about how the biblical performance is viewed by the audience. Do they understand the performance as a presentation of God's Word? Do they understand that the performance is an interpretation of a biblical passage by a local performer? All this is to say that performances of Bible translations are not monolithic. The following experiences in the Vuté community confirm this spectrum of performances.

As noted in the introduction to this book, my interests in Bible Translation and Africa stem from a considerable amount of experience with the Vuté New Testament project in Cameroon. Such involvement has led me to appreciate the fresh perspective of Bible Translation as contextualization. While working in the context of Africa I learned a great deal about the predominance of communication as oral performance. However, I was slow to integrate this communicative context into the activities of Bible Translation. In time, though, I grew to understand how oral performance offers contextual reshaping of the methods and results of Bible Translation. In turn I have learned how such reshaping reflects a shift in understanding Bible Translation as contextualization. As I combine the study of oral performance with biblical studies in general and Bible Translation in particular I find exciting opportunities for strengthening an appreciation of the mutual benefits of working on New Testament translation in preparation for performance. The resulting performances offer stimulating engagement with the Scriptures in contextually appropriate ways to communities. These performances, as sites of interpretation, contribute to broader appreciations of biblical compositions in terms of how they are expressed and the accompanying expectations of communities experiencing biblical performances.

This chapter involves an evaluation of earlier Vuté translation efforts in relation to the most recent translation activities that involve oral performance. Such a comparison highlights the differences in the theory and methods of translation as well as the significant effects that performance has on performers, audiences, and texts.

FROM ORALITY TO ORALITY
Translation for Performance among the Vuté People[3]

In June 2007 I spent three weeks in Yoko, Cameroon, with the Vuté community. During this trip, I worked with four Vuté Bible translators and several community-recognized performers. The translators included: Alfred Oumarou, Jean Nogoadjéré, Valentin Yakoura, and Rev. Justin Mvougnoh. The performers (besides the translators) included: Pim Samiyong, Paul Soumer, Oliver Mving, Jean Bosco Antangana.[4] Our goal was to prepare five pericopes from Mark's Gospel for public performance in a variety of contexts. These pericopes included: the cleansing of a leper; the healing of a paralytic; the exorcism of the Gerasene demoniac; the resurrection of Jairus' daughter and the healing of the woman with an issue of blood; and the eventual exorcism of the daughter of the Syro-Phoenician woman.[5] Interestingly, several encounters during my brief time in the Vuté community in June paralleled these Markan scenes: I spent time with an ostracized leper named Paul; one of the translator-performers, Valentin, is a victim of childhood polio that has left him partially paralyzed; one of the granddaughters of my son's Godmother presented herself numerous times in a mentally disturbed, "demonized" state; a dear friend of my wife's came to me to relate her continued struggle with chronic menstrual bleeding due to a tumor; I witnessed a child of one of my friends eating a meal outside where a neighborhood dog scrambled to get the crumbs that fell from the boy's meal. I mention these encounters because they not only form for me the background—the context—but they are similar to the sustained experiences of the Vuté community.

The various contexts for the performances included: an isolated hamlet, worship services at both Lutheran and Catholic churches, an evening concert at a Catholic church, a neighborhood weekly house meeting where folktales were told, and an evening gathering at the Vuté chief's compound where folktales were interspersed with performances from Mark's Gospel. These contexts shaped the style of performance. As noted above, the term performance is used here in the sense of a pub-

---

3. An earlier (and much shorter) version of this section was first published in a two-part article entitled "Performance Criticism and Its Implications for Bible Translation."

4. Each of the translators and performers is a man. There are female storytellers in Vuté communities. However, the translators selected no female performers. It is an important gap that needs to be addressed with future research.

5. The pericopes included Mark 1:40–45; 2:1–12; 5:1–20; 5:21–43; 7:24–30.

lic presentation. When a presentation occurred in a socially recognized formal setting such as a church service, there is an expectation that the performances will be more subdued. When biblical performances occur outside of this formal setting social constraints are generally loosened. Nonetheless, in no context were the biblical performances presented or received in a flippant way. The esteem attributed to the Bible in African contexts assured that performers, performances, and audience responses reflected this high regard for the Scriptures. The pericopes of the recently published New Testament were compared with fresh translations made specifically for these occasions of performance. These two written translations were compared to the transcripts of the actual (video-taped) performances in the various contexts.

Method and Text for Performance

My first objective was to discuss with the translators the viability of orality for communication. My opening remarks noted similarities in communication from two settings: Vuté culture and first-century Eastern Mediterranean culture—specifically Palestine. Of course the translators were not in the least surprised by the oral nature of their culture since they lived it daily—even as literate multilingual experts. However there was considerable surprise when the discussion turned to the predominantly oral setting of the New Testament. It was as if such knowledge validated their own orality. This immediately sparked discussion of the established literacy goals in relation to Vuté literature. I was quick to nuance the discussion that it was equally unhelpful to think in an exclusive binary way. Literacy clearly has its advantages and is well represented in Vuté communities. Nevertheless, orality has been relegated in translation to either a supplementary or substandard medium. This esteem of not only the Vuté language but also of Vuté orality was confirmed on several subsequent occasions as I listened to translators talk among themselves and to others about the validity of oral performances of biblical materials.

One important parameter that I discussed with the Vuté translators was the limits of translations for performance. By this I mean the distinction between the translation of the biblical compositions for performance on the one hand and storytelling that is inspired by and loosely related to biblical stories on the other hand. Harriet Hill distinguishes these by naming them "amplified text" and "Bible story," respectively.[6] In relation to performance of biblical texts, when has a performer gone beyond the text in order to make the biblical text relevant? This is not a new question; one is reminded of the continuum from a literal and dynamic translation to a paraphrase. Yet such a question is text-oriented, one that seeks to guard fidelity to a source text. In more functional approaches to translation, where loyalty to an audience is the aim, perhaps the question should be stated in terms of what is evoked in the experience of the audience. How does the performer help the audience to experience the message of the text? Are these experiences compatible to the first-century oral-derived texts? The tension involved with such questions is not easily resolved. Nonetheless, the aim that I communicated to the Vuté translators and performers was that the translations and performances would seek to be compatible with the biblical texts and potential experiences for the first-century audiences.

I presented to the Vuté translators fresh studies of the Markan pericopes that sought to bring into relief the oral features of the Greek text and the potential functional possibilities for their translation into Vuté. Beyond the features of the extant Greek I encouraged creative reflection of Vuté features of orality that might be used—even in places where such features are not evident in the Greek. Given the translators lack of understanding of Greek, they could not evaluate my assertions from the text for themselves. Rather, they were limited to several French translations: *Français Courant, Traduction Œcuménique de la Bible, Louis Segond, Parole de Vie,* and *Bible de Jérusalem.* The challenge with their use of these French translations is that most of them did not consider the auditory value of either the Greek text or of their translations into French. My counsel to the translators followed the general advice of Ernst Wendland and Kenneth Thomas in terms of seeking to maintain the functional artistry of the text.[7] This included a respect for the functionality of the form as has been discussed, for example, with lexical repetition. It was a nearly overwhelming step to go from previous neglect of form to pay such close heed to the form and its functions.

---

6. Hill, *The Bible at Cultural Crossroads*, 82–91.

7. Wendland, "A Literary Approach to Biblical Text Analysis and Translation; Wendland, *Translating the Literature of Scripture*; Wendland, *LiFE-Style Translating.* Thomas and Thomas, *Structure and Orality in 1 Peter.*

Bible Translation for Performance

Once the Markan passages were studied in depth, the translators drafted new translations for the purpose of performance. I discussed with the translators the possibilities of scripting the performance translation in a similar way to how I divided the Markan pericope in three columns as explained in chapter five: extralinguistic, text, paralinguistic. Although of interest to the translators they were not eager to prescribe the extra-textual choices. Their performance translations remained in paragraph form.[8] When they started drafting, they asked if they might have the previous (published) Vuté translation in front of them. I suggested that they wait until they had finished their translations before they began to compare. Later when I compared these two sets of translations—publication version and performance version—with the transcripts of actual performances, I recognized several distinctions.

Although the general order of events was the same in both translations, the choice of vocabulary varied. The lexical differences for the performance version did not seem to indicate a selection based on the auditory value as much as a demonstration of the rich lexical options of the language. There seems to be a richer selection of vocabulary that communicates emotive value in speech acts. For example, the leper begins in the performance version with a word of connoting respect towards a superior prior to making a request. In the publication version, the leper begins immediately with the conditional statement, "If you want to . . ." Later on in the story as performed, Jesus does not simply "say" to the healed leper to go show himself to the priest; rather, in the performance version Jesus "warns" the leper. In the exchange between Jesus and the Syro-Phoenician woman, after she has respectfully countered Jesus' proverb, the performance version inserts "Jesus had compassion on the woman because of this word." These emotive hues to the stories are not intended to stay within the story world. Rather, it seems that such use of emotion within the story is meant to evoke emotions within the listening audience. We are to sense the sternness of Jesus' warning to the cleansed leper. We are to appreciate the respectful woman in her challenge to Jesus and feel compassion towards her as we are told that Jesus has such a gracious response to her riposte. In the Gerasene demoniac story, the Greek text indicates to us that the gathered crowds are fearful when they find the former demoniac sitting, clothed, and in his right mind. The Vuté

---

8. See Table 4 near the end of this chapter where I have descriptively charted one of the performances using text, paralinguistic and extralinguistic.

translators thematicized this emotive evocation by stating in the performance version how the pig herders were likewise afraid when they saw their pigs perish in the sea. The same expression is used in both places in the performance version as a way to evoke within the audience a sense of awe and fear at the power of demons and the power of Jesus. Such an evocation for the audience rather than a description of emotion within the story world is characteristic of oral performances.[9]

A few other comments on the textual differences can be made when comparing the publication and performance versions. The performance version had fewer complex clauses. That is, there were a greater number of short simple clauses, whereas the publication version had a greater number of longer sentences that included subordinate clauses. According to sociolinguists, this distinction is descriptive of two types of registers: written with more complex sentences, and oral with short simple clauses.[10] In a similar way, complex verbal phrases in the publication version become two separate clauses in the performance version. For example, in the closing of the story of the Gerasene demoniac, the narrator relates that the former demoniac "went telling everywhere what Jesus had done for him." The performance version has two clauses: "This man went on. He began to proclaim what the Lord had done for him." Textual differences are also recognized with regard to reported and direct speech. There are several instances when a reported speech in the Greek and publication version are transformed into direct speech. For example, in the exchange between Jesus and the Gerasene demoniac, the Greek and publication version use reported speech: "He (the demoniac) pleaded with him (Jesus) wildly not to send him outside the country." The performance version has: "The man said: 'My name is multitude because we are many. But please, I beg you that you not send that demon far away.'" However, there are plenty of counterexamples of reported speech that remain reported speech in both the publication and performance versions. There is also at least one instance where both the Greek and performance version have reported speech but the publication version

---

9. This is precisely what Tedlock suggests with his anthropological research of performances: "What oral narrative usually does with emotions is evoke them rather than describe them directly . . ." (Tedlock, *The Spoken Word and the Work of Interpretation*, 51).

10. For example, Chafe, "Integration and Involvement in Speaking, Writing, and Oral Literature."

changes it to direct speech. Once again in the story of the Gerasene demoniac, when Jesus is leaving the Gerasene territory and climbing into the boat, the publication version changes it to direct speech by having the former demoniac say: "I want us to be together, you and me" whereas the performance version follows the Greek, "then the man spoke clearly that he wanted to be with him." Finally, in terms of a general word count, most of the performance translations were slightly longer.[11] This can be attributed to certain introductory comments, explanatory notes and the use of ideophones—those onomatopoetic expressions richly found in spoken African languages.[12]

Ideophones in Performance

In the translations for performance (as well as the actual performances) the translators (and performers) demonstrated a greater degree of liberty in the use of ideophones. Their use immediately energized the storytelling (and storyteller) and engaged the audience in following the actions of the characters in the stories. The translators had expressed the difficulty with which the four friends had as they tried to bring their paralytic friend to Jesus: *kpaaŋ kpaaŋ kpaaŋ*. When it comes to the action of the paralytic rolling up his mat as he stands and walks out in front of everyone, the performance translation script uses this expression: *hɔɔr hɔɔr hɔɔr*. Not all the performers used these ideophones in the actual performances. In the story of the Gerasene demoniac no ideophones are used in the performance translation. However, in some of the performances they are used—in fact, quite frequently with one of the performer-translators. For example, the manner in which the demoniac ran quickly to Jesus from the tombs when Jesus first climbed out of the boat: *ywàt ywàt ywàt*. This same expression is repeated in the same story before another ideophone that denotes the demoniac's action of falling before Jesus: *ywàt ywàt ywàt, gbùùr*. In the description of the demoniac's self abuse of cutting himself with stones, an ideophone is used that communicates how his body is covered with red from the blood

---

11. The performance text for the Gerasene pericope (Mark 5:1–20) had nine fewer words. The pericope containing the story of Jairus and the woman with the flow of blood did not get translated for performance. Performers used the publication version as a script for their performances.

12. Noss, "Ideas, Phones and Gbaya Verbal Art"; Noss, "The Ideophone in Bible Translation."

from the cuts: *njaàksàk*. And when the demons enter the pigs and cause them to rush towards the sea: *gɨr gɨr gɨr*. The high rate of actions of the pigs is accented by two other expressions: *fùkùùmndé* and then *kùrúk*—how the pigs fell into the water and then how they all perished. Other performers used ideophones at the same places in this story, but their expressions were not always identical to those cited above. Nonetheless, audiences understood and appreciated the action-words as they were performed. Questions remain as to whether certain stories or scenes with a story lend themselves to ideophones—action scenes, for example. As well, is the employment of ideophones dependent on the capacities of a performer and his or her ability to relate a story in an engaging way? Nevertheless, it is clear that very few ideophones were used in the publication translation. Considerably more were used for the performance translation with an abundant use—especially with certain performers—in the actual performances. Ideophones are one way that the performer engaged his audience.

Questions in Performance

This engagement with the audience was clearly a goal of the presenters. Questions in performance function on at least three levels. The first level involves questions that are contained already within the Greek text of Scripture. We often see these questions as demonstrating an interaction between characters within the story world. However, in performance, the boundaries of the story world are permeable. Questions posed to one group of characters can be understood as directed as well to the audience who is experiencing the performance of the Scriptural composition. Rhoads alludes to this crossing of boundaries when he discusses on-stage and off-stage distinction.

> By contrast, Tom Boomershine has argued that, in ancient performances, the performer always addressed the audience and made distinctions between characters without using on-stage focus at all. The difference is significant. In this latter scenario, the audience is always addressed, even when the characters speak. Hence, for example, when Jesus directly condemns the Pharisees, the narrator-as-Jesus addresses the audience directly—and thereby the audience "becomes" part of the drama by playing the Pharisees for Jesus. When Jesus teaches/ berates the disciples, the audience becomes the disciples being addressed. In this way,

then, the audience is led to identify with all the characters at one time or another.[13]

In the Vuté performances, after Jesus announces that the paralytic's sins are pardoned and the scribes are offended by such God-like assertions, Jesus asks the scribes which would be easier: to pardon the paralytic's sins or to say to him, rise, take up your mat, and walk. Yes, Jesus was asking the scribes. But when the performer asks the question, the audience could easily understand that they too were being queried. Is Jesus able to forgive sins? Will he have the authority and power to heal this paralytic?

In the Vuté performances, questions posed by the presenter to the audience often had the purpose of assuring the audience's comprehension. The questions often elicited verbal responses from the audience—both individually and as a whole group. There were no such questions in the published or performance translations. However, numerous examples are found in the transcripts of the live performances. At times the questions were intended to assure the performer that the audience was following the story: "You understand, don't you?" Such comprehension could be demonstrated by a response that the audience would infer correctly from the preceding exchanges of the story: "What happened as a result of that (the leper spread the news about Jesus cleansing him)?" Oftentimes, after hearing the responses of the audience, the performer would then give an answer to his own question. As a means of including the audience in the story, a question was often asked: "What would you have done in that situation?" Each of these types of questions underscores that the audience is not passive. The audience is meant to follow actively how the story unfolds. The performer checks throughout the performance to assure himself that what he is relating is being understood and appreciated by the audience.

Questions during the performance have other purposes as well. Oftentimes these questions underscore relevant passages or offer opportunities for the presenter to explain the relevancy of a particular piece of information. During one of the performances of the Gerasene demoniac, the performer poses the following question: "The one who is possessed by evil spirits does things like a crazy person, doesn't he?" Such a question engages the audience on several levels. The Vuté community often

---

13. Rhoads, "Performance Criticism—Part II, " 176.

explains the behavior of people who behave in socially odd ways as crazy. They attribute this behavior oftentimes to being bothered by evil spirits. The performer is connecting this distant story of a demoniac with Jesus to the everyday experiences of the audience with evil spirits and crazy people. Another performer presented a similar relevant question with the same story: "You know what demon-possessed people do?" Such a question immediately makes the story relevant to the life experiences of the Vuté audience. At other times the relevancy comes by an understanding of a word or phrase that may not be understood by the Vuté audience. This is the case with the question at the end of the story of the Gerasene demoniac, where the healed man goes off to the Decapolis and announces what Jesus has done for him. The question follows: "Do you know what Decapolis is?" The performer provides the answer to his own question: "It is ten cities within a region." Other examples of helping audiences find relevancy in biblical materials are discussed in the following section.

Relevance in Performances

Hill argues that the problem with comprehension in Bible Translation is not simply the result of a poor translation of words. Rather, based on Relevance Theory of communication, the audience does not have adequate context to infer accurately—given the social and religious gaps in their knowledge.[14] One practical solution to this challenge is to provide additional context for the audience that will permit them to infer accurately what was intended. Such context-building at times provides information that is lacking by the audience or steers them away from false inferences based on false assumptions—especially when there is potential religious-cultural dissonance between the biblical scenario and local culture. In written translations, such context building can occur outside of the body of the text in marginal footnotes or in a book's introduction or in glossaries, illustrations, or maps. Hill suggests that context building can also occur within the text. This is information that is not explicitly provided by the text but is implied and assumed of the original audiences. This distinction of information within or outside of text relates also with oral performance. Parenthetical comments or explanations can be understood as "outside the text" but they occur within the space and more accurately within the timing of the actual story. Hill looks at

14. Hill, *The Bible at Cultural Crossroads*.

Bible Translation for Performance

two ways of providing in-text context building with the Bible story and amplified text.[15] The Bible story type can involve simplification, conflation, omission, or reordering of events. Although there may be some minor reordering of Bible verses to correspond with the chronological order of events with the amplified text model, this second model limits its reconfiguration of the text to added contextual information with the goal of building context. The type of information provided and the way it is presented within the story is particular to a culture and audience. Below I present Vuté performances and how extra-textual material can be added.

Vuté storytellers would often set the scene for a pericope by summarizing what had happened immediately before the pericope or by a generalized account of Jesus' earthly ministry. In one context, after the Lutheran worship service, one of the performers began his performance of the leper's cleansing in this way: "You heard how the Pastor began by saying to you in the gospel reading, 'Jesus walked about a lot.' He didn't remain in only one village. He went often here and there; he walked around a lot. Well, one day . . ." Related to this was the choice by some of the performers to present themselves to the audience as one who had seen or heard the events he was about to present. In one such performance, the presenter began: "Now, you see me here. I've returned from Israel. It's because I have something to tell you that I came today. Since Jesus and I walked the same roads, I saw all that he was doing. When he healed the leper . . . I was following him." Such a self-introduction serves to validate the story that follows. Such accreditation of performer and subsequently the story corresponds with Speech-Act theory's understanding of the importance of who is speaking the words.[16]

In the story of the leper that approaches Jesus to be restored, the performance translation adds the parenthetic religious-cultural information for the Vuté audience: "At that time, a leper must not be with people in the village." The translators felt that the information about the communal separation due to impurity was not immediately available to the

---

15. Ibid., 72–91.

16. Austin, *How to Do Things with Words*, 14–15: "There must exist an accepted conventional procedure having a certain conventional effect, that procedure to include the uttering of certain words by certain persons in certain circumstances, and . . . the particular persons and circumstances in a given case must be appropriate for the invocation of the particular procedure invoked."

Vuté audience. This information reinforced the surprising act of Jesus to touch the leper. Within the same story, another performer gave his explanation of why the leper was directed by Jesus to go to the priest: to prove that the leprosy was truly gone, permitting the former leper to be socially reintegrated. The translators' and performers' addition of these pieces of information may be an influence of the exegetical study that I did with the translators and performers. There are several examples of how pieces of background information that were discussed in the exegetical study time were placed within the performance translation or the performance itself. Another cultural piece given was the difference of rooftops between those of first-century Palestine and the current Vuté construction—flat vs. pitched, respectively. Not only was this information placed in the performance translation of Mark 2:1–12, but each performer included this information in his performance as if it was critical to the audiences' understanding of the story. In fact, several performers enhanced the pithy explanation of the translation. One performer explained how people might spend time on their roofs to rest or to eat. At another performance, one of the audience members jokingly suggested that people used to climb up on the roof and drink palm wine together. The consistent and sometimes lengthy presentation of this cross-cultural information never seemed to interrupt the flow of the performance. Such an "in-text" option for context building seems to function well with oral performance.

Influence of Exegete, Translators, and Performers

The examples above demonstrate the influence that exegetes, translators, and performers have on a translation and its performance. However, other discussions of background material between the translators and performers had no overt effect on the translations or performances. During the discussions of the pericope of the Gerasene demoniac, I, as the exegete, suggested how some New Testament scholars had understood Mark's story as an attempt to subvert the Roman Empire.[17] Furthermore, I suggested that the colonial experience of first-century Palestine and the history of Cameroon might have points of similarity. The group found the similarities intriguing yet neither the translation nor any of the performances reflected any colonial references. Further research is needed to explain why this was the case. Nevertheless, it appears that nobody from

---

17. See, for example, Horsley, *Hearing the Whole Story*.

the group considered such information as relevant or potentially engaging to the audience. It could also be exemplary of the conditioning that the Vuté community has experienced with regard to a Christianity that separates the biblical narratives from politics. Another possible reason for this component's absence in the translation or performance is that such subversive subject matter continues to be communicated as the "hidden transcript" in sub-altern ways and not openly disclosed in public.[18]

Beyond my own exegetical influence on the translations and performances, I recognized within the performances (but not directly in the translation for performance) the influence of Vuté cultural values.[19] Gratefulness to someone who has helped you is a deep-seated value in Vuté culture. In at least two of the performances the performer underscored how people did not thank Jesus for his healing. In both cases the reasoning was the hurriedness of the character. The leper, finding that he was cleansed, quickly left Jesus to report his cleansing to the priest and freely announced it to all who would hear him. The Syro-Phoenician woman, having heard of her daughter's exorcism, quickly returns to her house without any further exchanges with Jesus. The performers inserted such information without my exegetical encouragement (and seemingly without textual support) to underscore an integral lesson of thankfulness. The Markan characters were not condemned by the performers but the audiences were reminded of their duty to show gratefulness.

A second example of performance additions involves humor, a common component of Vuté folktales. This creates interest for the audience and engages them in following closely the story and its lessons. This important component of folktales seems to be missing significantly from biblical performances. However, I do note a few examples where humor was used. These examples represent the performers' interpretation and insertion of added information. When one storyteller is explaining how first-century Palestinian houses with flat roofs differ from the Vuté construction, he suggests that one of the four friends of the paralytic listens

---

18. Discussions of such counter-colonial behavior are discussed in relation to the context of Africa and biblical texts in the following collections of articles: Draper, *Orality, Literacy, and Colonialism in Antiquity*; idem, *Orality, Literacy, and Colonialism in Southern Africa*; Horsley, *Oral Performance, Popular Tradition, and Hidden Transcript in Q*.

19. There could be some influence from the general biblical knowledge of the performers in relation to other gospel narratives—in particular the story of the ten lepers and the gratefulness of only one healed leper (Luke 17:11–19).

closely from the roof for Jesus' voice in the house before digging through the roof. The storyteller quickly assumes the role of those in the house as the roof is caving in. Despite this vandalizing, the owner keeps his attention on Jesus' teaching. Such a humorous presentation of the scene suggests how a Vuté person might object to the destruction of their roof and how (at least for the storyteller) such damage is of minimal importance in comparison to hearing the words of Jesus. As mentioned above, the Syro-Phoenician woman is quick to return to her daughter. One of the performers presents her as flitting about in excitement—to the humorous appreciation of the audience.

Some of the performers demonstrated a greater sense of liberty in adding to the translation script. These additions were sometimes spurred on by questions addressed to the audience followed by responses from the performer. When one performer asked what the audience would do if they were inside a house where people were breaking the roof, numerous responses were given. The performer responded to some of these by assuring the audience that there would be no need for fear because Jesus was there with them in the house. The same performer had a tendency to summarize a lesson communicated in the story. His conclusions were surprising to me in how he underscored at times issues of gratefulness or made the direct connection of Jesus representing God and God's power. Such cultural insertions as mentioned in the preceding examples underscore not only the (outsider's) exegetical influence on translation and performances but also the (insider) performers' influences on the performances. Those who do source-oriented translation are very reluctant to include such extra-textual additions. Audience-oriented translation encourages such relevancy. This tension is not readily resolved—especially when dealing with biblical translation for performance.

I have already discussed in earlier sections and chapters how translation involves interpretation and is not a neutral activity. Evidence for this assertion was found in the preparation of and presentation of translations for performance. My social location and exegetical studies shaped in part how the translation was prepared. The agency of the Vuté translators and performers was also in play as they shaped the translation by their selection of vocabulary, their use of ideophones, and their interaction with the audiences. The audiences themselves were active participants in this shaping as well in their reactions to the performances and their interactions with the performers.

Non-Verbal Features of Performance

I have described several performances in terms of the words used and their adherence to or deviation from the various translations prepared. However, as I have argued in previous chapters, as supported by Performance Criticism, performances are more than words. Performance involves para- and extra-linguistic means of communication. Paralinguistic communication was evident by the Vuté performers' use of vocal qualities and silence. At times a performers' voice became loud as he began speaking in character. Each of the performers who presented the story of the leper began the leper's pleading with a loud voice and an ideophone, *yée* (pleeeaaassse!) and likewise with another ideophone prior to Jesus' warning to the leper to show himself to the priest as Moses had prescribed, *kpab*! A raised voice also was evident when the performer was asking a question of the audience. At other times the speed of delivery of words increased while at other times there was a slow methodical pace. When the four friends of the paralytic came to the house that was full and no entrance was open, these descriptions are done in rapid succession. There is a type of rhythm with the description as words are repeated, "full ... full ... many ..." The next section in the same story is instruction to the audience on the difference between first-century Palestinian rooftops and Vuté rooftops. The pace at this point is slow and deliberate. Silence is used in many ways by the performers. Silence can indicate a change of scenes within the story. It can be an invitation for reflection to the audience or a way of underscoring an important part of the story. At one point a performer seemed to be using silence to help the audience imagine the actions in their mind's eye: with the introduction of the leper, the performer "falls before Jesus" and there is a brief silence. These are ways in which silence was used for dramatic effect.

Communication occurs in performance beyond the ear to the eye. All the performers made use of these visual effects of gestures and body posture. The Vuté performers often gesticulated with their hands. At times it was not clear how the gestures related to the words, but most often they were used either to reinforce words spoken or to indicate to the audience the positioning of invisible props or characters within the story. When the paralytic, was healed this occurred "in their eyes" (meaning in front of the whole crowd). This phrase was accompanied by the performer pointing with his index fingers to his own eyes. At another place where Jesus is telling the leper to go show himself to the priest, the performer is pulling at his own ear as a way of asking for obedience—"do you hear what I'm commanding you?!" Hand gestures and body posture of the performers helped the audience understand where we were in the story of the paralytic: first, down on the ground looking at the crowded house; next, up on the roof listening (the performer cups one hand to his ear as a gesture of listening closely) to locate Jesus in the house; third, back on the ground but inside the house, surrounded by scribes and other people. From my own experience with performing this scene, I recognize that making these settings clear to the audience is crucial, and each of the performers executed these gestures very effectively.

Other hand gestures involved pointing to characters in the story: "there were scribes sitting there . . ." When Jesus stretches out his hand and touches the leper, one performer adds an actual prop in the room and taps the back of a chair. With the story of the paralytic, the performer stomps his foot on the floor to give the sound effect of the four friends breaking through the roof in Capernaum. At other times the gestures enacted the events of the characters: the leper kneels before Jesus; the four friends carry the paralytic on a mat; when the leper is cleansed, the performer stretches out his hands and extends his fingers; he glances down at his feet to see the leprosy gone.

Beyond gestures and actions, but still within the area of visual aids, one of the performers was progressive in the way he dressed. In his first performance he wore a length of cloth tied over his shoulder. The next performance he carried a walking stick in his hand with the same cloth draped over his shoulder.[20] His third performance was the same attire, but he added living props to his story. For his final performance, around a fire at the chief's compound, he came into the crowd with the clothing and makeup of an old sage, ready to impart wisdom through storytelling. This performer was not only the most expressive with his appearance but in many other ways while performing. His skills in performing were not self-aggrandizing. He approached each performance with solemnity, with respect both to the time-honored Vuté manner of oral performance as well to the sacred Word of God. Were his performances entertaining? Yes. Did they offer fresh ways of infusing God's Word into the Vuté

---

20. Such attire, according to Jean Bosco Atangana, was meant to communicate that he was a first-century Judean.

community by performance? Yes. The attractive engagement of the Bible with the audience offers innovative opportunities for contextualization.

Beyond the performers' expressions, there is a synergy with the audience and the performer as they interacted through physical proximity, audience laughter and applause, and the questions exchanged between the performer and his audience. Some of the performers remained seated on chairs or benches when they recounted their stories. Others stood, walking back and forth across the stage while at times approaching the audience or withdrawing from them. The position of the performer on the stage changed throughout the story. One of the performers would look into the eyes of the audience when characters within the story were speaking and would then avert his eyes when the narrator took over the discourse. The actions of characters within the story would be played out by the performer who would walk towards the audience as the paralytic walked off in front of the scribes. At times the performer would turn his back to the audience as he was giving background information to the story.

Due to the embodiment of the performance, a more appropriate medium for discussing these Vuté stories would be to show excerpts from the video footage I took. Even so, the immediacy of the live performance would be lost. The ways in which the Vuté audiences influenced the performers would be frozen. We would be simply observers and not participants in such an experience. The challenges that performance presents to translation were encountered head-on with this recent Vuté research. It underscores the important need for BPC to continue its methodology of actual performances of biblical compositions. Below I follow the example from chapter five where I scripted one of my own performances. Here I present one of the Vuté performances. This description comes from a transcript of the performance and observations of the video-taped performance. Audience responses—including those of the "scribes" on stage—were not scripted but are spontaneous and are included in the extralinguistic column to demonstrate the participatory role of the audience. Obviously this performance was initially in the Vuté language and is translated into English. The context of the performance was the Catholic Church in Yoko during an evening music concert. After someone had explained to the audience the notion of oral performances of biblical texts, one of the performers, Jean Bosco Atangana, came out in front of the audience after several songs. He told the following story.

FROM ORALITY TO ORALITY

TABLE 4
English Script of Vuté Performance for Mark 2:1–12

Paralinguistic	Text	Extralinguistic
		Performer comes on to the scene dressed with a shoulder cloth and walking stick.
	I am in front of you. I was walking often with Jesus. I come from Israel.	Performer stops pacing and faces the audience; he points upwards (in the distance) to indicate that Israel is far away.
	After Jesus healed the leper, now he and I, we are going to Capernaum.	Performer continues pacing.
High pitched voice to accompany superlative.	We entered into a house. As soon as we entered in this house, since the people realized where he was, they came, very very numerous.	Hand gesture to indicate a great number of people.
Rhythmic flow of words accentuated with stress on the word "full."	Full in the house. Full outside. The space where you could enter and see Jesus was lacking.	Hand gestures to indicate multitude of people. Wag finger as a sign of negation.
	Well, as Jesus was teaching in this house, we saw some people carrying a paralytic.	There is a pause. Then as the performer turns aside with his stick in hand, four people enter the stage carrying a small boy on a mat. The crowd snickers and the four place the boy on the ground. Three of the carriers sit down on stools and become the scribes.
Speaks in raised voice over the crowd as they discuss the entrance of the four people carrying the boy on a mat.	Since those who were carrying the paralytic could not get kpaaŋ kpaaŋ kpaaŋ in front of Jesus.	
	Well, they remained like that, then they had an idea . . .	Pause for effect . . . so that audience wonders what the idea is.

Bible Translation for Performance

Paralinguistic	Text	Extralinguistic
	Look, in the country of Israel, there were Jews and their houses they built in a way that they were làktàk *(flat). It wasn't pointed like for us here; the grass roofs here.*	Gesture behind to indicate distance of Israel from the audience. Corresponding gestures with hands as to a flat vs. pointed roof.
	At that time they would climb up on the roof of the house. They would climb up high. They would stay there on top during the daytime, sometimes.	As performer explains the men climbing on to the roof, he turns his back to the audience and looks upwards to an invisible roof.
	When they got up above, somebody put his ear like that and began to listen to find out where Jesus was speaking.	Performer turns back towards the crowd and bends over looking at the floor and turns his ear to hear as if to locate Jesus.
	Then he said to the other: "break through here." They heard then the tab tab tab.	Performer stomps on the floor to indicate the four breaking through the roof.
	What does one do?	The crowd responds: "they are breaking the ceiling."
	Then you, the owner of the house, what would you do?	The response of the crowd is inaudible on the video.
	Everyone from the house must have been looking upwards but they knew that Jesus was also with them. Nothing could happen to them. "yirib" *(indicating a deep silence or complete calm).*	
	Then they let down carefully the paralytic in front of Jesus and placed the mat in front of him.	
	Then Jesus remained tranquil. He looked uu *(indicating a long time).*	Performer bends over and places his hand on the boy lying on the mat.
	He said, "my child, your sins are pardoned."	
Brief silence between questions.	*As he said this, the big scribes that you see here, here they are.*	The scribes are saying to each other: He mocks God. What is that? This is an insult to God, isn't it?

FROM ORALITY TO ORALITY

Paralinguistic	Text	Extralinguistic
	You, you know how Jesus was. He knew immediately what was in their heart. He knew what they were thinking.	
	He said to these people like this: What type of thoughts are you thinking in your hearts? Like that?	Performer motions to those in front of him on stage.
	He looked and said to them: "What I said to my child that his sins were pardoned or that he rise and return to his place, which is easier to say?"	
Brief silence.		Performer looks to his right and then left towards the crowd.
	Then Jesus said in front of them	Performer addresses himself to the child lying on the mat.
	"My son, arise."	The child rises.
	"Roll up your mat."	The child rolls up the mat.
	"Go home."	The child goes off running. The crowd applauds. The "scribes" leave the stage.
	As they saw this, those who stayed said "kei! (exclamation) truly the quality here we have never seen anything like it."	
Brief silence after question.	What moved them to say that?	Performer begins to pace. Audience laughs.
	You see, these things that we are doing is the Gospel. It is the book that the Lord wrote.	

Bible Translation for Performance

Performance as Song

Vuté performances are not restricted to speaking but include songs. As related in an earlier section, for several years the Catholic Church in the Vuté community has been involved in the composition and dissemination of Scripture-based songs. Community-recognized composers have often been invited to songwriting workshops where gospel texts are the basis of the lyrics for new songs. The criteria for these songs are twofold: the local style of music must be respected in the compositions; the lyrics for these songs are to follow closely the already translated texts, with limited creative licensing for revision. Audience participation with the composed songs is integral in that the congregations are expected to respond with a refrain. Two examples of such songwriting are mentioned here. First, I participated in a Catholic Mass while in Cameroon in June 2007. During the liturgy, one of the choir leaders sang a Scripture song from Luke 1:57–66, 80 – the lectionary text for that Sunday. It is the choir leader's voice alone that begins. However, at the first direct citation within the text (Zechariah's verbal response, "No, his name is to be John") the congregation joins in with several repetitions of the line. Several other refrains occur within the song (with two other direct quotes) as both performer and congregation join in with music now accompanied by the traditional drum. In comparing the lyrics of this song with the published translation, there is almost no deviation from the text. There are no cultural footnotes, no performer insertions. Such proximity to the text could be explained in part by the medium of the performance. Whereas the song leader could, he or she maintains the lines as originally composed. The lyrics are linked with the melody and rhythm. Furthermore the congregation who has participated in the song in the past would be aware of any deviation from what they know. Variation would disturb the audience's participation in the refrain. A second explanation for the song remaining close to the text is the setting: it was a performance within the Catholic liturgy on a Sunday morning in a church building. Formality of a ritual setting imposes restraints on performances (whether Christian or not). This is supported by *Skopotheorie's* prioritization of the audience (and broader context) determining the type of translation (and performance) done.

I filmed a second example of Scripture songs while I was in a small hamlet called Nazareth. The fifteen inhabitants and neighbors gathered to participate in biblical storytelling and singing. One of the story-songs

FROM ORALITY TO ORALITY

had been composed specifically for this encounter: the story of the Syro-Phoenician woman. The group had decided to have a narrator present the story with a song leader intervening when the woman spoke. At this point, the song leader directs the group in what became the refrain. The song sections were accompanied by a traditional drum, thumb piano, and hand shaker. Once again, the lyrics held closely to the translated text. Nevertheless, the emotion of the woman's pleading for her daughter was highlighted by the style and rhythm of the song. Minor changes were made so that the words matched the rhythmic syllabic space available. The context was far from a formal liturgy in a recognized place of worship. Rather, as the small group sat on bamboo benches in their hamlet's open courtyard, there was a continued adherence to the translated text.

In this performance the young storyteller begins with a somewhat stilted rendition of the first part of the story as related by Mark's narrator. He holds a paper (no doubt the written text in case he loses his place) in his hand.[21] The young man seldom looks up at the audience but looks concentrated on remembering the words. However, as soon as the Syro-Phoenician woman is introduced by him, he cedes the "stage" to the singer-storyteller, an older man who is recognized throughout the Vuté community as a gifted composer and singer. As the drums, thumb piano, and shaker begin, Martin keeps rhythm with both of his hands and then raises them in the culturally appropriate form of a plea that corresponds to the wording of the Syro-Phoenician woman. His feet move rhythmically to the music and after he finishes the initial words of the woman, he extends his hands in invitation to the group to sing with him the refrain. The group joins in seamlessly as they take on the voice of the woman pleading for her demon-possessed daughter. Appellations are exchanged as she addresses Jesus: Lord, Teacher, Respected Leader. The young storyteller regains the stage to give Jesus' initial response to the woman. In the background the rhythm instruments continue during his narration of events. The song leader then guides the group into the woman's riposte with a similar melody, yet with an additional accentuated rhythm that seems to my American ears as a smart reply led by the drums and the silence in between phrases of the singers. A final turn by the young storyteller finishes the story with the woman's daughter

---

21. As related in previous chapters, the presence of the written scroll can be understood as an authoritative symbol. This does not seem to be the case in the Vuté performance.

freed from her demons. The song leader completes the cycle by repeating both of the earlier refrains. During a meal after this evening of song and storytelling, the organizer of the event asked me if I had seen one of his neighbors at the gathering. He relates to me how his neighbor would never have stayed if the event had consisted of a traditional Bible reading where passages of Scripture were read from the written page. Yet, as the gospel compositions were sung and recounted, this neighbor stayed and participated. Had he heard God's Word proclaimed? Yes. Yet he experienced it in a culturally relevant and attractive way.

Conclusion

After all the performances had been completed on the final day, the translators, performers and I shared a meal together late into the night. I talked some, but mostly I listened as they shared spontaneously other stories or repeated folktales that we had heard in the previous performances. I heard them discuss how such a method of performance should be continued beyond this experimental stage. They affirmed each other in the validity of oral performance as they noted the similarities with the first-century oral communication context. They recognized how in time the Vuté audiences would grow more accustomed to such a reception of Scripture. There was an air of liberation, a liberation from an externally imposed literary bias. These talented Vuté people are not naïve in thinking that literacy does not play an important part in their lives. They do see, however, the value of hearing these biblical compositions and of experiencing a performance event. As the community comes together in performance, their identity is reinforced. At the same time, this identity is shifting as the community interacts with the biblical message. Community performances of biblical translations present the opportunity for liberation and identity-building as an expression of contextualization.

As for my understanding of Bible Translation and performance, I continue to reflect on the many issues involved. Preparation of translation for performance is much more extensive than the already lengthy process of literary translation. Performance of Bible Translation by its very nature cannot occur in isolation but incorporates many gifted people in the community. Audiences and settings deeply affect not only a performance but also the translation, as responses from the audience feed back into revisions of translations. This exchange underscores the potential for performance and interactions afterwards as sites of interpretation, sites for doing theology. In this way, the exchange foregrounds the social locations of exegetes, translators, performers, and audiences. As argued throughout this book, a performance's ultimate goal is transformation. I experienced such transformation—whether it was in the principles and methods of translation, or the transformation of people involved in the translation, or the transformation of the text as it was resurrected as the living word in performance.

CONCLUSION

THE WORD CONCLUSION IS A MISNOMER HERE. MY STUDIES and assertions have opened wide the way for further study. Many times my claims have limited experiential foundation. At other places the theories I advance are so fresh that time will determine the direction they will eventually take. Nevertheless, this study has made some important claims that should be considered in discussions of missiology, theology, Bible Translation, biblical studies, and anthropology.

It is helpful to understand the predominant assumptions of Bible Translation. In terms of theology, Bible Translation has often been understood as a conservative tool of evangelism or a means of providing communities with a way to measure faithful allegiance to the Scriptures. In such thinking, expressions of contextualization are compared to the scriptural plumb line. In so doing, one no longer questions the contextual influence on the interpretation of Scripture (whose plumb line is used!); rather, it is often the dominant (but latent), northern hemisphere's array of interpretations that is used to measure acceptability. Similar in motivation to this view of Scripture is how Bible Translation is viewed as a benevolent way for so-called developing churches to grow in their Christian faith. Both views understand Bible Translation as a unilateral activity: from the established northern hemispheric source to the developing southern hemispheric target. Others, not satisfied with these views of Bible Translation, turn an indifferent or critical back to Bible Translation's role in mission and theology.

My proposal is that Bible Translation as contextualization offers an alternative to this. Bible Translation is a mutual engagement of north and south in a way that benefits all parties. Insights from new translations emanating from fresh linguistic categories and worldviews are offered by southern hemisphere communities. This active participation by host communities in Bible Translation establishes and maintains identity

Conclusion

within the community and offers liberation from dominance: linguistically, socially, and theologically.

Although such a paradigm for Bible Translation can be viewed in many contexts around the world, I have predominantly been considering the African context in this study. Given this delimitation I have looked at the rich and varied discussions of (published) African theologians. These women and men are the ones who have set my agenda for how to understand Africa and its relation to the Bible. Their voices and views are by no means monolithic but they are united in seeking African responses to their challenges. These Africans are the ones who have (unknowingly) suggested to me the components of Bible Translation as contextualization as they offer discourses on anthropological pauperization, liberation, identity, reconstruction, postcolonialism, and so on. It is also these African voices that have lifted up the richness of African oral performance through their extensive verbal art, including epics, proverbs, and folktales. Bible Translation in Africa that ignores these verbal art forms cannot be contextual.

Presuppositions of communication have also linked Bible translation efforts in recent centuries to unilateral northern dominance. Bible Translation efforts that unquestionably link the task to literacy and denigrate the predominantly oral cultures around the world do not follow the model of contextualization. Such a biased view of communication is also found in biblical studies which has until recently been minimally affected by an understanding of first-century contexts as orally biased. My study places Bible Translation as a mediator between two contexts of orality: first-century Mediterranean world and twenty-first century Africa. Prompted by contextual theology's method of discovering (rather than bringing) in the local, I note the predominance of oral communication today in Africa as it interfaces with the written and printed word—most often in dominating world languages. Although issues of orality are relatively recent to New Testament studies, they offer those involved in Bible Translation insights into the intentional composition of the New Testament to be heard. Orality features have been delineated by several scholars. Studies of the general oral context of the first-century offer insights into how the New Testament was communicated orally in communal settings that resist interpretations of individual, silent reading. Furthermore, this communal understanding of orality brings to the forefront not only the location of meaning but the source of authority.

Conclusion

This insightful understanding of the auditory intentions and implications of biblical communications, however, is limited. It is not that orality studies have gone too far in their research of biblical materials, but rather that they have not gone far enough. First-century presentations were not simply heard, they were viewed. Moreover they were experienced. Biblical Performance Criticism permits us to enlarge our understanding of the interaction of the performer and his or her audience. In relation to the Bible, performance helps us to understand the communal interactions not only of the one who composes the message but also of the ones who perform the message. Performance refuses rigidity. Instead of discussing the original text one must talk of early performances and the oral-derived scripts that remain. Each of these assertions not only challenges more established literary-biased views of Scripture but is also provocative in opening up creative ways of appreciating host communities who cherish oral performance. The challenge for Bible Translation is not simply how to translate a text from one language to another, but how to translate a biblical performance script into an appropriate form for performance. This immediately challenges the bifurcation of form and meaning. It disputes the loci of meaning and monovalence. Translating performances requires more appropriate communication models that are sufficiently robust to engage multi-form communications.

The challenges for performance translation are enormous and have only been lightly addressed in this study. My intent was not to limit such discussions to theory but to place the challenge in a concrete setting: the Vuté community of central Cameroon. In many ways Bible Translation efforts in the Vuté context began as traditional, with assumptions of literacy and the main goal of a printed text. However, the Vuté context by its unfailing use of oral performance continued to challenge such presuppositions. With a published New Testament the translators are beginning to rethink how their efforts are affected by understanding the New Testament in oral performance parameters. It is the Vuté community who are the agents of such inquiries and pursuits. Initial explorations of re-translations for performance with multiple performances and settings demonstrate the challenge—no, the impossibility—of separating translation from interpretation. In fact, the very acts of translation and of performance become theological enterprises. Bible Translation, then, becomes contextualization by the local community as they reshape biblical performances in local contexts.

Conclusion

This study has aimed at looking at Bible Translation in the context of the twenty-first century. It addresses the critiques made against Bible Translation as a literary-biased strategy of dominance. The translation of biblical compositions for performance goes from one orality to another orality. Ultimately, the value of understanding Bible Translation as contextualization and performance must be measured by host communities who are the agents for translation and contextualization.

BIBLIOGRAPHY

Abraham, K. C., editor. The "African Report" presented at the Second General Assembly of EATWOT held in Oaxtepec, Mexico, in 1986. In *Third World Theologies: Commonalities and Divergences*. Maryknoll, NY: Orbis, 1990.

Achtemeier, Paul. "*Omni Verbum Sonat*: The New Testament and the Environment of Late Western Antiquity." *Journal of Biblical Literature* 109 (1990) 3–27.

Aitken, Ellen Bradshaw. *Jesus' Death in Early Christian Memory: The Poetics of the Passion*. Novum Testamentum et Orbis Antiquus 53. Göttingen: Vandenhoeck & Ruprecht, 2004.

Anderson, Allan H. *African Reformation: African Initiated Christianity in the 20th Century*. Trenton: Africa World Press, 2001.

Appiah, Kwame Anthony. "Topologies of Nativism." In *In My Father's House: Africa in the Philosophy of Culture*, 47–72. New York: Oxford University Press, 1992.

Appiah-Kubi, Kofi, and Sergio Torres, editors. *African Theology en Route: Papers from the Pan African Conference of Third World Theologians, December 17–23, 1977, Accra, Ghana*. Maryknoll, NY: Orbis, 1979.

Arichea, Daniel C. "Theology and Translation: The Implications of Certain Theological Issues to the Translation Task." In *Bible Translation and the Spread of the Church: The Last 200 Years*, edited by Philip C. Stine, 40–67. Studies in Christian Mission 2. Leiden: Brill, 1990.

Aslam, Rekha. *Linguistic Differences in Speaking and Writing: With Special Reference to Involvement and Detachment Strategies*. New Delhi: Northern Book Centre, 1990.

Assmann, Jan, "Form as a Mnemonic Device." In *Performing the Gospel: Orality, Memory and Mark*, edited by Richard A. Horsley, Jonathan A. Draper, and John Miles Foley, 67–82. Minneapolis: Fortress, 2006.

Austin, J. L., *How to Do Things with Words*. Edited by J. O. Urmson and Marina Sbisa. Oxford: Oxford University Press, 1975 [1962].

Bailey, Kenneth. "Informal Controlled Oral Tradition and the Synoptic Gospels." *Asia Journal of Theology* 5.1 (1991) 34–54.

———. "Middle Eastern Oral Tradition and the Synoptic Gospels." *Expository Times* 106 (1995) 363–67.

Bailey, Randall C., and Tina Pippen, editors. "Race, Class, and the Politics of Biblical Translation," *Semeia* 76. Atlanta: Scholars, 1996.

Baker, Mona, editor. *Routledge Encyclopedia of Translation Studies*. New York: Routledge, 1998.

Bar-Ilan, Meir. "Illiteracy in the Land of Israel in the First Centuries C. E." In *Essays in the Social Scientific Study of Judaism and Jewish Society*, Vol. 2, edited by Simcha Fishbane et al., 46–61. Hoboken, NJ: Ktav, 1992.

Bibliography

Barrett, David B. *Schism and Renewal in Africa: An Analysis of Six Thousand Contemporary Religious Movements.* Nairobi: Oxford University Press, 1968.

———. "AD 2000–350 Million Christians in Africa." *International Review of Mission* 59.233 (1970) 39–54.

Barton, Stephen C. "New Testament Interpretation as Performance." *Scottish Journal of Theology* 52 (1999) 179–208.

Bartsch, Carla. "Oral Style, Written Style, and Bible Translation." *Notes on Translation* 11 (1997) 41–48.

Bauman, Richard. "Folklore." In *Folklore, Cultural Performances, and Popular Entertainments: A Communications-centered Handbook,* edited by Richard Bauman, 29–40. New York: Oxford University Press, 1992.

———, editor. *Folklore, Cultural Performances, and Popular Entertainments: A Communications-centered Handbook.* New York: Oxford University Press, 1992.

———. "Performance." In *Folklore, Cultural Performances, and Popular Entertainments: A Communications-centered Handbook,* edited by Richard Bauman, 41–49. New York: Oxford University Press, 1992.

———. *Story, Performance, and Event: Contextual Studies of Oral Narrative.* Cambridge: Cambridge University Press, 1986.

———. *Verbal Art as Performance.* Prospect Heights, IL: Waveland, 1984 [1977].

Bediako, Kwame. "African and Christian Identity: Recovering an Ancient Story." *The Princeton Seminary Bulletin* 25 (2004) 153–61.

———. "Biblical Exegesis in the African Context—The Factor and Impact of the Translated Scriptures." *Journal of African Christian Thought* 6.1 (2003) 15–23.

———. *Christianity in Africa: The Renewal of Non-Western Religion.* Maryknoll, NY: Orbis, 1995.

———. "The Doctrine of Christ and the Significance of Vernacular Terminology." *International Bulletin of Missionary Research* 22 (1998) 110–11.

———. "Editorial." *Journal of African Christian Thought* 5.1 (2002) 1–3.

———. "Scripture as the Hermeneutic of Culture and Tradition." *Journal of African Christian Thought* 4.1 (2001) 2–11.

Bediako, Kwame, Hans Visser, and Gillian Bediako. *Jesus and the Gospel in Africa: History and Experience.* Maryknoll, NY: Orbis, 2004.

Berleant, Arnold. *The Aesthetic Field: A Phenomenology of Aesthetic Experience.* Springfield, IL: Thomas, 1970.

Bevans, Stephen. *Models of Contextual Theology.* 2nd ed. Maryknoll, NY: Orbis, 2003.

———, and Roger Schroeder. *Constants in Context: A Theology of Mission for Today.* Maryknoll, NY: Orbis, 2004.

Bhabha, Homi K. *The Location of Culture.* London: Routledge, 1994.

Biber, Douglas. *Variation Across Speech and Writing.* Cambridge: Cambridge University Press, 1988.

Birch, Bruce C., and Larry L. Rasmussen. "The Nature and Role of Biblical Authority." In *Bible and Ethics in the Christian Life,* 141–58. Minneapolis: Augsburg, 1989.

Boomershine, Thomas. "Biblical Megatrends: Towards a Paradigm for the Interpretation of the Bible in Electronic Media." In *Society of Biblical Literature Seminar Papers* 26, edited by K. Richards, 144–57. Atlanta: Scholars, 1987.

———. "Biblical Translation and Communication Technology." *United Bible Societies Bulletin* 160/161 (1991) 14–19.

Bibliography

———. "Jesus of Nazareth and the Watershed of Ancient Orality and Literacy." *Semeia* 65 (1995) 7–36.
———. "Mark the Storyteller: A Rhetorical-Critical Investigation of Mark's Passion and Resurrection Narrative." PhD diss., Union Theological Seminary, New York, 1974.
———. "Peter's Denial as Polemic or Confession: The Implications of Media Criticism for Biblical Hermeneutics." In *Orality Aurality and Biblical Narrative, Semeia* 39, edited by Lou H. Silberman, 47–68. Atlanta: Society of Biblical Literature, 1987.
———. "A Transmediatization Theory of Biblical Translation." *United Bible Societies Bulletin* 170/171 (1994) 49–57.
Borgman, Paul. *The Way according to Luke: Hearing the Whole Story of Luke-Acts*. Grand Rapids: Eerdmans, 2006.
Bosch, David. J. *Transforming Mission: Paradigm Shifts in Theology of Mission*. Maryknoll, NY: Orbis, 1991.
Botha, Eugene. "Pragmatic Models of Text Interpretation and Bible Translation: Speech-Act Theory and Non-Verbal Communication." Paper presented in Sibiu, Romania, at SNTS, July 2007.
Botha, Pieter J. J. "Greco-Roman Literacy as Setting for New Testament Writings." *Neotestamentica* 26 (1992) 195–215.
———. "Letter Writing and Oral Communication in Antiquity: Suggested Implications for the Interpretation of Paul's Letter to the Galatians." *Scriptura* 42 (1992) 17–34.
———. "Living Voice and Lifeless Letters: Reserve Towards Writing in the Graeco-Roman World." *Hervormde Teologiese Studies* 49 (1993) 742–59.
———. "Mark's Story as Oral Traditional Literature: Rethinking the Transmission of Some Traditions about Jesus." *Hervormde Teologiese Studies* 47 (1991) 304–31.
———. "Mute Manuscripts: Analyzing a Neglected Aspect of Ancient Communication." *Theologia Evangelica* 23 (1990) 35–47.
———. "The Verbal Art of the Pauline Letters: Rhetoric, Performance and Presence." In *Rhetoric and the New Testament: Essays from the 1992 Heidelberg Conference*, edited by Stanley Porter and T. H. Olbricht, 409–28. Journal for the Study of the New Testament Supplement Series 90. Sheffield: Sheffield Academic, 1993.
Brenner, Athalya, and Jan Willem van Henten, editors. *Bible Translation on the Threshold of the Twenty-First Century: Authority, Reception, Culture and Religion*. Journal for the Study of the Old Testament Supplement Series 353. New York: Sheffield Academic, 2002.
Byrskog, Samuel. "A New Perspective on the Jesus Tradition: Reflections on James D. G. Dunn's 'Jesus Remembered.'" *Journal for the Study of the New Testament* 26 (2004) 459–71.
Carr, David M. *Writing on the Tablet of the Heart: Origins of Scripture and Literature*. Oxford: Oxford University Press, 2005.
Carruthers, Mary. *The Book of Memory: A Study of Memory in Medieval Culture*. Cambridge Studies in Medieval Culture 19. Cambridge: Cambridge University Press, 1990.
Chafe, Wallace L. "Integration and Involvement in Speaking, Writing, and Oral Literature." In *Spoken and Written Language: Exploring Orality and Literacy*, edited by Deborah Tannen, 35–53. Norwood: Ablex, 1982.
Comaroff, John and Jean Comaroff. *Of Revelation and Revolution*, Vol. 1, *Christianity, Colonialism, and Consciousness in South Africa*. Chicago: University of Chicago Press, 1991.

Bibliography

———. *Of Revelation and Revolution*, Vol. 2, *The Dialectics of Modernity on a South African Frontier*. Chicago: University of Chicago Press, 1997.

Cosgrove, Charles H., editor. *The Meanings We Choose: Hermeneutical Ethics, Indeterminacy and the Conflict of Interpretation*. London: T. & T. Clark, 2004.

Daar, John A. *On Character Building: The Reader and the Rhetoric of Characterization in Luke-Acts*. Literary Currents in Biblical Interpretation. Louisville: Westminster John Knox, 1992.

Davis, Casey Wayne. *Oral Biblical Criticism: The Influence of the Principles of Orality on the Literary Structure of Paul's Epistle to the Philippians*. Journal for the Study of the New Testament Supplement Series 172. Sheffield: Sheffield Academic, 1999.

de Saussure, Ferdinand. *Course in General Linguistics*. Edited by C. Bally and A. Reidlinger. Translated by W. Baskin. New York: Philosophical Library, 1966 [1915].

de Vries, L. "Bible Translation and Primary Orality." *The Bible Translator* 51 (2000) 101–14.

de Waard, Jan, and Eugene Nida. *From One Language to Another: Functional Equivalence in Bible Translating*. Nashville: Nelson, 1986.

Dean, Margaret E. "Textured Criticism." *Journal for the Study of the New Testament* 70 (1998) 79–91.

Dedji, Valenmtin. *Reconstruction and Renewal in African Christian Theology*. Nairobi: Acton Publishers, 2005.

Derico, T. M. "Upgrade and Reboot: A Re-Appraisal of the Default." Paper presented at the Society of Biblical Literature annual conference, 2004.

Derrenbacker, R. A., Jr. *Ancient Compositional Practices and the Synoptic Problem*. Bibliotheca Ephemeridium theologicarum Lovaniensium 186. Leuven: Leuven University Press, 2005.

Dewey, Joanna. "Mark as Interwoven Tapestry: Forecasts and Echoes for a Listening Audience." *Catholic Biblical Quarterly* 53 (1991) 221–31.

———. "Oral Methods of Structuring Narrative in Mark." *Interpretation* 43 (1989) 32–44.

———. "Textuality in Oral Culture: A Survey of the Pauline Traditions." *Semeia* 65 (1995) 37–65.

Dickson, Kwesi A. *Theology in Africa*. Maryknoll, NY: Orbis, 1984.

Douglas, Mary. *Edward Evans-Pritchard*. Harmondsworth, UK: Penguin, 1980.

———. "Primitive Worlds." In *Purity and Danger: An Analysis of Concept of Pollution and Taboo*, 91–116. New York: Routledge Classics, 2002.

Draper, Jonathan A. "Confessional Western Text-Centered Biblical Interpretation and an Oral Residual Context." *Semeia* 73 (1996) 59–78.

———. "Many Voices, One Script: The Prophecies of George Khambule." In *Performing the Gospel: Orality, Memory and Mark*, edited by Richard A. Horsley, Jonathan A. Draper, John Miles Foley, 44–63. Minneapolis: Fortress, 2006.

———, editor. *Orality, Literacy, and Colonialism in Antiquity*. Semeia Studies 47. Atlanta: Society of Biblical Literature, 2004.

———, editor. *Orality, Literacy, and Colonialism in Southern Africa*. Semeia Studies 46. Atlanta: Society of Biblical Literature, 2003.

———. "Practicing the Presence of God in John: Ritual Use of Scripture and the *Eidos Theou* in John 5:37." In *Orality, Literacy, and Colonialism in Antiquity*, edited by Jonathan A. Draper, 155–68. Semeia Studies 47. Atlanta: Society of Biblical Literature, 2004.

Bibliography

———. "Recovering Oral Performance from Written Text in Q." In *Whoever Hears You Hears Me: Prophets, Performance, and Tradition in Q*, Richard A. Horsley with Jonathan A. Draper, 175–94. Harrisburg, PA: Trinity, 1999.

Dube, Musa W. "Consuming the Colonial Cultural Bomb: Translating *Badimo* into Demons in the Setswana Bible (Matt. 8:28–34; 15:22; 10:8)." *Journal for the Study of the New Testament* 73 (1999) 33–59.

———, editor. *HIV/AIDS and the Curriculum: Methods of Integrating HIV/AIDS in Theological Programmes*. Geneva: WCC Publications, 2003.

———. *Postcolonial Feminist Interpretation of the Bible*. St. Louis: Chalice, 2000.

———. "Readings of *Semoya*: Batswana Women's Interpretations of Matt. 15:21–28." *Semeia* 73 (1996) 111–30.

———. "Villagizing, Globalizing, and Biblical Studies." In *Reading the Bible in the Global Village: CapeTown*, edited by Justin S. Ukpong and others, 41–64. Global Perspectives on Biblical Scholarship 3. Atlanta: Society of Biblical Literature, 2002.

———. "'What I Have Written, I Have Written' (John 19:22)?" In *Interpreting the New Testament in Africa*, edited by Mary N. Getui, Tinyiko Maluleke, and Justin Ukpong, 145–64. Nairobi: Acton, 2001.

Dube, Musa W., and Musimbi R.A. Kanyoro, editors. *Grant Me Justice!: HIV/AIDS and Gender Readings of the Bible*. Maryknoll, NY: Orbis, 2004.

Dudrey, Russ. "1 John and the Public Reading of Scripture." *Stone-Campbell Journal* 6 (2003) 235–55.

Dundes, Alan, editor. *Sacred Narrative: Readings in the Theory of Myth*. Berkeley: University of California Press, 1984.

Dunn, James D. G. "Altering the Default Setting: Re-envisaging the Early Transmission of the Jesus Tradition." *New Testament Studies* 49 (2003) 139–75.

———. *Jesus Remembered: Christianity in the Making*. Vol. 1. Grand Rapids: Eerdmans, 2003.

Edwards, Viv, and Thomas J. Sienkewicz. *Oral Cultures Past and Present: Rappin' and Homer*. Oxford: Blackwell, 1990.

Eisenstein, Elizabeth L. *The Printing Press as an Agent of Change: Communications and Cultural Transformations in Early Modern Europe*. Cambridge; New York: Cambridge University Press, 1979.

Ela, Jean-Marc. *African Cry*. Translated by Robert R. Barr. Maryknoll, NY: Orbis, 1986.

———. *My Faith as an African*. Translated by John Pairman Brown and Susan Perry. Maryknoll, NY: Orbis, 1988.

———. *Repenser la théologie africaine: Le Dieu qui libère*. Paris: Karthala, 2003.

Ellingworth, Paul. "Orality and Bible Translation." Paper presented in Aberdeen, Scotland at SNTS, 2006.

Elliott, Scott S. "'The Word' in Text, Sound, and Image: The American Bible Society's New Media Bible and the Research Center for Scripture and Media." *Bulletin/CSR* 30.3 (2001) 65–67.

Escobar, Samuel. "The Role of Translation in Developing Indigenous Theologies—A Latin American View." In *Bible Translation and the Spread of the Church: The Last 200 Years*, edited by Philip C. Stine, 81–94. Studies in Christian Mission 2. Leiden: Brill, 1990.

Fabian, Johannes. *Power and Performance: Ethnographic explorations through proverbial wisdom and theater in Shaba, Zaire*. Madison: University of Wisconsin Press, 1990.

Bibliography

Fine, Elizabeth C. *The Folklore Text: From Performance to Print*. Bloomington: Indiana University Press, 1984.

Fine, Elizabeth C., and Jean Haskell Speer, editors. *Performance, Culture, and Identity*. Westport, CT: Praeger, 1992.

Finnegan, Ruth. *Literacy and orality: studies in the technology of communication*. New York: Blackwell, 1988.

———. *Oral Literature in Africa: Backgrounds, Character, and Continuity*. Bloomington: Indiana University Press, 1970.

———. *Oral Poetry: Its Nature, Significance, and Social Context*. Bloomington: Indiana University Press, 1992.

———. *Oral Traditions and the Verbal Arts: A Guide to Research Practices*. ASA Research Methods in Social Anthropology. New York: Routledge, 1992.

Foley, John Miles. *How to Read an Oral Poem*. Urbana: University of Illinois Press, 2002.

———. *Immanent art: from structure to meaning in traditional oral epic*. Bloomington: Indiana University Press, 1991.

———. "Indigenous Poems, Colonialist Texts." In *Orality, Literacy, and Colonialism in Antiquity*, edited by Jonathan A. Draper, 9–36. Semeia Studies 47. Atlanta: Society of Biblical Literature, 2004.

———. "Memory in Oral Tradition." In *Performing the Gospel: Orality, Memory and Mark*, edited by Richard A. Horsley, Jonathan A. Draper, and John Miles Foley, 83–96. Minneapolis: Fortress, 2006.

———, editor. *Oral Tradition in Literature: Interpretation in Context*. Columbia: University of Missouri Press, 1986.

———. *The Singer of Tales in Performance*. Bloomington: Indiana University Press, 1995.

———. *The Theory of Oral Composition: History and Methodology*. Bloomington: Indiana University Press, 1988.

Fowler, Robert. *Let the Reader Understand: Reader-Response Criticism and the Gospel of Mark*. Minneapolis: Fortress, 1991.

———. "Why Everything We Know about the Bible Is Wrong: Lessons from the Media History of the Bible." In *The Bible in Ancient and Modern Media: Story and Performance*, edited by Holly E. Hearon and Philip Ruge-Jones, 3–18. Biblical Performance Criticism Series 1. Eugene: Cascade Books, 2009.

Fox, Everett. *The Five Books of Moses: A New Translation with Introduction, Commentary, and Notes*. New York: Schocken, 1995.

Franklin, Karl. "Oral Societies and our Textual Bias." *Word & Deed* 2.3 (2003) 47–58.

Fry E. M. "An Oral Approach to Translation." *The Bible Translator* 55 (2004) 506–10.

Furniss, Graham. *Orality: the power of the spoken word*. New York: Palgrave Macmillan, 2004.

Furniss, Graham, and Liz Gunner, editors. *Power, marginality and African oral literature*. Cambridge: Cambridge University Press, 1995.

Gamble, Harry Y. *Books and Readers in the Early Church: A History of Early Christian Texts*. New Haven: Yale University Press, 1995.

Geertz, Clifford. *The Interpretation of Cultures*. New York: Basic Books, 1973.

Gerhardsson, Birger. "The Secret of the Transmission of the Unwritten Jesus Tradition." *New Testament Studies* 51 (2005) 1–18.

Getui, Mary N., Tinyiko Maluleke, and Justin Ukpong, editor. *Interpreting the New Testament in Africa*. Nairobi: Acton, 2001.

Bibliography

Getui, Mary and Matthew Theuri, editor. *Quests for Abundant Life in Africa*. Nairobi: Acton, 2005.

Getui, Mary N. and E. Obeng, editor. *Theology of Reconstruction: Exploratory Essays*. 2nd ed. Nairobi: Acton, 2005.

Gibellini, Rosino, editor. *Paths of African Theology*. Maryknoll, NY: Orbis, 1994.

Giles, Terry and William J. Doan. *Twice Used Songs: Performance Criticism of the Songs of Ancient Israel*. Peabody, MA: Hendrickson, 2008.

Gilliard, Frank. "More Silent Reading in Antiquity: *Non Omne Verbum Sonabat*." *Journal of Biblical Literature* 112, no. 4 (1993) 689–96.

Gilliland, Dean S., editor. *The World among Us: Contextualizing Theology for Mission Today*. Dallas: Word, 1989.

Gittins, Anthony. "Beyond Liturgical Inculturation: Transforming the Deep Structures of Faith." *Irish Theological Quarterly* 69 (2004) 47–72.

———, editor. *Life and Death Matters: Doing Inculturation in Africa*. Nettetal, Germany: Steyeler, 2000.

González, Justo L. *Christian Thought Revisited: Three Types of Theology*. Rev. ed. Maryknoll, NY: Orbis, 1999.

Goody, Jack. *The Domestication of the Savage Mind*. Themes in the Social Sciences. Cambridge: Cambridge University Press, 1977.

———. *The Interface Between the Written and the Oral*. Studies in Literacy, Family, Culture, and the State. Cambridge: Cambridge University Press, 1987.

———. *The logic of writing and the organization of society*. Studies in Literacy, Family, Culture, and the State. Cambridge: Cambridge University Press, 1986.

———. *The Myth of the Bagre*. Oxford Library of African Literature. Oxford: Clarendon, 1972.

———. *The Power of the Written Tradition*. Smithsonian Series in Ethnographic Inquiry. Washington: Smithsonian Institution Press, 2000.

———, and Ian Watt. "The Consequences of Literacy." In *Literacy in Traditional Societies*, edited by Jack Goody, 27–68. Cambridge: Cambridge University Press, 1968.

Graham, William A. *Beyond the Written Word: Oral Aspects of Scripture in the History of Religion*. New York: Cambridge University Press, 1987.

Greenfield, P. M. "Oral and Written Language: The Consequences for Cognitive Development in Africa, the United States and England." *Language and Speech* 15 (1972) 169–78.

Gutt, Ernst-August. *Translation and Relevance: Cognition and Context*. Manchester, UK: St. Jerome Publishing, 2000.

Güttgemanns, Erhardt. *Candid Questions Concerning Gospel Form Criticism: A Methodological Sketch of the Fundamental Problematics of Form and Redaction Criticism*. Trans. William G. Doty. Pittsburgh Theological Monograph Series 26. Pittsburgh, PA: Pickwick, 1979.

Halliday, M. A. K. *Spoken and Written Language*. 2nd ed. Language Education. Oxford: Oxford University Press, 1989.

Harris, William. *Ancient Literacy*. Cambridge: Harvard University Press, 1989.

Harvey, John D. *Listening to the Text: Oral Patterning in Paul's Letters*. Grand Rapids: Baker Books, 1998.

———. "Orality and Its Implications for Biblical Studies: Recapturing an Ancient Paradigm." *Journal for the Evangelical Theological Society* 45 (2002) 99–109.

Bibliography

Hastings, Adrian. *The Construction of Nationhood: Ethnicity, Religion and Nationalism.* Cambridge: Cambridge University Press, 1997.

Havelock, Eric. *The Muse Learns to Write: Reflections on Orality and Literacy from Antiquity to the Present.* New Haven: Yale University Press, 1986.

———. *Preface to Plato.* Cambridge: Harvard University Press, 1963.

Hearon, Holly E. *The Mary Magdalene Tradition: Witness and Counter-Witness in Early Christian Communities.* Collegeville, MN: Liturgical, 2004.

———. "The Implications of Orality for Studies of the Biblical Text." In *Performing the Gospel: Orality, Memory and Mark,* edited by Richard A. Horsley, Jonathan A. Draper, and John Miles Foley, 3–20. Minneapolis: Fortress, 2006.

———, and Philip Ruge-Jones, editors. *The Bible in Ancient and Modern Media: Story and Performance.* Biblical Performance Criticism Series 1. Eugene: Cascade Books, 2009.

Heliand, The: The Saxon Gospel. Translated by G. Ronald Murphy, SJ. New York: Oxford University Press, 1992.

Henaut, Barry W. *Oral Traditions and the Gospels: The Problem of Mark 4.* Journal for the Study of the New Testament Supplement Series 82. Sheffield: Sheffield Academic, 1993.

Henderson, Ian H. "Didache and Orality in Synoptic Comparison." *Journal of Biblical Literature* 111 (1992) 283–306.

Hermanson, Eric A. "'Badimo a ba robale ka kagiso' Let the ancestors rest in peace: Colonization or Contextualization in the Translation of the Bible in Setswana (Matthew 8:28–34; 15:22; 10:8)." Paper read at the Post Conference Studiorum Novi Testamenti Societas, Hammanskraal Campus, University of Pretoria, August 9, 1999.

Hezser, Catherine. *Jewish Literacy in Roman Palestine.* Texts and Studies in Ancient Judaism 81. Tübingen: Mohr/Siebeck, 2001.

Hiebert, Paul G. "Critical Contextualization." *International Bulletin of Missionary Research* 11, no. 3 (1987) 104–12.

Hill, Harriet. *The Bible at Cultural Crossroads: From Translation to Communication.* Manchester, UK: St. Jerome Publishing, 2006.

Hodgson, Robert, and Paul Soukup, editors. *From One Medium to Another: Basic Issues for Communicating the Scriptures in New Media.* New York: American Bible Society, 1997.

Hollander, Harm W. "The Words of Jesus: From Oral Traditions to Written Record in Paul and Q." *Novum Testamentum* 42 (2000) 340–57.

Hope, E. R. "A Text-Linguistic Model for Media Scriptures." *The Bible Translator* 55 (2004) 441–48.

Horsley, Richard A. *Hearing the Whole Story: The Politics of Plot in Mark's Gospel.* Louisville: Westminster John Knox, 2001.

———. "Mark as Oral." In *Hearing the Whole Story: The Politics of Plot in Mark's Gospel,* Richard A. Horsley, 53–78. Louisville: Westminster John Knox, 2001.

———. "The Oral Communication Environment of Q." In *Whoever Hears You Hears Me: Prophets, Performance, and Tradition in Q,* Richard A. Horsley with Jonathan A. Draper, 123–49. Harrisburg: Trinity, 1999.

———, editor. *Oral Performance, Popular Tradition, and Hidden Transcript in Q.* Semeia Studies 60. Atlanta: Society of Biblical Literature, 2006.

Bibliography

Horsley, Richard A., and Jonathan A. Draper, *Whoever Hears You Hears Me: Prophets, Performance, and Tradition in Q*. Harrisburg, PA: Trinity, 1999.

Horsley, Richard A., Jonathan A. Draper, and John Miles Foley, editors. *Performing the Gospel: Orality, Memory and Mark*. Minneapolis: Fortress, 2006.

Hymes, Dell. "Breakthrough into Performance." In *Folklore: Performance and Communication*, edited by Ben-Amos and Goldstein 11–74. Approaches to Semiotics 40. The Hague: Mouton, 1975. Reprinted in Hymes, *"In Vain I Tried to Tell You": Essays in Native American Ethnopoetics*, 79–141. Studies in Native American Literature 1. Philadelphia: University of Pennsylvania Press, 1981.

———. *Foundations in Sociolinguistics: An Ethnographic Approach*. University of Pennsylvania Publications in Conduct and Communication. Philadelphia: University of Pennsylvania Press, 1974.

———. "Models of the Interaction of Language and Social Life." In *Directions in Sociolinguistics*, edited by J. J. Gumperz and Dell Hymes, 35–71. New York: Holt, Rinehart & Winston, 1972.

———. *Now I Know Only So Far: Essays in Ethnopoetics*. Lincoln: University of Nebraska Press, 2003.

Irvin, Dale T., and Scott W. Sunquist. *History of the World Christian Movement: Volume I: Earliest Christianity to 1453*. Maryknoll, NY: Orbis, 2001.

Iser, Wolfgang. *The Act of Reading: A Theory of Aesthetic Response*. Baltimore: John Hopkins University Press, 1978.

Jahandarie, Khosrow. *Spoken and Written Discourse: A Multi-disciplinary Perspective*. Stamford, CT: Ablex, 1999.

Jakobson, Roman. "Closing Statement: Linguistics and Poetics." In *Style in Language*, edited by T. A. Sebeok, 350–77. New York: Wiley, 1960.

Jenkins, Philip. *The Next Christendom: The Coming of Global Christianity*. New York: Oxford University Press, 2002.

Jinbachian, Manuel M. "The History, Base Text(s), and Translation Techniques of the Armenian Bible." *The Bible Translator* 55 (July 2004) 364–75.

Joubert, Annekie. "Defining and Working in an Oral Culture: Between Oral and Written Transmission—The Problems of Textualising Performance Events." Paper presented at SNTS, 2004.

———. *The Power of Performance*. Trends in Linguistics: Studies and Monographs 160. Berlin: Mouton de Gruyter, 2004.

Jousse, Marcel. "Études de Psychologie Linguistique: Le Style Oral, Rhythmique et Mnémotechnique chez les Verbo-Moteurs." *Archives de Philosophie* II/4. Translated by Edgard Sienaert and Richard Whitaker. New York: Garland, 1990.

Katongole, Emmanuel. *African Theology Today*. African Theology Today Series 1. Scranton, PA: University of Scranton Press, 2002.

Kelber, Werner. "The Case of the Gospels: Memory's Desire and the Limits of Historical Criticism." *Oral Tradition* 17.1 (2002) 55–86.

———. "Introduction." In *The Oral and the Written Gospel* Philadelphia: Fortress, 1997.

———. *The Oral and the Written Gospel: The Hermeneutics of Speaking and Writing in the Synoptic Tradition, Mark, Paul, and Q*. Philadelphia: Fortress, 1983.

———. "Orality, Scribality, and Oral–Scribal Interfaces: Jesus—Tradition—Gospels, Review and Present State of Research." Paper delivered at the SNTS conference in Halle, Germany, August 2005.

Bibliography

———. "The Works of Memory: Christian Origins as MnemoHistory—A Response." In *Memory, Tradition, and Text: Uses of the Past in Early Christianity*, edited by Alan Kirk and Tom Thatcher, 221–48. Semeia Studies 52. Atlanta: Society of Biblical Literature, 2005.

Kennedy, George. *New Testament Interpretation through Rhetorical Criticism*. Chapel Hill: University of North Carolina Press, 1984.

Kirk, Alan. "Social and Cultural Memory." In *Memory, Tradition, and Text: Uses of the Past in Early Christianity*, edited by Alan Kirk, and Tom Thatcher, 1–24. Semeia Studies 52. Atlanta: Society of Biblical Literature, 2005.

———, and Tom Thatcher, editors. *Memory, Tradition, and Text: Uses of the Past in Early Christianity*. Semeia Studies 52. Atlanta: Society of Biblical Literature, 2005.

Kobia, Samuel. *The Courage to Hope: The Roots for a New Vision and the Calling of the Church in Africa*. Geneva: WCC Publications, 2003.

Kraft, Charles. *Christianity in Culture: A Study in Dynamic Biblical Theologizing in Cross-Cultural Perspective*. Maryknoll, NY: Orbis, 1979.

Lachenaud, Michel. "Histoire Des Vuté d'après leurs traditions orales." Unpublished manuscript, author's collection, n.d.

Lakoff, George. *Women, Fire, and Dangerous Things: What Categories Reveal about the Mind*. Chicago: University of Chicago Press, 1987.

Leach, E. R. "Ritualization in Man in Relation to Conceptual and Social Development." *Philosophical Transactions of the Royal Society of London* 251 (1966) 403–8.

Lévi-Strauss, Claude. *La Pensée Sauvage*. Paris: Plon, 1962.

———. *Tristes Tropiques*. Translated by Hohn and Doreen Weightman. Harmondsworth, UK: Penguin, 1976.

Levy, Shimon. *The Bible as Theatre*. Brighton: Sussex Academic, 2002.

Lévy-Bruhl, Lucien. *Les Fonctions Mentales dans les Sociétés Inférieures*. Paris: Alcan, 1910.

Loba-Mkole, Jean-Claude. "Bible Translation and Inculturation Hermeneutics." In *Biblical Texts and African Audiences*, edited by Ernst R. Wendland and Jean-Claude Loba-Mkole, 37–58. Nairobi: Acton, 2004.

———. "The New Testament and Intercultural Exegesis in Africa." *Journal for the Study of the New Testament* 30 (2007) 7–28.

———. *Triple Heritage: Gospels in Intercultural Mediations*. Pretoria: Sapientia, 2005.

Loba-Mkole, Jean-Claude, and Ernst R. Wendland, editors. *Interacting with Scriptures in Africa* Nairobi: Acton, 2005.

Lode, Kare. *Appelés à la Liberté—Histoire de l'Eglise Evangélique Luthérienne du Cameroun*. Amstelveen, Pays-Bas: IMPROCEP éditions, 1990.

Lord, Albert Bates. *Epic Singers and Oral Tradition*. Myth and Poetics. Ithaca: Cornell University Press, 1991.

———. "The Gospels as Oral Traditional Literature." In *The Relationships among the Gospels: An Interdisciplinary Dialogue*, edited by W. O. Walker Jr., 33–92. Trinity University Monograph Series in Religion 5. San Antonio: Trinity University Press, 1978.

———. *The Singer of Tales*. 2nd ed. Edited by Stephen Mitchell and Gregory Nagy. Cambridge: Harvard University Press, 2000 [1960].

Loubser, J. A. (Bobby). "How Do You Report Something That Was Said with a Smile?—Can We Overcome the Loss of Meaning when Oral-Manuscript Texts of the Bible Are Represented in Modern Printed Media?" *Scriptura* 87 (2004) 296–314.

Bibliography

———. "Invoking the Ancestors, Some Socio-rhetorical Aspects of the Genealogies in the Gospels According to Matthew and Luke." *Neotestamentica* 39 (2005) 127–40.

———. "Moving Beyond Colonialist Discourse: Understanding Oral Theory and Cultural Difference in the Context of Media Analysis." In *Orality, Literacy and Colonialism in Antiquity*, edited by Jonathan A. Draper, 65–82. Semeia Studies 47. Atlanta: Society of Biblical Literature, 2004.

———. "New Possibilities for Understanding Ancient Gospel Performances." Paper presented at SBL's annual meeting in the section, Bible in Ancient and Modern Media, 2005.

———. "The Oral Christ of Shembe: Believing in Jesus in Oral and Literate Societies." *Scriptura* (1993) 70–80.

———. "Orality and Literacy in the Pauline Corpus, Some New Hermeneutical Implications." *Neotestamentica* 29 (1995) 61–74.

———. *Orality and Manuscript Culture in the Bible*. Stellenbosch: Sun, 2007.

———. "Orality and Pauline 'Christology': Some Hermeneutical Implications." *Scriptura* 47 (1993) 25–51.

———. "Possession and Sacrifice in the NT and African Traditional Religion: The Oral Forms and Conventions Behind the Literary Genres." *Neotestamentica* 37 (2003) 221–45.

———. "Reconciling Rhetorical Criticism with its Oral Roots." *Neotestamentica* 35 (2001) 95–110.

———. "What is Biblical Media Criticism? A Media-critical Reading of Luke 9:51–56." *Scriptura* 80 (2002) 206–19.

Louw, J. P., editor. *Sociolinguistics and Communication*. United Bible Society Monograph Series 1. Stuttgart: United Bible Societies, 1986.

Magesa, Laurenti. *Anatomy of Inculturation: Transforming the Church in Africa*. Maryknoll, NY: Orbis, 2004.

Malinowski, Bronislaw. "The Problem of Meaning in Primitive Languages." In *The Meaning of Meaning: A Study of the Influence of Language upon Thought and of the Science of Symbolism*. New York: Harcourt, Brace, 1927.

———. *A Scientific Theory of Culture and Other Essays*. Chapel Hill: University of North Carolina Press, 1944.

Maluleke, Tinyiko Sam. "African Christianity, the Bible, and Theology." In *Bible Translation & African Languages*, edited by Gosnell L. O. R. Yorke and Peter M. Renju, 161–76. Nairobi: Acton, 2004.

———. "The Bible and African Theologies." In *Interpreting the New Testament in Africa*, edited by Mary N. Getui, Tinyiko Maluleke, and Justin Ukpong, 165–76. Nairobi: Acton, 2001.

———. "Black and African Theologies in the New World Order: A Time to Drink from Our Own Wells." *Journal of Theology of Southern Africa* 96 (1996) 3–19.

———. "Half a Century of African Christian Theologies: Elements of the Emerging Agenda for the Twenty-first Century." *Journal of Theology of Southern Africa* 99 (1997) 4–23.

———. "'A Morula Tree between Two Fields': The Commentary of Selected Tsonga Writers on Missionary Christianity." D.Th. diss., University of South Africa, 1995.

———. "The Next Phase in the Vernacular Bible Discourse: Echoes from Hammanskraal." *Missionalia* 33 (2005) 355–74.

Bibliography

———. Review of *The Zionist Christian Church in South Africa: A Case-Study in Oral Theology*, by Piet Naudé. *Missionalia* 24 (1996) 101–2.

Martey, Emmanuel. *African Theology: Inculturation and Liberation*. Maryknoll, NY: Orbis, 1993.

Marxsen, Willi. *Mark the Evangelist: Studies on the Redaction History of the Gospel*. Translated by James Boyce et al. Nashville: Abingdon, 1969.

Maxey, James A. "Ideology and Translation." In *Dictionary of Bible Translation*, edited by Philip Noss. Rome: Edizioni di Storia e Letterature, forthcoming.

———. "New Testament and African Orality: Implications for Exegesis and Orality." Paper presented at the New Testament Discipline Group of the Association of Chicago Theological Schools, 2005.

———. "Oral Evocations of the *Kerygma*: An Orality-Performance Study of 1 Corinthians 15:1–11." Unpublished manuscript, 2005.

———. "Performance Criticism and its Impact on Translation and Theology." Paper presented at the Translation Track of the Forum of Bible Agencies—International, October, 2006.

———. "Performance Criticism and Its Implications for Bible Translation. Paper presented in Sibiu, Romania, at SNTS, July 2007, and SBL 2007 in the section of the Bible in Ancient and Modern Media.

———. "Performance Criticism and Its Implications for Bible Translation, Part I: Oral Performance and New Testament Studies." *The Bible Translator* 60 (2009) 37–49.

———. "Performance Criticism and Its Implications for Bible Translation, Part II: Challenges and Experiences." *The Bible Translator* 60 (2009) 165–82.

———. "Relative Clauses in Vuté." MA thesis, University of Texas at Arlington, 1994.

———. "Translating Philemon: Oral, Rhetorical, Social, and Discourse Considerations." Unpublished manuscript, 2005.

Mbiti, John S. *African Religions and Philosophy*. New York: Praeger, 1969.

———. *Bible and Theology in African Christianity*. Nairobi: Oxford University Press, 1986.

———. "The Bible in African Culture." In *Paths of African Theology*, edited by Rosino Gibellini, 27–39. London: SCM, 1994.

———. "Do You Understand What You Are Reading? The Bible in African Homes, Schools, and Churches." *Missionalia* 33 (2005) 234–48.

McGrath, Alister E. *In the Beginning: The Story of the King James Bible and How It Changed a Nation, a Language, and a Culture*. New York: Doubleday, 2001.

McLuhan, Marshall. *The Gutenberg Galaxy: The Making of Typographic Man*. Toronto: University of Toronto Press, 1962.

———. *Understanding Media: The Extensions of Man*. New York: New American Library, 1964.

———, and Quentin Fiore. *The Medium Is the Massage*. New York: Random House, 1967.

Metzger, Bruce M. *The Bible in Translation: Ancient and English Versions*. Grand Rapids: Baker Academic, 2001.

"Mission and Evangelism in Unity Today." In *"You Are the Light of the World": Statements on Mission by the World Council of Churches 1980–2005*. Geneva: WCC Publications, 2005. WCC conference, 2005. Online: http://www.oikoumene.org/Preparatory-Paper-N-1-M.795+B6Jkw9MA__.o.html

Bibliography

Mojola, Aloo Osotsi, and Ernst Wendland. "Scripture Translation in the Era of Translation Studies." In *Bible Translation: Frames of Reference*, edited by Timothy Wilt, 1–25. Manchester, UK: St. Jerome Publishing, 2003.

Mosala, Itumeleng J. *Biblical Hermeneutics and Black Theology in South Africa*. Grand Rapids: Eerdmans, 1989.

———. "The Use of the Bible in Black Theology." In *Unquestionable Right to Be Free*, edited by Itumeleng J. Mosala and Buti Tlhagale, 175–99. Maryknoll, NY: Orbis, 1986.

Mugambi, J. N. K. *The African Heritage and Contemporary Christianity*. Nairobi: Longman Kenya, 1989.

———. *Christian Theology and Social Reconstruction*. Nairobi: Acton, 2003.

———. "Foundations For An African Approach to Biblical Hermeneutics." In *Interpreting the New Testament in Africa*, edited by Mary N. Getui, Tinyiko Maluleke, and Justin Ukpong, 9–29. Nairobi: Acton, 2001.

———. *From Liberation to Reconstruction: African Christian Theology after the Cold War*. Nariobi: East African Education Publishers, 1995.

———. "Oral and Textual Expression in Worship and Personal Testimony within an African Context." Paper presented at SNTS meeting, Aberdeen, Scotland, section "NT, Orality and Translation," 2006.

———. "Pioneer Bible Translations: Some Pros and Cons." Paper presented at SNTS meeting, Halle, Germany, section "NT, Orality and Translation," 2006.

———, and Laurenti Magesa, editors. *The Church in African Christianity: Innovative Essays in Ecclesiology*. Nairobi: Initiative Publishers, 1990.

Muken, André Kabasele, Jean-Claude Loba-Mkole, and Dieudonné P. Aroga Bessong, editors. *Cultural Readings of the Bible in Africa*. Yaoundé, Cameroon: Clé, 2007.

Mveng, E., and R. J. Z. Werblowsky, editors. *Black Africa and the Bible / L'Afrique Noire et la Bible*. The Jerusalem Congress on Black Africa and the Bible, April 24–30, 1972.

Naudé, Piet. "Theology with a New Voice? The Case for an Oral Theology in the South African Context." *Journal of Theology for Southern Africa* 94 (1996) 18–31.

———. *The Zionist Christian Church in South Africa: A Case-Study in Oral Theology*. New York: Melien, 1995.

Neef, Martin, Anneke Neijt, and Richard Sproat. *The Relation of Writing to Spoken Language*. Tübingen: Niemeyer, 2002.

Ngũgĩ Wa Thiong'o. *Decolonizing the Mind: The Politics of Language in African Literature*. Nairobi: Heinemann Kenya, 1986.

Nicolson, Adam. *God's Secretaries: The Making of the King James Bible*. New York: HarperCollins, 2003.

Nida, Eugene A., editor. *Book of a Thousand Tongues*. Rev. ed. New York: United Bible Societies, 1972.

———. *Toward a Science of Translating, with Special Reference to Principles and Procedures Involved in Bible Translating*. Leiden: Brill, 1964.

———, and Charles R. Taber. *The Theory and Practice of Translation*. Helps for Translators 8. Leiden: Brill, 1969.

Nord, Christiane. "Basic Concepts of *Skopostheorie*: Skopos, Aim, Purpose, Intention, Function and Translation Brief." In *Translating as a Purposeful Activity: Functionalist Approaches Explained*. Manchester, UK: St. Jerome Publishing, 1997.

———. *Translating as a Purposeful Activity: Functionalist Approaches Explained*. Manchester, UK: St. Jerome Publishing. 1997.

Norris, Frederick W. *Christianity: A Short Global History*. Oxford: Oneworld, 2002.

Bibliography

Noss, Phil. "Ideas, Phones and Gbaya Verbal Art." Presented at: International Symposium on Ideophones Cologne: Institute of African Studies, University of Cologne, 1999.

———. "The Ideophone In Bible Translation: Child Or Stepchild." *The Bible Translator* 36 (1985) 423–30.

———. "The Oral Story and Bible Translation." *The Bible Translator* 32 (1981) 301–18.

Oduyoye, Mercy Amba. *Daughters of Anowa: African Women and Patriarchy*. Maryknoll, NY: Orbis, 1995.

———. *Hearing and Knowing: Theological Reflections on Christianity in Africa*. Maryknoll, NY: Orbis, 1986.

———. *Introducing African Women's Theology*. Introductions in Feminist Theology 6. Sheffield: Sheffield Academic, 2001.

———, and Hendrik M. Vroom, editors. *One Gospel, Many Cultures: Case Studies and Reflections on Cross-Cultural Theology*. Currents of Encounter 21. New York: Rodopi, 2003.

Okpewho, Isidore. *African Oral Literature: Backgrounds, Character, and Continuity*. Bloomington: Indiana University Press, 1992.

Olick, Jeffrey K., and Daniel Levy. "Collective Memory and Cultural Constraint: Holocaust Myth and Rationality in German Politics." *American Sociological Review* 62 (1997) 921–36.

Olson, David. "From Utterance to Text." *Harvard Educational Review* 47 (1977) 257–81.

———. "Literacy and Objectivity: The Rise of Modern Science." In *Literacy and Orality*, edited by David R. Olson and Nancy Torrance, 149–64. Cambridge: Cambridge University Press, 1991.

———. *The World on Paper: The Conceptual and Cognitive Implications of Writing and Reading*. Cambridge: Cambridge University Press, 1994.

Olson, David, and Nancy Torrance. "Introduction." In *Literacy and Orality*, edited by David R. Olson and Nancy Torrance, 1–7. Cambridge: Cambridge University Press, 1991.

———, editors. *Literacy and Orality*. Cambridge: Cambridge University Press, 1991.

Olson, David, Nancy Torrance, and Angela Hidyard. *Literacy, Language, and Learning: The Nature and Consequences of Reading and Writing*. Cambridge: Cambridge University Press, 1985.

Ong, Walter J. *Orality and Literacy: The Technologizing of the Word*. London: Routledge, 1982.

———. *The Presence of the Word: Some Prolegomena for Cultural and Religious History*. New Haven: Yale University Press, 1967.

———. *Ramus: Method and the Decay of Dialogue*. Cambridge: Harvard University Press, 1958.

Orlinsky, Harry M., and Robert G. Bratcher. *A History of Bible Translation and the North American Contribution*. Biblical Scholarship in North America. Atlanta: Scholars, 1991.

Parratt, John, editor. *A Reader in African Christian Theology*. TEF Study Guide 23. London: SPCK, 1987.

———. *Reinventing Christianity: African Theology Today*. Grand Rapids: Eerdmans, 1995.

Parry, Milman. "Studies in the Epic Technique of Oral Verse-Making, I: Homer and Homeric Style." *Harvard Studies in Classical Philology* 41 (1930) 73–147.

Bibliography

———. "Studies in the Epic Technique of Oral Verse-Making, II: The Homeric Language as the Language of Oral Poetry." *Harvard Studies in Classical Philology* 43 (1932) 1–50.

———. "Whole Formulaic Verses in Greek and Southslavic Heroic Songs." *Transactions of the American Philological Association* 64 (1933) 179–97.

Payne, David. "Oral Bible Translation and Chronological Bible Storying." *Word & Deed* 2.3 (2003) 41–46.

Pemberton, Carrie. *Circle Thinking: African Women Theologians in Dialogue with the West*. Studies of Religion in Africa 25. Leiden: Brill, 2003.

Peterson, Derek. "The Rhetoric of the Word: Bible Translation and Mau Mau in Colonial Central Kenya." In *Missions, Nationalism and the End of Empire*, edited by Brian Stanley, 165–79. Grand Rapids: Eerdmans, 2003.

Phemister, Marilyn. *Audio Greek New Testament: Westcott & Hort Greek New Testament*. Grand Rapids: Christian Classics Ethereal Library, 2003.

Pobee, John S. "Bible Study in Africa: A Passover of Language." *Semeia* 73 (1996) 161–80.

———. *Exploring Afro-Christology*. Studies in the Intercultural History of Christianity 79. Frankfurt: Lang, 1992.

———. "Oral Theology and Christian Oral Tradition: Challenge to our Traditional Archival Concept." *Mission Studies* 6 (1989) 87–93.

———. *Toward an African Theology*. Nashville: Parthenon, 1979.

Quarshie, B.Y. "Doing Biblical Studies in the African Context—The Challenge of Mother-tongue Scriptures." *Journal of African Christian Thought* 5 (2002) 4–14.

Rhoads, David. *Biblical Performance Criticism: An Emerging Discipline in New Testament Studies*. Biblical Performance Criticism Series. Eugene: Cascade Books, forthcoming.

———. *The Challenge of Diversity: The Witness of Paul and the Gospels*. Minneapolis: Fortress, 1996.

———. "Performing the Gospel of Mark." In *Reading Mark, Engaging the Gospel*, 176–201. Minneapolis: Fortress, 2004.

———. "Performance Criticism: An Emerging Methodology in Second Testament Studies—Part I." *Biblical Theology Bulletin* 36 (2006) 1–16.

———. "Performance Criticism: An Emerging Methodology in Second Testament Studies—Part II." *Biblical Theology Bulletin* 36 (2006) 164–84.

Rhoads, David, Joanna Dewey, and Donald Michie. *Mark as Story: An Introduction to the Narrative of a Gospel*. 2nd ed. Minneapolis: Fortress, 1999.

Richards, E. Randolph. *Paul and First-Century Letter Writing: Secretaries, Composition and Collection*. Downers Grove, IL: InterVarsity, 2004.

Robbins, Vernon K. *Exploring the Texture of Texts: A Guide to Socio-rhetorical Interpretation*. Valley Forge, PA: Trinity, 1996.

———. "Interfaces of Orality and Literature in the Gospel of Mark." In *Performing the Gospel: Orality, Memory and Mark*, edited by Richard A. Horsley, Jonathan A. Draper, John Miles Foley, 125–46. Minneapolis: Fortress, 2006.

———. "Oral, Rhetorical, Literary Cultures: A Response." *Semeia* 65 (1995) 75–91.

———. "Progymnastic Rhetorical Composition and Pre-Gospel Traditions: A New Approach." In *The Synoptic Gospels*, edited by Camille Focant, 111–47. Leuven: Leuven University Press, 1993.

Russell, James C. *The Germanization of Early Medieval Christianity: A Sociohistorical Approach to Religious Transformation*. New York: Oxford University Press, 1994.

Bibliography

Said, Edward. *Orientalism*. New York: Pantheon, 1978.

Sanneh, Lamin. "The African Transformation of Christianity: Comparative Reflections on Ethnicity and Religious Mobilization in Africa." In *Religions/Globalzations: Theories and Cases*, edited by Dwight N. Hopkins et al., 105–34. Durham: Duke University Press, 2001.

———. "Christian Missions and the Western Guilt Complex." *Christian Century* (April 1987) 331–34.

———. "Domesticating the transcendent: the African transformation of Christianity: comparative reflections on ethnicity and religious mobilization in Africa." In *Bible Translation on the Threshold of the Twenty-first Century: Authority, Reception, Culture and Religion*, edited by Athalya Brenner and Jan Willem van Henten, 70–85. Journal for the Study of the Old Testament Supplement Series 353. London: Sheffield Academic, 2002.

———. *Translating the Message: The Missionary Impact on Culture*. Maryknoll, NY: Orbis, 1989.

———. *Whose Religion Is Christianity? The Gospel beyond the West*. Grand Rapids: Eerdman, 2003.

Sanneh, Lamin O., and Joel A. Carpenter. *The Changing Face of Christianity: Africa, The West, and the World*. Oxford: Oxford University Press, 2005.

Sapir, Edward. "The Status of Linguistics as a Science." In *E. Sapir (1958) Culture, Language and Personality*, edited by D. G. Mandelbaum, 160–66. Berkeley: University of California Press, 1929.

Schaaf, Ype. *L'Histoire et le Rôle de la Bible en Afrique*. Lavigny, Switzerland: Editions des Groupes Missionnaires, 1994.

———. *On Their Way Rejoicing: The History and Role of the Bible in Africa*. Carlisle, UK: Paternoster, 1994.

Scherer, James. *Gospel, Church and Kingdom: Comparative Studies in World Mission Today*. Minneapolis: Augsburg, 1987.

———, and Stephen B. Bevans. *New Directions in Mission and Evangelization*, vol. 3: *Faith and Culture*. Maryknoll, NY: Orbis, 1999.

Schineller, Peter. *A Handbook on Inculturation*. New York: Paulist, 1989.

———. "Inculturation and Syncretism: What Is the Real Issue?" *International Bulletin of Missionary Research* 16.2 (1992) 50–53.

Schreiter, Robert. *Constructing Local Theologies*. Maryknoll, NY: Orbis, 1985.

———. "Defining Syncretism: An Interim Report." *International Bulletin of Missionary Research* 17.2 (1993) 50–53.

———, editor. *Faces of Jesus in Africa*. Faith and Culture Series. Maryknoll, NY: Orbis, 1991.

———. *The New Catholicity: Theology between the Global and the Local*. Faith and Culture Series. Maryknoll, NY: Orbis, 1997.

———. "Tradition and Christian Identity." In *Constructing Local Theologies*, 95–121. Maryknoll, NY: Orbis, 1985.

Scobie, Alex. "Storytellers, Storytelling, and the Novel in Greco-Roman Antiquity." *Remisches Museum für Philologie* 122 (1979) 229–59.

Scott, Bernard Brandon. "A New Voice in the Amphitheater: Full Fidelity in Translating." In *Fidelity and Translation: Communicating the Bible in the New Media*, edited by Paul A. Soukup, SJ and Robert Hodgson, 101–18. New York: American Bible Society, 1999.

Bibliography

———, and Margaret E. Dean. "A Sound Map of the Sermon on the Mount." In *SBL Seminar Papers*, edited by Eugene H. Lovering, 672–725. Atlanta: Scholars, 1993.

Scribner, Sylvia, and Michael Cole. *The Psychology of literacy*. Cambridge: Harvard University Press, 1981.

Shaw, R. Daniel, and Charles E. Van Engen. *Communicating God's Word in a Complex World: God's Truth or Hocus Pocus?* Lanham, MD: Rowman & Littlefield, 2003.

Shiell, William David. *Reading Acts: The Lector and the Early Christian Audience*. Biblical Interpretation Series 70. Boston: Brill Academic, 2004.

Shiner, Whitney. "Memory Technology and the Composition of Mark." In *Performing the Gospel: Orality, Memory and Mark*, edited by Richard A. Horsley, Jonathan A. Draper, John Miles Foley, 147–65. Minneapolis: Fortress, 2006.

———. *Proclaiming the Gospel: First-Century Performance in Mark*. Harrisburg, PA: Trinity, 2003.

Shorter, Aylward. *Toward a Theology of Inculturation*. Maryknoll, NY: Orbis, 1988.

Sibinga, Joost Smit. "1 Cor 15:8/9 and Other Divisions in 1 Cor 15:1–11." *Novum Testamentum* 39 (1997) 54–59.

Sim, Ronald J. *Retelling Translation: A Course Book*. Unpublished manuscript, 2005.

Smalley, William A. *Translation as Mission: Bible Translation in the Modern Missionary Movement*. The Modern Mission Era, 1792–1992. Macon, GA: Mercer University Press, 1991.

Sölle, Dorothee. *Thinking about God: An Introduction to Theology*. Philadelphia: Trinity, 1990.

Soukup, Paul A., SJ, and Robert Hodgson, editors. *Fidelity and Translation: Communicating the Bible in the New Media*. New York: American Bible Society, 1999.

Sterk, Jan P. "Translation and Media: How Different Can We Be and Still Be Equivalent (or at Least Similar)?" In *Similarity and Difference in Translation: Proceedings of the International Conference on Similarity and Translation*, edited by Stefano Arduini and Robert Hodgson Jr., 127–51. Rimini, Italy: Guaraldi, 2004.

Stewart, Charles, and Rosalind Shaw, editors. *Syncretism/Anti-syncretism: The Politics of Religious Synthesis*. European Association of Social Anthropologists. London: Routledge, 1994.

Stine, Philip C., editor. *Bible Translation and the Spread of the Church: The Last 200 Years*. Studies in Christian Mission 2. Leiden: Brill, 1990.

———. *Let the Words Be Written: The Lasting Influence of Eugene A. Nida*. Biblical Scholarship in North America 21. Atlanta: Society of Biblical Literature, 2004.

Stock, Brian. *The Implications of Literacy: Written Language and Models of Interpretation in the Eleventh and Twelfth Centuries*. Princeton: Princeton University Press, 1983.

———. *Listening for the Text: On the Uses of the Past*. Middle Ages Series. Philadelphia: University of Pennsylvania Press, 1996.

Stocking, George W., Jr., editor. *The Shaping of American Anthropology 1883–1911: A Franz Boas Reader*. New York: Basic Books, 1974.

Street, Brian V., editor. *Cross-cultural Approaches to Literacy*. Cambridge Studies in Oral and Literate Culture 23. Cambridge: Cambridge University Press, 1993.

———. "Introduction: New Literacy Studies." In *Cross-cultural Approaches to Literacy*, edited by Brian V. Street, 1–21. Cambridge Studies in Oral and Literate Culture 23. Cambridge: Cambridge University Press, 1993.

———. *Literacy in Theory and Practice*. Cambridge Studies in Oral and Literate Culture 9. Cambridge: Cambridge University Press, 1983.

Bibliography

Sugirtharajah, R. S. *The Bible and Empire: Postcolonial Explorations.* Cambridge: Cambridge University Press, 2005.

———. *Postcolonial Criticism and Biblical Interpretation.* Oxford: Oxford University Press, 2002.

———, editor. *Vernacular Hermeneutics.* Bible and Postcolonialism 2. Sheffield: Sheffield Academic, 1999.

Sundersingh, Julian. "Toward a Media Based Translation: Communicating Biblical Scriptures to Non-Literates in Rural Tamilnadu, India." PhD diss., Fuller Theological Seminary, School of World Mission, 1999.

Tannen, Deborah, editor. *Spoken and Written Language: Exploring Orality and Literacy.* Advances in Discourse Processes 9. Norwood, NJ: Ablex, 1982.

Tedlock, Dennis. *Finding the Center: The Art of the Zuni Storyteller.* 2nd ed. Lincoln: University of Nebraska Press, 1999.

———. *The Spoken Word and the Work of Interpretation.* University of Pennsylvania Publications in Conduct and Communication. Philadelphia: University of Pennsylvania Press, 1983.

———. "Translator's Introduction." *Alcheringa: Ethnopoetics* 1.1 (1975).

Thatcher, Tom, editor. *Jesus, the Voice, and the Text: Beyond The Oral and the Written Gospel.* Waco, TX: Baylor University Press, 2008.

Thomas, Kenneth J., and Margaret Orr Thomas. *Structure and Orality in 1 Peter: A Guide for Translators.* United Bible Societies Monograph Series 10. New York: United Bible Societies, 2006.

Thomas, Linda E. "The Outsider's Role in Socially Engaged Scholarship on African Religion." In *Living Stones in the Household of God: The Legacy and Future of Black Theology,* edited by Linda E. Thomas, 107–15. Minneapolis: Fortress, 2004.

Thomas, Rosalind. *Literacy and Orality in Ancient Greece.* Key Themes in Ancient History. Cambridge University Press, 1992.

Thwing, Rhonda R. "The Vuté Noun Phrase and the Relationship between Vuté and Bantu." MA thesis, University of Texas at Arlington.

Turner, Victor. *The Forest of Symbols: Aspects of Ndembu Ritual.* Ithaca: Cornell University Press, 1967.

Ukpong, Justin S. "Bible Reading with a Community of Ordinary Readers." In *Interpreting the New Testament in Africa,* edited by Mary N. Getui, Tinyiko Maluleke, and Justin Ukpong, 188–212. Nairobi: Acton, 2001.

———. "Developments in biblical interpretation in Africa: Historical and hermeneutical directions." *Journal of Theology for Southern Africa* 108 (2000) 3–18.

———. "Inculturation Hermeneutics: An African Approach to Biblical Interpretation." In *Bible in a World Context,* edited by Walter Dietrich and Ulrich Luz, 17–32. Grand Rapids: Eerdmans, 2002.

———. "New Testament Hermeneutics in Africa: Challenges and Possibilities." *Neotestamentica* 35 (2001) 147–67.

———. "The Parable of the Shrewd Manager (Lk 16:1–13) An Essay in the Inculturation Biblical Hermeneutic." *Semeia* 73 (1996) 189–210.

———. "Popular Readings of the Bible in Africa and Implications for Academic Readings: Report on the Field Research Carried out on Oral Interpretation of the Bible in Port Harcourt Metropolis, Nigeria under the Auspices of the Bible in Africa Project, 1991–94." In *The Bible in Africa: Transactions, Trajectories, and Trends,* edited by Gerald O. West and Musa W. Dube, 582–94. Leiden: Brill, 2000.

Bibliography

———. *Reading the Bible in the Global Village: Cape Town.* Global Perspectives on Biblical Scholarship 3. Atlanta: Society of Biblical Literature, 2002.

Upton, Bridget Gilfillan. *Hearing Mark's Endings: Listening to Ancient Popular Texts through Speech Act Theory.* Biblical Interpretation Series 79. Leiden: Brill, 2006.

van Niekerk, Attie, and C. J. Pauw. "Understanding and/or Participation? The Goal of Making the Bible Available in Oral Context." *Scriptura* 74 (2000) 249–57.

Vansina, Jan. *Oral Tradition as History.* Madison: University of Wisconsin Press, 1985.

Villumstad, Stein. *Social Reconstruction in Africa: Perspectives from Within and Without.* Nairobi: Acton, 2005.

Walls, Andrew F. *The Missionary Movement in Christian History: Studies in Transmission of Faith.* Maryknoll, NY: Orbis, 1996.

———. "Towards Understanding Africa's Place in Christian History." In *Religion in a Pluralistic Society: Essays Presented to Professor C. G. Baëta in Celebration of His Retirement from the Service of the University of Ghana, September 1971 by Friends and Colleagues Scattered over the Globe,* edited by J. S. Pobee, 180–89. Studies in Religion in Africa 2. Leiden: Brill, 1976.

———. "The Translation Principle in Christian History." In *The Missionary Movement in Christian History: Studies in the Transmission of Faith,* 26–42. Maryknoll, NY: Orbis, 1996.

Wendland, Ernst R. "The Drama of James: The Oral Performance of a NT Epistle and its Implications for Bible Translation, with Special Reference to James 2:14–26." Paper presented in Sibiu, Romania, at SNTS, July 2007.

———. "Duplicating the Dynamics of Oral Discourse in Print." *Notes on Translation* 7.4 (1993) 26–44.

———. *Language, Society and Bible Translation.* Cape Town: Bible Society of South Africa, 1985.

———. "A Literary Approach to Biblical Text Analysis and Translation." In *Bible Translation: Frames of Reference,* edited by Timothy Wilt, 179–230. Manchester, UK: St. Jerome Publishing, 2003.

———. "Oral-aural Dynamics of the Word, with Special Reference to John 17." *Notes on Translation* 8 (1994) 19–43.

———. *LiFE-Style Translating.* Dallas: SIL International, 2006.

———. *Translating the Literature of Scripture: A Literary-Rhetorical Approach to Bible Translation.* Dallas: SIL International, 2004.

Wendland, Ernst R., and J. P. Louw. *Graphic Design and Bible Reading: Exploratory Studies in the Typographical Representation of the Text of Scripture in Translation.* Capetown: Bible Society of South Africa, 1993.

Wendland, Ernst R., and Jean-Claude Loba-Mkole, editors. *Biblical Texts and African Audiences.* Nairobi: Acton, 2004.

West, Gerald O. "African Biblical Hermeneutics and Bible Translation." In *Interacting with Scriptures in Africa,* edited by Jean-Claude Loba-Mkole and Ernst R. Wendland, 3–29. Nairobi: Acton, 2005.

———. "Contextual Bible Study in South Africa: A Resource for Reclaiming and Regaining Land, Dignity and Identity." In *The Bible in Africa: Transactions, Trajectories and Trends,* edited by Gerald O. West and Musa W. Dube, 596–610. Leiden: Brill, 2000.

———. "Indigenous Exegesis: Exploring the Interface Between Missionary Methods and the Rhetorical Rhythms of Africa; Locating Local Reading Resources in the

Bibliography

Academy." In *Redirected Travel: Alternative Journeys and Places in Biblical Studies*, edited by R. Boer and E. Conrad. Journal for the Study of the Old Testament Supplement Series 382. Sheffield: Sheffield Academic, 2003.

———. "Mapping African Biblical Interpretation: A Tentative Sketch." In *The Bible in Africa: Transactions, Trajectories and Trends*, edited by Gerald O. West and Musa W. Dube, 29–53 Leiden: Brill, 2000.

———. "On the Eve of an African Biblical Studies: Trajectories and Trends." *Journal of Theology for Southern Africa* (1999) 99–115.

———. "Reading the Bible Differently: Giving Shape to the Discourse of the Dominated." *Semeia* 73 (1996) 21–42.

———. "Unpacking the Packages that is the Bible in Africa Biblical scholarship." In *Reading the Bible in the Global Village: Cape Town*, edited by Justin S. Ukpong et al., 65–94. Leiden: Brill, 2002.

West, Gerald O., and Musa W. Dube, editors. "Reading with African Overtures." *Semeia* 73 (1996).

West, Gerald O., and Musa W. Dube, editors. *The Bible in Africa: Transactions, Trajectories and Trends*. Leiden: Brill, 2000.

Whorf, B. L. "Science and Linguistics." In *B. L. Whorf (1956) Language, Thought and Reality*, edited by J. B. Carroll. Cambridge, MA: MIT Press, 1940.

Wilson, Victor M. "Oral Typesetting: Seeing by Ear in the Ancient World." In *Divine Symmetries: The Art of Biblical Rhetoric*, 35–57. Lanham, MD: University of Press of America, 1997.

Wimbush, Vincent L. "The Bible and African Americans: An Outline of an Interpretative History." In *Stony the Road We Trod: African American Biblical Interpretation*, edited by Cain Hope Felder, 81–97. Minneapolis: Fortress, 1991.

Winger, Thomas M. "Orality as the Key to Understanding Apostolic Proclamation in the Epistles." PhD diss., St. Louis: Concordia Seminary, 1997.

Wire, Antoinette Clark. *Holy Lives, Holy Deaths: A Close Hearing of Early Jewish Storytellers*. Studies in Biblical Literature 1. Atlanta: Society of Biblical Literature, 2002.

Yaghjian, Lucretia B. "Ancient Reading." In *The Social Sciences and New Testament Interpretation*, edited by Richard L. Rohrbaugh, 206–30. Peabody, MA: Hendrickson, 1996.

Yates, Frances. *The Art of Memory*. Chicago: University of Chicago Press, 1966.

Yorke, Gosnell. "Bible Translation in Anglophone Africa and Her Diaspora: A Postcolonialist Agenda." *The Bible Translator* 22 (2004) 153–66.

———. "Grace and Peace in the Pauline Corpus and the Portuguese Bible: Implications for Translating 'Grace' in Lusophone Africa and a 'Peace' Proposal for UBS Handbooks." *The Bible Translator* 54 (2003) 332–46.

———. "Hearing the Politics of Peace in Ephesians: A Proposal from an African Postcolonial Perspective." *Journal for the Study of the New Testament* 30 (2007) 113–27.

Yorke, Gosnell L. O. R., and Peter M. Renju, editors. *Bible Translation and African Languages*. Nairobi: Acton, 2004.

Young, Robert J. C. "Culture and the History of Difference." In *Colonial Desire: Hybridity in Theory, Culture and Race*. New York: Routledge, 1995.

INDEX

Aesthetic, 16, 85–86, 91, 95, 100, 111–12, 120, 125, 130, 157, 160, 168
Agent, agency, 5, 20, 33, 37, 57–58, 60, 63–64, 68, 72–73, 75, 142, 167, 182, 195–96
Agenda, 1, 16, 20, 47, 58, 60–61, 73, 88, 136, 194
Alliteration, 135, 145, 147
Anachronistic, 16, 109–10, 116, 126, 134
Anthropological, anthropologist, anthropology, 1, 5, 14–15, 21, 25, 27, 29, 33, 35, 37, 40, 45, 47, 72, 74, 76, 79, 82, 84, 86–87, 92, 95, 104, 118, 133, 193
Anthropological pauperization, 5, 53, 194
Antiquity, 71, 97, 108–13, 116, 118, 131, 146, 151
Artistry, 86, 153, 172
Audience, 9–11, 13, 16–18, 29, 42, 70, 79, 83, 85, 89, 91–92, 97–102, 105, 112, 121–22, 125, 129–30, 134–50, 152–53, 156–61, 163–66, 168–69, 171–92, 195
Auditory, 8, 95, 117, 120, 122–23, 130–31, 172–73, 195
Aural, 9, 13, 83, 94, 96, 108, 112–13, 120, 124, 128, 131, 135, 151, 153, 165
Authority, authoritative, 17, 99, 106, 111, 114, 116, 118, 126–28, 131, 140, 142, 151, 154, 162–63, 165–66, 177, 190, 194

Bible Society, 6, 8, 30, 67, 151–52, 156, 165
Biblical languages, 35, 55, 146, 160

Biblical Performance Criticism (BPC), 17, 131–35, 137–40, 142–44, 146, 149–50, 157, 159, 165–66, 185
Biblical studies, 2, 14, 16, 17, 34, 50–51, 63–64, 69–72, 78, 96, 102, 105–6, 114, 116, 125, 131, 133, 144, 151, 166, 169, 193–94

Cameroon, 5–9, 148, 166–67, 169–70, 180, 189, 195
Catholic, 6–7, 11–13, 20–21, 23, 25–26, 31, 46, 170, 185, 189
Church growth, 2, 19, 30
Cognitive, 15, 45, 72, 82, 101, 157
Colonial, (neo)colonialism, 3, 15, 20, 24, 35–36, 47, 53, 55, 58–59, 61, 63, 66, 69, 70, 72–73, 142, 180
Communal, 1, 112, 117, 125, 130, 134, 136, 140, 142–43, 151, 155, 164–66, 179, 194, 195
Communication, 1–3, 9, 15–17, 25–26, 32–34, 36, 44–45, 47, 65, 69, 70, 73–75, 78–91, 93–94, 99–102, 104, 106, 108–13, 116–18, 123–25, 127–28, 130–32, 134, 136–37, 143–44, 151–52, 154, 158, 160–61, 168–69, 171, 178, 183, 191, 194–95
Composition, 11–13, 16–17, 75, 85, 96, 104–8, 111–12, 118–20, 122–23, 125, 127, 130–31, 133–35, 138, 143–47, 149–50, 154–55, 157, 164, 166, 169, 171, 176, 185, 189, 191, 194, 196
Conservative, 20, 29, 40, 193
Contextual theology(ies), 4, 14–15, 20, 25, 49, 54, 62, 64, 69, 168, 194
Conversion, 3–4, 34, 75

Index

Dominant, 1–2, 22, 31, 46, 55, 57, 74, 100, 128, 157, 193
Drama, dramatic, dramatizing, 2, 11, 13, 42, 60, 90, 119, 141, 144, 156–57, 162, 176, 183
Dynamic, 4, 23, 26–27, 29, 33–35, 44–45, 47–48, 54, 56–57, 64, 84, 89–90, 92, 100–101, 124, 137, 139–40, 148, 151, 153–56, 158–59, 172

Ecumenical, 7, 13, 20, 23,
Education, 5, 95, 110, 116
Embodiment, 2, 43, 166, 185
Emotion, 16, 90, 112, 135, 138, 144, 148, 173–74, 190
Engagement, 54, 56–57, 148, 169, 176, 185, 193
Epistemological, 52, 71, 91, 100, 132
Ethnocentric, 79, 87, 143
Ethnography, 86, 92, 102
Ethnopoetics, 16–17, 78, 84–86, 88, 91, 93, 97, 102, 135, 139, 143–44, 160
Ethos, 3, 8, 36, 47, 74–75, 121–22, 126, 132, 134–36
Evangelical, 5, 20–23, 27, 29, 33, 40, 43
Evangelism, evangelization, evangelistic, 2, 4, 19, 23–24, 28, 30, 32, 34–35, 47, 74–75, 193
Exegete, exegetical, 6, 10, 18, 29, 55, 116, 120, 123, 147, 155, 180–82, 192
Expatriate, 6, 33, 57
Extralinguistic, 158, 162–64, 173, 185–88

Facial expressions, 17, 92, 135, 145, 147, 149
Fidelity, faithful, 17, 27–28, 33, 41, 69, 100, 120, 159, 161, 172, 193
First-century, 1, 9, 16, 47, 104–6, 108, 111, 114, 116–17, 120, 123–28, 131, 134–38, 141, 144–46, 159, 161, 171–72, 180–81, 183, 191, 194–95
Folktales, folklore, folklorist, 8, 10–11, 15–16, 60, 78, 86, 91, 93, 102, 127, 135, 144, 170, 181, 191, 194
Form, 9, 11, 15, 17, 23–26, 28, 34, 37, 43–44, 64, 69, 85, 86–91, 93–96, 101, 104–8, 120, 124, 129, 131, 133, 138, 140–42, 152–53, 156, 158–60, 166, 170, 172–73, 190, 194–95
Functional, 74, 93, 101, 152, 154–56, 158–59, 172

Genre, 61, 82, 84–86, 91–92, 95, 97, 104, 119–20, 122
Gesture, 10, 17, 33, 77, 89, 92, 98, 135, 144–45, 149, 162–63, 183–84, 186–87
Global, globalization, 19, 25–26, 45, 49, 56, 165
Gospel of Mark, 6–7, 17, 105–6, 118, 122, 141, 144, 148–49, 170
Great-divide, 15, 78, 80–82, 102, 104, 116

Hear, hearer, 1, 9, 11–17, 34, 41–42, 50, 55–56, 62–64, 69–70, 74–75, 100, 104, 112, 117, 120–22, 124–26, 129–30, 135, 145–47, 155–56, 177, 179, 181–82, 184, 187, 191, 194–95
Hegemonic, hegemony, 36, 58, 72, 79, 99
Hermeneutic, 15, 28, 39, 45, 53, 59–60, 62–65, 71, 75–76, 105–6, 119, 128, 131, 139, 154
Host, 5, 17, 29, 73–76, 84, 90–91, 93, 131, 154–56, 160, 168–69, 193, 195–96
Humor, 13, 168, 181, 182

Identity, 1–2, 5, 16–17, 19, 24–25, 28, 32, 37, 40, 44–45, 52, 54–55, 69, 77, 85, 88, 100, 129–30, 138, 147, 165, 168, 191, 193–94
Ideology, ideological, 3, 15, 17, 34, 52, 59, 68, 73, 78, 81, 93, 119, 121, 125, 127, 133, 139, 142
Ideophone, 154, 175–76, 182–83
Illiteracy, illiterate, 69, 112–13, 142
Immanent Art, 98, 101–2, 140, 165
Impact, 10, 13, 16, 18, 20, 30, 36–37, 44, 56, 65, 71, 75, 80, 84, 86, 90–91, 93, 95, 101–2, 107, 121–22, 125, 134, 136, 138, 141
Incarnation, 14, 28, 30–31, 44, 47, 74
Indeterminacy, 99, 102, 139–40, 158–59
Indigenous, 21, 35–37, 40, 43–45, 58, 61, 65, 68, 93, 142, 164

218

Index

Interface, interplay, 3, 15–16, 47, 69, 74, 95–96, 100, 104, 110, 114, 117, 123, 126, 132, 139, 142, 164–65, 194
Interpretive, 9, 60, 64, 70, 95, 97, 113, 164
Intersemiotic, 16, 91–92
Intonation, 83, 89, 92, 135, 141, 155–56, 163

Letter, epistle, 11, 16, 65, 89, 96, 111, 113, 116–17, 119–20, 122–24, 128, 130, 134, 138, 147, 155–57, 161, 166
Lexical, 67, 83, 135, 145, 156–57, 160, 172–73
Liberal, 38–40
Liberation, 39–45, 47–48, 52–56, 58, 61–64, 69, 71, 77, 81, 132, 142–43, 168, 191, 194
Linguistic, 4, 9, 16, 23, 25–26, 30–31, 34–35, 41–43, 45–46, 48, 53–54, 56, 66, 73–74, 82–83, 86–87, 92–94, 101, 112, 123, 133, 138, 142, 146–47, 153, 161, 193–94
Literacy, 1, 3, 6, 8–11, 14–16, 36, 47, 69–72, 74–75, 77–82, 84, 86, 95, 102, 104, 108–11, 113–16, 119, 125–27, 129, 131–32, 134, 142, 171, 191, 194–95
Literary, 1, 3, 11, 15, 60–61, 64–65, 75–76, 79, 82–83, 85–86, 89, 98, 100, 102, 105, 106–7, 109–10, 115, 119–21, 123, 125–26, 128, 130, 132–34, 137, 142–43, 152, 154–55, 191, 195–96
Local, 2, 4, 6, 10, 15, 24–26, 30–31, 33, 37, 42, 44–45, 47, 49, 51, 57, 63–66, 69, 73, 75–76, 142–43, 165, 168–69, 178, 189, 194–95
Lutheran, 5–7, 12–13, 170, 179

Manuscript, 7, 78, 108, 111, 114–15, 118, 128, 152, 195
Meaning, 9, 17, 23, 29, 35–36, 39–40, 56, 88, 94, 97–99, 101–2, 111, 120, 122, 124, 127, 129, 130, 137, 139–41, 145, 151–54, 157–59, 165–66, 183, 194

Media, multimedia, 15–16, 78, 94, 104–5, 110, 113, 115–17, 129, 131, 134, 150–52, 164
Mediterranean, 1, 46, 71, 108, 127, 134, 141, 161, 171, 194
Memory, social memory, 17, 79, 99–100, 112, 129, 147, 149, 156, 165
Mentality, 24, 78–79, 151
Methodology, 9–10, 14–15, 17, 92–93, 101, 121, 123, 133, 149, 185
Metonymic, 98, 100, 102, 122, 127, 129, 130, 147
Missiology, 3–4, 13–15, 20, 29–30, 32–33, 46–47, 49, 68, 76, 193
Missionary, 4, 21–23, 27, 30, 34, 35–37, 57–59, 61–63, 65–66, 72–74
Mnemonic, 100, 124, 129, 149, 157
Mutual, 4, 18, 19, 32, 44, 48, 56–57, 63, 74, 169, 193

Narrative(s), 39, 42, 60, 86–90, 98, 100, 118–20, 126, 129–30, 133–35, 138, 141, 143, 147, 151, 165, 181
Neutral, 2–3, 10, 15, 27, 32, 52, 60, 70, 73–74, 116, 128, 147, 182
Northern hemisphere, 2, 14, 49, 193

Objective, 10, 33–34, 51, 99, 146, 167, 171
Onomatopoeic, 90, 159, 160, 175
Oppressive, 2–3, 53, 57–58, 62–63, 69, 137
Oral bias, 114, 116, 126
Oral biblical criticism, 123–24, 127, 135
Oral performances, 10–11, 13, 16, 18, 76, 78, 89–90, 107, 131, 143–44, 166, 171, 174, 185
Oral poetry, 96–99, 102, 144
Oral society, 47, 108, 124
Oral tradition, 16, 60, 70, 95–99, 105–7, 122, 129, 130, 140, 164, 166
Oral-derived, 99, 127, 139, 140, 172, 195
Orality, 15, 50, 54, 63–64, 70, 75, 139, 142–43
Original, 6, 9, 12, 23, 43, 55, 90–93, 106, 118, 122, 133, 143, 151–53, 155–56, 161, 178, 189, 195

Index

Paradigm, 2–5, 14, 15, 19, 35, 37–38, 40, 44–45, 47, 49, 54–55, 57, 59–60, 62, 69, 72, 75–77, 85, 105, 132, 194

Paralinguistic, 85, 89–90, 92, 135, 137, 144, 158, 162–64, 173, 183, 186–88

Pluralism, 49, 54

Poetic(s), 42, 85, 87–88, 154, 157

Political, 6, 15, 22, 34, 41, 53–54, 56, 81, 116, 125–26

Poor, poverty, 22, 40, 41, 52, 64, 178

Postcolonial(ism), 3–4, 20, 33–35, 45, 47, 50, 59, 61, 67–70, 72, 74–75, 81, 142, 194

Power, 3, 5, 9, 11, 15, 35–36, 41, 63, 65, 71, 73, 81–82, 85, 97, 98, 111, 116, 124–27, 132, 141, 142, 168, 174, 177, 182

Print, print-bias, 7, 11, 13, 16, 43, 69, 78, 86, 88, 91–94, 108–10, 112, 114–16, 128, 137, 150–52, 155, 157, 159–60, 194–95

Proclaim, 40, 69, 163, 174, 191

Proximity, proxemics, 17, 94, 135, 147, 185, 189

Psychodynamics, 78, 106

Punctuation, 83, 111, 155, 160

Reader, 9, 15, 17–19, 28, 41, 50, 54, 56, 62–65, 70, 75–76, 92, 98, 108, 112–13, 117, 133, 136, 138–43, 155–58

Receptionalism, 98, 101, 139–40

Reconfiguration, 17, 115, 132, 136, 138–39, 141, 149–50, 166, 179

Registers, 83, 174

Relevance, 28, 52, 56, 101–2, 151–52, 154, 158, 165, 178

Rhetoric, rhetorical, 16, 34, 90–91, 93, 102, 105, 112, 114–15, 117, 120–23, 125, 130, 133–34, 138, 140–41, 143–44, 147, 153–56, 161

Rhythm, 43, 83, 121–22, 129–30, 135, 145, 147, 153, 155–56, 160, 164, 183, 186, 189–90

Scribe, 10, 111–13, 125, 177, 184–88

Script, 17, 89–90, 93, 111, 115, 131, 144, 158, 160–62, 164, 173, 175, 182, 185–86, 195

Scriptures, 4, 6, 8, 10–11, 13, 22, 25–33, 36–41, 43–44, 50, 52, 55–57, 61, 73, 118, 123, 126–28, 152–55, 165–66, 169, 171, 176, 189, 191, 193, 195

Scroll, 110–11

Semiotic, 25, 151–52

Silence, 21, 89–90, 112, 145, 149, 183, 187–90

Skopostheorie, skopos, 168–69

Social location, 3, 5, 51, 68, 73, 75, 93, 125, 136, 143, 164, 182, 192

Sociolinguistics, 15–16, 78, 82, 84, 94–95

Song, songwriter, 10–13, 69, 96, 164, 185, 189, 190–91

Sound, 13, 116, 120–22, 124, 135, 152–53, 156, 159, 160–61, 184

Source, 17, 23, 38, 47, 52, 57, 59, 61, 70, 73, 84, 87, 88, 90–91, 93, 104–5, 108, 142, 159–60, 172, 182, 193–94

Southern hemisphere, 2, 4, 14, 18, 24, 49, 193

Spectrum, 96, 102, 169

Speech-act, 129, 136–37, 138, 141, 179

Spoken, 2, 11, 30–31, 42, 69, 82, 84, 102, 108, 111–12, 120

Scriptio continua, 111–12

Stage, 8, 13, 53, 89, 107, 135, 149, 162–63, 176, 185–86, 188, 190–91

Storyteller, 10, 128, 144, 175, 179, 181–82, 190

Structural, structure, 2, 16, 20, 24, 26, 53, 62–63, 69, 81, 84–86, 98–99, 104, 112, 119–20, 122–25, 127, 129–30, 137, 140, 153, 155–58, 160, 166

Syncretism, 25–28

Text, textual, 8–14, 16–18, 34–36, 39, 60, 62, 64–70, 72, 87, 91–96, 99–100, 102, 104–6, 108, 110, 112–13, 116–18, 120–23, 126–27, 131, 133–36, 138–40, 142–47, 149, 151–58, 160, 163, 165–67, 169, 171–74, 176, 178–82, 185–90, 192, 195

Index

Tradition(al), 11, 13, 16–17, 20, 24–26, 28, 37, 39, 56–57, 60, 69, 70, 80, 85, 87, 89–91, 94, 96–100, 102, 106–7, 118–20, 127–30, 140, 142, 147, 157, 164–66, 189–91, 195

Transcribe, transcript, 16, 18, 87–88, 89, 95, 102, 107, 111, 128, 135–36, 144, 161, 171, 173, 177, 181, 185

Transformation, 11, 26, 44, 46, 48, 61, 64–65, 138, 148, 165, 168

Translation principle, 9, 56, 157

Transmediatization, 151

Transmission, 1, 16, 58, 104–8, 119, 131, 150, 154, 166

Type C (liberation) theology, 40–41, 43

Typology, 38, 40

Unilateral, 32–33, 35, 56, 73–74, 139, 193–94

Universal, 20–22, 31, 36, 56, 85, 156

Verbal art, 1–2, 16, 86–87, 91, 98, 138, 143–45, 194

Vernacular, 30–32, 36–37, 42–43, 45, 51, 54–57, 59, 63–64, 66, 68, 74–75, 146, 153, 165

Voices from the past, 96, 102

Vulgate, 46, 121

Vuté, 5, 6–13, 17, 162, 167–73, 177–86, 189–91, 195

Womanist, feminist, 15, 50, 54 59–62, 70

Workshop, 8, 10–13, 189

World Christianity, 46, 48–49, 57, 73

Worldview, 25, 45, 55–57, 69, 86, 193

www.ingramcontent.com/pod-product-compliance
Lightning Source LLC
Chambersburg PA
CBHW022013220426
43663CB00007B/1066